Hospitalised with a broken back (compounded with Tuberculosis) at the age of three, John McBarron ("Barney") relates his rite of passage in Glasgow's poverty-stricken East-end.

Emerging after four years of treatment in the years leading up to World-War II, all of the gritty reality, violence, yet indefatigable humour that is woven into the "Glesca" cultural fabric is recorded faithfully.

In a not-too-distant world that had no television and little radio, "ra peepul" relied on their own self-made entertainment, the occasional cinema trip, but especially the weekly tribal battles known as the "fitba" and "ra dancin".

Alternately moving and laugh-out-loud funny, the author perfectly conveys the mood of the times and the character and spirit with which every Scot can identify.

Bob de Vaatt

John McBarron was born in 1928 into a family that fared no better than others in the poverty-stricken East End of Glasgow. He left school at the age of 14 and joined his father in the family grocery store (the wee shop) just down from Celtic Park. At barely 17 he became seriously frustrated with his limited life and with a hunger to improve his limited education he developed a passion for reading. In his mid-twenties he chose to forego the opportunity to join Glasgow University on the grounds of his father's illness requiring family support in the shop.

At the age of 32 he went to London to explore its cosmopolitan culture and whether his thoughts on becoming a writer had any merit. Some 25 years later he took early retirement from the Gillette Company, Boston, as a Senior International Consultant in Corporate Management Information Systems. He now lives happily in Glasgow not far removed from Celtic Park.

Ah b'lang tae
Glasgow

John McBarron

http://www.jmcbs-glasgow.co.uk

Published by

Premier Print (Scotland) Limited
2 Camlachie Street,
Glasgow G31 4JH

Book Jacket designed by
Robert McDonald
Graphic Designer
robbo.mac@virgin.net

Pen and Ink Illustrations by
Michael McBarron

ISBN: 0-9547626-0-6

This book is dedicated to a memorable evening in
Frenchman Bay, Australia,
in the company of my dear friends,
Phil and Pat,

Their selfless attention to my rambling commentary,
combined with their persuasive prompting,
begot this book.

My heartfelt thanks to my soulmates
Michael and Cathie.

Their respect and love will always be
my touchstone.

Contents

Ah b'lang tae Glasgow

Prologue

In the early 20th century the country was in a serious economic depression. It was at its high in the years following the first world war. The period from 1918 to 1938 was a particularly dark time with over 2,000,000 people unemployed. Strikes were on the increase and widespread suffering and deprivation were the order of the day. As the crisis continued to worsen the Lloyd George's coalition government was brought down.

Glasgow's heavy industry took a beating at this time and unemployment was common place. Living conditions, already among the worst in Europe, were deteriorating rapidly. In particular the insanitary outhouse-toilets and backcourts of the older tenements were in a deplorable state of grime and vermin. It was so endemic that it became a way of life.

It was the bedrock for disease to flourish. In particular, tuberculosis grew to rampant levels and soon became the scourge of the tenements. Almost out of control, Glasgow Corporation were forced to set in motion a hospital building program that was aimed specifically at treating the disease and with the wider aim of bringing it under control. These new hospitals were to be appropriately referred to as sanitoriums. The last one to be built was Mearnskirk, which was to be dedicated to the treatment of children under fifteen years.

Their program worked and in the course of the succeeding decade tuberculosis was brought under control. However, it was not until 1943 when Selman A. Waksman discovered Streptomycin that an effective cure could be prescribed.

Chapter I

A Change of Haven

Mearnskirk

Homecoming

Oor Hoose

The Part y

A Change of Haven - Mearnskirk

Mearnskirk Hospital, Glasgow, June 26, 1935; I was released as cured. To this day I still remember it as the end of one life and the beginning of another. I had entered the sanitorium when I was three years old and was now leaving at the wondrous age of seven going on eight. In a span of 4 years I had lived a dream like existence in a world that always seemed to be bathed in the warmth and light of summer. My home was a large dormitory, which was referred to as a Pavilion and shared by others of a similar age. Our beds were separated by French doors leading on to a ground level veranda. These doors were a byword for fresh air and, as we were constantly reminded of, an essential requirement for our "getting better". Hence, to ensure that we heavily dosed our lungs with this elixir, they always seemed to be more open than closed.

On days when the sun was oozing warmth the nurses would wheel our beds out on to the veranda where, still restricted to our kip, we would be left to look up and ponder the passing clouds and fantasise. I remember in one particular dream I fell off the top of the Empire State Building (I had seen it in a comic) only to wake up on the veranda with a bump on my head and a sore shoulder. Those Nurses; they did make a rigmarole of it. But any kind of knock, or bruise, or rise in temperature and they would be fussing all over you. I always protested and rejected their attentions and if they persisted I would just curl up in a ball. But this would only invite the inevitable poke and tickle, which quickly broke down any resistance and lead to the war cry for a truce - keys! Keys!

These loving people filled my early memories. They also embodied the rules of the house; the proscribed crimes and punishments; the "Do's and Don'ts"; the rewards and the penalties. All of which would be strictly enforced with the highest degree of communal fun and laughter in mind. Another maxim for "getting better"; or, you may "spare the rod but not the sweeties". The chief enforcer of this justice and many other such maxims was the senior nurse, called Jean McDonald. As I remembered her then, she was a tall and pretty girl whose soft brogue adorned her mischievous personality. Always smiling and encouraging others to do likewise. I remember on one visiting day my dad jokingly "pulled her up for it".

"You let this lot git away wi' murder", he said.

"I do, don't I", she replied. "But be assured, John", she added, "we all have a line that is never crossed. Isn't that right John", she said, poking her finger into me.

She seemed always to be at the centre of any major happenings in the ward. On the daily medication round she would walk up and down the centre of the ward feigning a serious look on her face. Should anyone grimace at the taste of their medicine she would mockingly wave a threatening finger and stare them into submission. "You did enjoy it; didn't you"?

"Yes! Jean".

The dinner round was when she really sparkled. She had a repertoire of tricks she could perform with cups and plates. My favourite, which always had me in stitches, was when she took a plate of food from the trolley and strode up the centre of the floor as if to serve someone. Suddenly she would feign a foot trip, stagger as if falling, and then, with a muted scream, and legs apart, she would slowly slide to the floor to perform a perfect exhibition of the splits. Gracefully retrieving the situation she would always blame one of us for causing her accident. Her piece de resistance, only performed on special occasions, was also with a dinner plate of food balanced in the palm of her hand. Again, she would begin with a feigned trip and stagger. But in the course of this she would turn the plate under her arm, and with amazing dexterity, contort her wrist in such a way as to perform a circle with the plate above her head and bring it back to where it started without spilling a drop. It always drew a loud cheer, which she would modestly accept with a regal curtsey and an appropriate hand gesture.

And so the day arrived when I was to take my leave of this cosseted world. It began as normal with breakfast in bed followed by our morning dip in the tub. It was soon after this that Jean came up to my bed with a bigger than usual smile on her face.

"Today's the day, John. In an hour or so you will be home among your brothers and sisters where you're going to be spoilt rotten."

With the exception of Agnes, who occasionally accompanied my mother on her visits, I knew little or nothing about my brothers and sisters hence, I just politely nodded in agreement. She obviously sensed the sadness that her comment had aroused in me. But for the moment she chose to ignore it.

"Now let's start getting dressed. You know the rules. You've got your clean pants and simmet on. What always comes next?"
"My jacket" I replied.
"Good boy."
She gently lifted my face to look her straight in the eyes.
"There will come a day in the future when you'll be able to throw your jacket away. Till then, promise me that you'll always put it on first thing in the morning."
"I promise, Jean." And with that she gave me a cuddle.

The jacket consisted of a square piece of leather, which covered the whole of my back. At the outer edges it housed two lightweight metal bars which were intended to prevent you from bending your spine. To put the jacket on you slid your arms through armholes formed by leather straps. You then had two lower soft straps at the bottom of the jacket, which you pulled round your waste and tied. When fully fitted you could only bend from the hip and hence it was generally known as a straightjacket. At the time the jacket was the only clue I had to my being in Mearnskirk. The answer to this question, however, was of no concern to me. My earliest memory was that of always having to wear a jacket hence, I had no conscious awareness of it. I could run, jump, and fall over with the best of my pals without any reaction, other than from those fussing nurses. Nevertheless I was aware of the added pleasure I got when I curled up in bed at night without it.

Now resplendent in my new homecoming suit Jean looked me over. She then beckoned over two other nurses. "What do you think?" She asked them. "Don't you think there is something missing?"
Both nurses looked at me, then at each other and shook their heads.
"No, we think he looks great," They said

"I've got it." Jean said. And with that she suddenly produced a handkerchief. Strange to say, it was already folded and seemed to fit exactly into my top pocket. "That's it." She said with pride. "Now you look like a gentleman." She then took me into the centre of the ward and gestured to all my pals. "What do you think of him now?" This brought forth a hail of embarrassing remarks from every bed. "Ok. Enough's enough. What about a proper send off?" Jean called out.

Amid the clapping and the jeering kidology I walked round and shook everyone's hand. I then looked back up the ward and waved a final goodbye. Hand in hand we then walked through the nurses area and out into the grounds of the hospital. The grounds always looked enormous to me with resplendent lawns and walkways connecting to the other pavilions. Each pavilion seemed to stand alone in its own little oasis of ground. I remember their bright red brick and white corner stone, which seemed to frame them against the rural background. We walked towards the main building of the hospital where we expected to meet my mother and father. We paused at one of the bench seats set at intervals along our path.

"Let's sit down for a moment and have a wee chat." she said. "How do you feel?" She asked

'I'm a bit afraid" I replied.

She took hold of my hands and looked at me fondly. "I know you are," she said. "But this will pass; I promise. But right now I want to see that cheeky self-confidence back; that need-to-know spark in your eyes; not to forget your stubbornness. I want you to feel tall and not to leave here without any frailties of your own making." All of these words held little meaning for me. But like all such pronunciations from Jean, the implicit care and love always made me feel good.

She stood up at this. "Are we agreed?" she asked.

Imitating one of her thumbs-up gestures. "We are agreed". I proudly responded.

"Then let's go and meet your mother and father."

"Jean?"

"Yes John?"

"What's a frailty?"

"You do ask them, don't you? A frailty is a weakness; a burden; a nuisance problem you want to be rid of. I remember an uncle of mine who once said I had a frailty because I laughed too much."
"Don't be daft" I said, "How can you laugh too much?"
"Well, maybe that was my uncle's frailty," she replied with a knowing smile.
As the main building came into view I could see my mother and father standing in the entrance.
"Can I go on, Jean?" I asked. "Of course you can" she replied. With that I ran the twenty or so yards and threw my arms round my mother's waist.
She bent over and hugged me. "Aye, yae look lovely in your new suit, John. Ur yae lookin' forward to go'n hame?"
Before I could answer my father took over.
"Of course yae ur; urn't yae?"
At this point Dr Dale arrived. As I remember him, he was a tall well-built man with dark hair and a small moustache that seemed to suit him. In his presence everyone was always very quiet and zealously respectful.
For my part I was always in awe of him. I remember being told by my mother that I owed my life to him and, while I never understood why, it did not in the least surprise me. He was something of a father figure to me. There was authority in all he said and done; and I was very trusting and comfortable with him.
"Well, John, the time has come for you to leave us. Not for good though. I want to keep an eye on you for a while longer." he said.
His words made me feel good and very important.
"I have spoken to your father and mother on this and they have agreed to bring you back every three months so that we can have a chat.
Is that Ok by you?"
"Yes Sir" I replied with undisguised glee.
"Come then and I will walk the three of you down to the gates"
"Can I say goodbye to Jean"
"Of course, you can"
I turned round and there she was a couple of steps behind us, her arms beckoning. "Come here" she said. She dropped down on to her

heels and hugged me. "Now, what was it you agreed to always remember" she asked
"To always feel tall and have no frailties"
She kissed me on the cheek and stood up.
"Off you go now; no more goodbyes"
I ran down to rejoin my mother and father. Dr Dale bid us farewell and left us. As we walked through the gates I turned to have a last look. I expected Jean to be still there waving, but she was gone.
I wasn't to realise it at the time, but the Mearnskirk culture and environment was a defining period - not least in terms of language: I was already "talkin' wi' a bool in ma mooth"

A Change of Haven - Mearnskirk

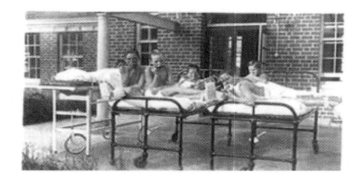

There's nae place like hame

Chapter I

A Change of Haven

A Change of Haven - Homecoming

As we walked through the gates we were met by a very friendly looking man whom, by his casual nod of familiarity to my parents, was clearly a friend or family relative. He must also have had some knowledge of me as he warmly singled me out.

"Hello, John. You don't know me but I'm here to give you a lift hame."

Dad intruded at this point. "This is Walter...Walter McLaughlen. A very good friend of me and yer mither. He's come to drive us hame in his new motor caur." Having occasionally seen a motor car in the hospital grounds the thought of being given a lift in one gave me a tingle of excitement. It also thrilled me to know that my parents had such a great friend.

"I've been thinkin'," said mum with a studied pause. "Havin' come all this way, I think wi should take John to Rouken Glen Park for a quick visit. It's jist doon the road from here. Yae don't mind, Walter, dae yae?"

"The truth is, Aggie, ah've got tae be back in the shop for 12; ah've goat a couple oí travellers comin' in to see me aboot some stock an ah've only got an hour to spare. Yae know how it is John?" he said, looking to dad for support.

"It's nae problem, Walter, yer business comes furst", dad said. He then quickly turned to mum. Is that no right Aggie'?" he asked, looking for confirmation.

"Course it's aw right" said mother. "It wis mer than good o' yae, Walter, to bring us up in the furst place. It's jist that a waant tae spen' a bit mer time wi' ma boy before we go hame to the family. Yae know whit it's like there. We can get a tram caur from Rouken Glen to Glesga Cross, an' wan from there tae Bri'geton"

"Look Aggie" said Walter, "yae don't hiv tae explain tae me. A'll tell yae wit ah'll dae. Get yer sel's in tae the caur an ah'll drive yae all doon tae the park an' buy yae all a double nugget ice cream. Or, looking down at me with a smile, "miby wee John wid prefer a poky-hat wi lots of maccalum instead of a nugget?"

Having no understanding of what the previous conversation had been about, and being unsure of what a macallum meant, I just nodded my head in agreement.

A Change of Haven - Homecoming

We drove down, what later became known to me as, the Kilmarnock Road, the main trunk road between Glasgow and the Ayrshire coast. The journey lasted about 5 minutes and there we were, outside the gates of Rouken Glen Park. Walter parked the car, got out, and beckoned me to follow him. Just a few yards along the pavement I had my first sight of an ice cream hand cart. Brightly painted in primary colours with the owner's name proudly displayed, they were a common sight in those days.

Glasgow had always been famous for the quality and flavour of its ice cream. Primarily due, it is said, to its introduction in the nineteenth century by Italian immigrants from the Ciociara district in Italy. Pushing their carts to all parts of the city their infectious cry of "Gelati, ecco un poko!" would have us kids plaguing our parents for a halfpenny. It was this cry that got them the name of the 'Hokey Pokey men', and from there the favourite of every kid, a 'Poky-Hat' - an ice cream cone, usually smothered in macallum (a scarlet coloured raspberry juice).

Have you ever tasted a flake, John? Asked Walter. "No", I replied. "Stick a flake in the poky-hat", he told the vendor.
By now Walter was beaming all over himself and looked very much like a man who had bought himself out of an unwanted obligation. Mind you, he was right about the flake. It was my introduction to a Glaswegian delight on a warm sunny day. A flaky stick of chocolate embedded upright into a large pokey-hat of ice cream. For me it was a unique experience that was to be often repeated in my youthful years. It would take my father's entire handkerchief to dry my face out when it was finished.

Walter took his leave and got into his car. He called out to me that he would see me again, and waved his hand. Holding up my ice cream by way of repeating my thanks, I waved back. We walked into the park and sat ourselves down on the first bench we came to. This was a welcome aid to the management of an ice cream flake as there was an obvious conflict between keeping control of the melting ice cream with your tongue and having a bite of the delicious chocolate.

Glancing up at mum and dad I was pleased to see that they were
having the same problem.

"Whit wis that all aboot back there?" dad asked mum. "Whit dae yae
mean?" responded mum.

"Yae know whit a mean. Walter went oot o' his way to drive us up
here an' take us back and you didnae appear to be aw that grateful"

"Yae'r right John. Ah know he's a nice man. His heart's in the right
place an' ah know he's bin a good friend to you. It's jist that he keeps
goin' on aboot that bliddy motor caur of his. But yae'r right, and am
sorry. A'll speak tae him. Don't worry aboot it. But ah still believe
the kid'll enjoy a ride in the tram caur a lot better than in a stuffy
motor."

"Yae'r absolutely right, Aggie. It's a sunny day an' we'll get 'im
hame soon enough."

With that said he looked down at me with a grin on his face. As I
quickly came to learn, my dad did not smile often, but he grinned a
lot, and when he was content his grin could be infectious.

"Ok, son, let's get yae cleaned up before we go any further".

As we walked back through the gates there was a very arresting
sound of a double clang of a muffled bell. Dad ran towards its source
vigorously waving his hand. My eyes immediately followed him and
a little excitedly I pulled at mother's hand and pointed. "What's that?
I asked

"It's a tram caur" she replied with amusement.

There it stood, in the middle of the road; its wand pressed against the
overhead lines; my first sight of a tramcar. It was huge and
stunningly colourful with a lower and upper level for passengers. Its
lower tier was painted with a band of vivid orange and, in exact
proportion to its lower tier, the upper level was painted a gleaming
blue. As was later confirmed it was a gloriously new machine
straight from the depot that morning on its maiden journey. It was
mid morning and such was the time of day there were very few
passengers on it. But, as far as I was concerned, this tram had been
specially laid on for me. I stood there in awe of it for what seemed

like forever. My trance was broken by a further clang of the tram's
bell.

"C'mon, John, we hiv tae git oan, the driver's waitin' fur us." said
dad.

With that they both gripped a hand and partly pulled me up the two
steps on to the platform. Still holding onto their hands we walked in
to the lower deck. There was a further clang on the bell and with a
slight jerk the tram took off. As we sat down my mind was racing
frantically. I was initially locked into the changing whine of the
electric motor as the tram picked up speed. I was impatient to
explore and stood up with the intention of walking down the carriage
towards the driver. As I did so I almost lost my feet and had to grab
the nearest pole. Almost simultaneously my mother had grabbed me
by the waist.

"Where're yae gaun, John. The tram's too shoogly; yae'll fall on yer
face."

Seeing the reassuring fun on both their faces I took hold of the grab
bar at the back of the seat and braved a few more steps forward.

 "I want to see the driver. Please!" I begged.

My dad nodded his head in sympathy; bent over and picked me up.

"Ok" he said "Haud own tight and we'll go an see the driver."

With a few deft shuffles of his feet to combat the random shoogle of
the car and aided by the grab bars of the seats we got there. He stood
me down in front of the door, who's upper half was made of glass.
He placed my hand on the door handle and urged me to hold on tight.
I had no sooner done this when the tram shoogled on a bend. With
that I gave a little stagger and pulled on the door that caused it to
slide open a little. Dad quickly wedged his foot against it, which
stopped any further movement.

"Yae're quite safe" he assured me with a grin.

With that I settled down to watch the driver with great intent. He
stood in front of an oval shaped iron box whose height reached his
waist. It was capped with a highly polished brass plate on the center
of which was mounted the car's drive control. This consisted of a
brass lever fixed to a central spindle at one end and to a wooden ball
at the other end, which provided a handgrip for the driver. After
some minutes of intense scrutiny of the driver's actions I felt that I

could drive the car. In my mind I replayed the driver's movements. To start the car you pushed the lever round (just a little) in a clockwise direction. To increase the speed you would push the lever a little bit more. There always seemed to be a pause between each push. To stop the car you would push the lever in the opposite direction but this time it was in one continuous movement. I wondered at the time as to what would happen if the same continuous movement was used when starting the car. In addition to the main drive lever there was also a smaller lever protruding from the left side of the box. The driver seemed to rest his hand on this lever which he only occasionally moved.

"What's that other lever for?" I asked dad.

"That's the brake" he replied. "He pulls on that when he wants tae check the speed of the caur, or when he waants tae stop all tae gether. Look, we're now comin' to a tram stop. He's now pulling on the brake to slow up. And now watch for the final pull. See it?"

With that the car came to a halt exactly at the tram stop. At this point my mother intervened.

"We're gettin' closer tae the toon and it's startin' to get busy doon here. So why don't we take John upstairs whir he can see a lot mer." Without waiting for a reply she slid open the door separating us from the driver."

"Sorry driver" she said "Yae don't mind us takin' the boy upstairs, dae yae?"

"Go on." he said with a smile and an upward nod of his head."

With that my dad lifted me up in his arm and quickly whisked me up the spiral stairs to what was the forward compartment of the tram. Like the driver's position below it was separated from the other passengers by a sliding door. The compartment could seat 5 passengers and had the most spectacular view I had ever seen in my life. My disappointment with the enforced movement upstairs was soon forgotten. Stretched out before me (Pollokshaws Rd.) was an amazing sight! A seemingly unending line of red stone tenement buildings on either side of the road. Their windows rose to three, and sometimes four, levels. From my position I had an unrestricted view of the first level windows and when the car came to halt at the tram stop

A Change of Haven - Homecoming

I could see clearly into the rooms. On one occasion I could see people sitting round a table eating and drinking.
"Do people live there?" I asked my dad with some wonderment.
"Of course they dae" my mother responded. "We live in a hoose jist like that" she added.
This statement seemed to confuse me for a moment as I suddenly realised I was going home. But what was home? And where was home? As there was no way of me answering these questions I immediately dismissed them and returned to my fascination with these new found wonders.

All of these shapes and sounds were new to me. And I had never seen so many people; some standing, some walking, and some hurrying. Most of them with a carrier bag over one arm. The most fascinating sight, though, were the shops. They were the ground level frontages of the tenements. Separated only, it seemed, by the access closes leading to the houses above. They were, as I later came to understand, the commercial lifeblood of Glasgow. A never-ending bazaar of goods and people with all manner of signage above the shops proclaiming their trading name and wares.

On this section of the journey I plagued the life out of my parents with a multitude of questions. Most of them they considered amusing and ignored, others they tried to answer as best they could. For my part I think I learned or acquired the gist of three new words: Buy, Sell, and Shop. As I was to further learn they covered an area that my mother and father had more than a passing interest in.

The tram route took us down to Eglinton Toll where we veered right to join Cathcart Rd. We then passed through the Gorbals which, as I remember, only differed from the previous part of the trip by the darker colour of its tenements, and on to the Albert Bridge where I had my first view of the River Clyde. It could only have been a few stops after this that we arrived at Glasgow Cross where we had to change trams. We left the tram at the corner of Saltmarket and the Trongate. As the tram pulled away from the stop it left us with a clear view of the majestic Tollbooth Steeple. It stood in the center of the crossroads comprising the High St, Gallowgate, London Road, Saltmarket, and the Trongate.

We stood at the corner of the Trongate and took in the crossroads, which was said to be the busiest intersection in Glasgow. By way of trying to clarify the confusion of movement and noise, my parents pointed out a few landmarks. Looking left along Trongate, mother said that this was the start of Argyle St.
"What you cannae find there disnae exist." she enthused. Not to be left out of it dad pointed my eyes across the road to the start of the High St.
"If yae take the first street on the left yae're in the fruit market." He went there most mornings, he added, to buy fresh fruit and veg for the shop. There was a relish in their voice that reflected the close associations they had with this part of Glasgow. With even more relish, though, they now pointed to the far right hand corner of the crossroad. Over there, they said was the start of the Gallowgate. And just a few minutes walk along its way was the best-known shopping area in Glasgow - 'The Barras'. Throughout their commentary they continually looked at me to ensure that I was suitably enthralled by their wisdom and knowledge of Glasgow. Truth be told, whilst it was a wondrous experience I very quickly gave up on trying to absorb their well-intentioned aims. It did occur to me that the only problem with all this parental education was that it always presupposed you to have a knowledge and learning capacity commensurate with their own. As a consequence, one willingly defers to their superior wisdom and switches off. Thankfully, though, some of that early learning did stick.

Eventually, the comment was made that I might be getting a bit tired and that maybe it was time to get me home. With that, and with a little to-ing and fro-ing, we took ourselves across to the other side of the Saltmarket. From there and with much less trouble, we crossed to the other side of the London Road where we waited at the tram stop for the red car going to Bridgeton. This duly arrived and we were on our way. The tram was fairly busy, and therefore, of necessity, we had to sit downstairs. Again, the journey time was taken up by gazing at the passing shop frontage and when the car halted at its appointed stop I would continue to marvel at the goods displayed in their window. We passed through Bridgeton Cross, which, as my dad pointed out, was famous for its wrought iron umbrella. It was originally donated by George Smith & Co. in 1874 and was now used as a general meeting place for the locals who, if not working, would gather for a blether with like-minded intellects. As ever, in Glasgow, the place abounded with the bustle of people.

The tram took a right off the London Rd, went partly round the umbrella, and then took a left into Dalmarnock Rd. We were nearly home, I was told. After two stops from the crossroads the character of Dalmarnock Road dramatically changed. On the left side the tenements and their ground level shops continued but on the right side they were replaced with lower level buildings that were subdued in character and showed no signs of habitation or commercial usage. A few stops later and just as dramatically, it all changed again.

We get off at the next stop, my dad said. Gripping their hands we waited till the car came to a complete stop. Again, I was more lifted than walked down the stairs. We walked only a short distance when we came to the corner of Nuneaton St. and turned into it. I stared in amazement at the unbroken line of tenements on both sides of the street. This was my first view of them from street level. There was a gallery of windows on both sides. They were four stories high and they looked huge! With one exception both sides had an unbroken line of shops. The exception was a cinema right at the beginning of the street on the other side. I immediately spotted it and knowing that it could not be a shop I asked my dad what it was.
"It's the Dalmarnock picture hoose. They show fillums there." he said
A multitude of questions poured out, the answers to which were utterly meaningless to me. We walked very slowly so that I could pause and gaze into the shop windows; it was all so unreal. Half way along Nuneaton St. it was intersected by another street. Its name was Baltic St. We turned into it and had only walked a few yards when my parents stopped, turned, and pointed to the close across the road.

"We're here, John", my mother said.

Even before she spoke I knew. The close number was 307, and we were home.

There was a group of people standing around the entrance. I heard my name being called and immediately recognized my sister Agnes. I had grown fond of her in the course of her occasional visits to the hospital in the company of my parents. She was quite small and cute, I thought, and with her dark hair and neat dressing she always looked pretty to me.

She was excitedly jabbing her finger in the air and calling for me to look up. There were coloured buntings draped across the top of the close and white card hanging below which displayed the message, "Welcome home, John." She ran across the street and greeted me with an affectionate hug.

"Look," she said pointing up at a window two storeys high, "I did that. Dae yae like it?"

There was even more bunting pinned around a double window. Draped from its sill was another message card that was unreadable at this height. Carried away with her excitement I gleefully nodded my head. She took my hand and, visibly trying to suppress her pride, we crossed the street towards the gathering crowd of people at the closehead. She pointed out my brothers Bill, and Bert, who waved to me and disappeared up the close. Holding tightly to sister Agnes's hand, I blushed with self importance, as all these people made all sorts of welcoming calls and gestures. As I passed through them there were many affectionate ruffles of my hair, a very Glaswegian trait.

As we walked up the close I became aware of a dank smell; this was my first meeting with the aroma of the tenements. I looked up at Agnes's smiling face for reassurance and immediately the smell dropped into the background. My mother and father who were behind us called out for us to stop at the foot of the stairs. I looked up the staircase and could see Bill and Bert peering round the top of its inner wall and making meaningless gestures to me. Mother called out some kind of warning to them and they disappeared.

"Ah'll gie yae a coal cerry upstairs, John," said dad, as he bent over to pick me up.

"I want to walk up with Agnes." I pleaded.

Yae'll need to practice first," said my mother. But don't worry! We'll hive yae runnin' up an' doon before long."

My father ignored my plea and picked me up and swung me on to his shoulder. As he did so a feeling of fear came over me. It passed quickly but it left me with a feeling that I had been carried up these stairs before. Yet, to my certain knowledge I had never seen a tenement building, let alone its staircase, prior to that day. Despite a good memory of those early years I am still bereft of recall prior to my time in Mearnskirk.

As we walked up the stairs my dad moved towards the outer wall to counter the narrowing of the steps on the inner wall, as they spiraled back on themselves (past the communal toilet) to a straight upward passage to the first landing. There were a few neighbourly people standing in front of the three doors on the landing. There were calls of welcome home and some more ruffling of my hair. With little pause my dad carried on upstairs to the next landing which had three similarly positioned doors. Two to the left, and one to the right. The one to right was fully open and Agnes, with a big grin on her face, stood beckoning. There was no doubt as to whose house this was.

Glasgow Cross

Bridgeton Cross

Chapter I

A Change of Haven

Mearnskirk

Homecoming

<u>Oor Hoose</u>

The Party

Agnes by now had taken over and was determined to show me round every nook and cranny of the house. Our front door from the landing opened into a lobby, which had doors into the back and front rooms.

The Front Room had a south facing double window, which made it reasonably bright. It had a great view of the street below and an even better one of the facing tenement, whose windows, as if seeking more light, were uncurtained or fully drawn back. Their only privacy was a small lace curtain (de rigueur for a tenement window) that covered the lower half of the window and in some instances not even that.

The decor in our front room was fairly spartan. A small wrought iron fireplace in the center of the wall provided heating for the room. It was flanked on the window side with a high recessed cupboard, and on the other side a dressing table. To the right of this, and butting into the corner of the back wall, was an alcove whose space contained a double bed suspended on the inner walls by wooden supports. It looked gloomy, and my first thought on seeing it prompted the hope that it was not to be mine. Backing on to the wall to the right of the alcove was yet another bed, which Agnes claimed was hers.

Identical in shape to the front, the Back Room was the main living area with a double window looking on to the Backcourt. The window was flanked on both sides by folded wooden panels reaching from the sill to the roof. Sitting beneath the panels was a cupboard, which housed the 'Sink', a square iron basin with a brass water tap shaped like a swan's neck positioned at its head. It was also referred to as the 'jawbox'. It provided great drinking water and sustained all of our washing and cooking needs. The room also had an alcove, which backed on to the one in the front room and housed another suspended double bed, which I quickly learnt, was the domain of my parents.

Dramatically dominating everything in the room, though, was the fire place. A large, heavily blacked range that strutted its ornate oven and grated hearth. A symbol of warmth and security, but ugly, with a never-ending need to belie its fading looks with blacking polish. Sitting in the middle of the room was the table for all occasions. Very modern and very polished. It had flaps which, when folded down, caused it to take up the minimal of floor space. Given that the room also contained a sideboard spanning a large part of one wall and the 'Kumfynite Cabinet' standing against the other wall, I thought the table flaps were clever.

The 'Kumfynite', which I later learnt was bought specifically for my homecoming, was to become my favorite furniture. At first look it was like a box-shape cabinet with paneled frontage topping a large drawer just above floor level. It had a hinged lid on top, which I could barely reach. I remember my mother encouraging me to get a chair and lift the lid. With great excitement I slowly did so, and was absolutely stunned by what I saw. It contained a multitude of compartments each one a different size. There were many bits and pieces, which I could not identify; some sparkling (my mother's earrings and other jewellery); some were gifts for me; absolute magic, the source of many later fantasies.

"This is also yer bed," my Dad said with a big grin

I remember me looking at him with disbelief. But before I could answer he lifted me down and pushed the chair to one side. He then gripped the handles on either side of the cabinet with his fingers and, with his thumbs, he pressed the button above each handle and slowly pulled the panel along the floor. Trailing behind the panel, to my amazement, was an unfolding bed.

"Dae yi like it"? Mother asked.

Confusion reigned and pushed me to tears. I threw my arms round her waist and hugged her. They responded to my tears with humorous banter that soon brought me round. On doing so my first reaction was to get the chair back in position and continue with my exploration of the Kumfynite.

"Haud on, Haud on!" my mother said. "Yae'll hiv aw the time in the world tae dae that tomorrow. Right noo we're goin' to get the place ready fur yir comin' hame party. Take 'im next door to one of the neighbours Agnes, an' give his face an' haunds a quick wash. Also take 'im doon tae the toilet. And do be careful" she warned. "A'll git things started here." she added.

"Dae yae need to go to the lavatory now?" Agnes asked.

"I need a pee" I answered.

"Ok" she said opening the front door on to the landing. As she did so she unhooked a large black key from a bunch of other keys hanging on the wall beside the door. Taking me by the left hand she positioned me close to the left-hand wall at the top of the staircase.

"Now, yae must always be careful when usin' the stairs" she warned. She pointed out the dangers of the sloping curve on the center edge of each step, which was caused by years of usage. They can be very slippy in the winter she stressed. And again she emphasised the importance of always keeping close to the outer wall. We walked down to where the stairs spiralled round the central wall and there was a door straddling the outer curve. I had previously noticed it as a curiosity when I was being carried upstairs by dad. Agnes located the key and opened the door. Given that the only lavatory I had ever previously used was located within the confines and hygiene controls of Mearnskirk, what was now being presented to me was something of a culture shock. I just stood there for a few moments not knowing what to do. Agnes pointed to the floor with some pride and told me that mother had made her give the place a special cleaning for my homecoming.

"Look at how white the pipeclay boarder roon' the edges of the fler are" she enthused. "The whiter the chalk looks, the more recently it has been cleaned" she added, looking quite pleased with her self.

The lavatory bowl looked clean enough but its wooden seat, which was hinged back against the wall, looked decrepit and long since insanitary. The cistern sat on two brackets positioned above a partly opened window to the rear of the bowl. It was made of iron and heavily rusted at its base by condensation. A long chain dangled from its flushing lever. That dank smell, the aroma of the tenement, had returned. I stood there, absolutely stunned.

"Are yae alright, John?"

I just nodded in response.

"Hiv yer pee, then. I promise I wulnae look," she added with a mischievously knowing smile, whose purpose was lost on me.

Chapter I

A Change of Haven

Mearnskirk

Homecoming

Oor Hoose

The Party

A Change of Haven - The Party

On the pretence that my mother needed some time to prepare the house for the party, Agnes took me next door to one of our neighbours. There, under Agnes's supervision, I was allowed to wash up and comb my hair. All spruced up, I was now more than eager to return our own house. But for some reason Agnes seemed intent on thwarting my wish by chattering on to the neighbours about my former life style in Mearnskirk. It was a very Glaswegian example of the art of gossip, where a little knowledge expands to fill available time. In this case it seemed more like a device to delay our return. By way of easing my boredom with all of this I was offered a 'sweetie' by our neighbour who was a bit gushing and unduly pleased with my presence. Before I could accept her offer Agnes intervened on the unconvincing grounds that I would be having my dinner shortly. It was this final deprivation that prompted my plea to go home. By now Agnes sensed that any further attempt at prevention would do more harm that good.

"Ok", she said, and turned to thank our neighbour. This was sanction enough for me. I made a beeline for the door and scurried across the landing to our own door, which was open only to find that the door to the back room was locked. A feeling of isolation welled in me, which prompted me to blame it on Agnes. In sheer frustration I was about to bang it with my fist when Agnes arrived. But, before she could say or do anything the door suddenly opened from within.

To my astonishment the room was packed with people and they were all staring at me. There was a momentary quiet followed by applause and calls of welcome home. I had never seen any of these people in my life yet they each announced themselves as uncles, aunts, or cousins. I even met for the first time my other sister, May.

The table, with its flaps fully open, filled the center of the room and, as a consequence everyone was standing. There was a strong smell of alcohol everywhere. I remembered this smell from the medicine cabinet in Mearnskirk, but not as strongly as this.

My mother steered me round everyone and asked me to shake hands. Some of them pressed money into my hand for which I thanked them and put it in my trouser pocket. The formalities over, I was then sat at the head of the table by mother. It was only then that I took in the size of the table; its bright white cover cloth, and the variety of food spread out on plates. Dominating everything, however, and positioned in front of me, was an awesome example of Glasgow's finest treat. A clooty dumpling bedecked with seven candles.

"Blow them oot," said mother.

"But it's not my birthday." I protested.

"Naw, but it is a special occasion," she said.

Without further encouragement I bent over and blew, and blew, then blew again to finish them off.

"Now, before we slice the dumpling," said mother, "you, yer brothers and sisters," who by now had taken a seat at the table, "are goin' to eat some dinner. Ok?"

We all nodded our head in agreement. Two neighbours (I presumed) then entered with plates of hot food.

"Great!" Said Bert "It's ma favourite."

I received the first plate containing mince beef, sausage roll, and beans. This was followed by a large dollop of mashed potatoes. It was also one of my favourites and I was a bit hungry. Noticing the lack of cutlery I impatiently called out to my mother.

"Where's my knife and fork?"

"Git, the wee man! Where wir yae brought up?" said Uncle Harry.

He was the only one whose name I could remember from the earlier introductions. I think this was because he had a twisted nose and also gave me the most money. Everyone laughed loudly at his remark, which I could not understand. It did seem to me at the time that he must be one of those important people who every one always agrees with. It was also noticeable that he called for his glass to be filled more often than the others did and that my dad was eager to do so.

The knifes and forks now in place the dinner was quickly scoffed. As the plates were being removed my brothers left their seats and joined me at the top of the table.

"Yae know there's money in the dumpling." Bert said.

"You're kidding." I said.

"No he's not." Said Bill

"I heard a neighbir say that there wis a haulf a croon in it." Said Bert.

"Jist watch them, John. They'll try 'n cheat you." Shouted Agnes.

"Not, if am watchin'." said mother as she reappeared smiling, with a bread knife in her hand.

"Before I slice it, John, I want tae explain a few things. Furstly, yes, there is money in it. But it's wrapped up in silver paper and yae've got tae be careful that it disnae cut yer mooth. Now, there's also farthin's, hae'penys, pennies, and tanners in it. An' be careful with the tanners and farthin's as yae can easily swalli' them. There's also a haulf a croon which is in a special part of the dumplin.'"

With a united yell, my brothers and sisters immediately started pointing to different parts of the dumplin' and pleaded to have their selected slice.

A Change of Haven - The Party

"Ok," said mother, giving us each a paper flag with a pin in it. "Each of yae select yae'r slice an' pin yer flag tae it. But, we take it in turns which I'll call out."

By now everyone had come closer to the table to add to the excitement.

"Ok, John tae go furst," said mother.

No sooner had she spoken, than everyone, headed up by Uncle Harry's louder voice, cried out for me to plant it on the top. Without hesitation I planted it as directed.

"Dae yae wan' tae change yer mind?" mother asked with the knife poised in the cutting position.

I responded with a brief, vigorous shake of the head.

"One last chance." she called.

Another shake of the head started her slowly cutting a nice thick slice of the top.

"An' whit dae we hiv here?" she said, as she slowly turned it over and placed it on a plate in front of me. There were immediate shouts of approval as I eased the wrapped coin from the dumpling and peeled back the silver paper. It was indeed a half crown, and the biggest coin I had ever seen, I murmured in a mute voice. It was almost as if everything was suddenly becoming too much for me. I watched on as the game played itself out to an anticlimax. There was the occasional screech when first Agnes, and then May, unwrapped a sixpence. I found one myself as I ate my way through part of my slice. My head was now nodding. The last thing I can remember of that day was holding my arms tightly round my mother neck.

Furget the food, let's hiv the clootie dumplin'

Ah b'lang tae Glasgow

Chapter II

My New World

The Family

The Shop

Granny and Granda

My New Pals

My first School

My New World - The Family

I remember waking up for the first time in what was now 'my house'. I remember it being very quiet; that I was lying in a strange bed; and that I was a little fearful. The clouded light coming through the rain-splattered window struggled to overcome the darkness. It was a depressing sight to wake up to. My slowly waking mind struggled to identify this gloomy image. The head of the bed seemed as if it protruded from a box-like structure. It also had a high square structure at its foot screening off the lower part of the window. Lying very still, my eyes randomly explored the blank space above my head. Memory returned and I knew it to be my 'Kumfynite' bed.

My fear subsided a little but the gloom still troubled me. There was a slight rustling sound to my left and almost immediately I had a picture in my mind of the alcove that housed my parents bed. Supported on my elbows I partly raised myself and continued to explore with my eyes. I could see my straightjacket hanging on a nearby chair but little else. Still a little fearful, I peeled back the bed covers and placed my feet on the linoleum-covered floor. On doing so, I instinctively looked left towards my parents' bed and was a little startled but instantly joyous to see my mother backed up against the edge of the bed and smiling down at me.
"Did yae sleep well in yer new bed?"
Without an answer I stood up and threw my arms around her waist. She bent over and kissed me on the head. All was well again and my fear had gone. I then noticed that my father was nowhere to be seen.
"Where's daddy?" I asked.
"He's gon' to open the shop. He has to earn oor pennies, yae know. Ah'll take yae to see him in a wee while. Now, we hiv to get you dressed. Remember the rule that Jean taught yae? It must be the first thing yae dae when yae git up in the mornin'?"
I confidently nodded my head and unhooked my straightjacket from the back of the chair. I slid my hands through its armholes and positioned it squarely on my back.
"Do yae want me to fasten the buckle for yae?" She said, referring to the lower strap.
"No, I can do it myself." I protested with pride.
Mum then partly opened the room door and shouted along the lobby.

My New World - The Family

"Agnes! May! Give those two buggers a shout or they'll be late for school!"

Thus began the morning ritual in the McBarron household. One that would only vary with the school holidays. Mother then directed me to the sink and pointed out where the soap, cloth, and towel were.

"Now, gee yer haunds an' face a good wash, an' git yersel' dressed. Dae yae need a haun'?"

"No, I can manage." Having said that, I then struggled to turn on the water which was not helped by the icy cold feel of the tap. But this was nothing compared to the sharpness of the running water which caused me to blurt out in shock and pull my hands away quickly. With a grin on her face my mother apologized for exposing me without warning to washing with cold water. "If it's too cold for you I'll heat up some water." she added. But not wanting to be seen as being different from the rest of the family, I proudly refused the offer.

"Have you got a clean shirt for me?" I asked

"Och, that wan'll dae yae for noo. Don't be so fussy." she said with amusement.

As I quickly learned, there was no compulsion to change your clothing more than once a week unless it was damaged or soiled from outdoor activities, or was deemed to be unrepresentative of mother's pride, and standing with the neighbours.

Having washed and dressed I took a seat at the table which now had one flap raised and covered with a glistening coloured material called an oil cloth. I sat there and watched as Mum opened the seal of a pre-sliced loaf of bread. She then brought from the pantry a selection of packs containing sliced ham, corned beef, and other spreading edibles, such as butter, and jam. With amazing deftness she then buttered and sliced them into halves, which she stacked on three plates. She then produced a pack of paper bags and laid them beside the plates.

"What are they for?" I asked.

"It's for packing' their playpieces. They jist choose the pieces they want an' put them in a bag."

She then brought a pot full of tea from the stove and placed it on a heatproof tablemat. Agnes appeared at this point and gave me an affectionate hug. She then went to the pantry and got out the teacups.

"Ur they up yit?" mum asked Agnes.

"Yeh, they shouldnae be long" she answered.

After some five minutes Mum gave them another shout from the lobby. With some helpful prompting from Agnes I was soon scoffing into a jam sandwich supported by a cup of tea (two sugars). May then appeared and sat down beside me. She looked quite neat in her white shirt and black skirt. She did not say anything. This, as I came to know her, was a character trait that earned her the title of the 'quiet one of the family.' Shortly after Bill, then Bert appeared.

"A good night?" asked Bill, to which I nodded with a mouthful of bread.

"How's it gon' wee man?" Bert mumbled. He looked as if he was still half-asleep, and my cheery smile in response did nothing to improve his tired appearance.

As we sat eating breakfast mum, with a wag of her finger, drew the attention of Agnes.

"Look, I want yae to look after John, today. Yer dad's goin' to be busy this mornin' an' ah'll hiv tae run the shop. We'll take John round to see the shop, then you can take him tae meet his Granny and Granda'." Agnes nodded in agreement. Mum then turned her attention to the others.

"C'mon now, get yourselves off to school or yae'll be late."

May immediately responded, and as she left she waved to me.

"See you later, John." she said with a cheery smile.

"Jist wait fir yer brothers." mum reminded her. It took another timely reminder from Agnes, before Bill and Bert unwillingly took their leave.

"See yae later, John" they called out as they left.

"Clear the table and wash up those few dishes, Agnes, and we'll git oan oor way." said Mum. She then turned her attention to me and told me to put on my jacket. "We're going to meet up with your faither in the shop", she added. Day two, and my next adventure had begun.

Chapter II

My New World

The Family

The Shop

Granny and Granda

My New Pals

My first School

My New World - The Shop

"Look, I'll go on ahead, Agnes. I want to hiv a quick word wae Peggy. See yae doonstairs." mum said. She then gave my face a fondle and dashed off.

Agnes quickly finished her few chores. She then ushered me out on to the landing and locked the door behind her. Taking me by the hand she positioned me at the start of the staircase. She then went back over the dangers that the stairs posed and the dire need for me to stay close to the outside wall where the stairs would be at their widest when we walked round the spiral. She led me down one step at a time, which required me to pause and lead with my right foot. When we got to the lower landing Agnes paused to check that I was still comfortable. Apart from the smell, which I was adjusting to, I was ok, and the remaining stairs down to the close were no problem. Mum was standing at the front of the close waiting for us. I released myself from Agnes and ran down the close and grabbed her hand. I always needed to be close to her in those early days, it made me feel comfortable and confident. Unlike with Agnes my excitement was tinged with uneasiness.

The rain had stopped and the sun was trying to break though. To the right of the closehead I immediately identified Nuneaton St cutting across Baltic St. I remember feeling pleased and reassured by this. To the left, some twenty or so yards away I could see another street cutting across. This was Mordaunt Street. This gave me my first bearings on where we lived. I fixed it as a section of Baltic Street lying between these two streets. I looked up at the facing tenement windows. There were people propped up on their elbows leaning out and peering at all and sundry. There was a wave from someone who must have known us. It was strangely exciting and very friendly. "Ok, let's go an' see yer daddy in the shop", mum said fondly. We turned left out of the close and walked along Baltic Street. We crossed Mordaunt then under the Railway Bridge. On the other side of the bridge, to the right, a wall stretching some fifty yards replaced the tenements. I never came to know what lay behind this wall. At its end was the start of another line of tenements that stretched as far as the eye could see along the length of Baltic Street. On our side as we walked was the railway embankment fenced off by a short stretch of upright railway sleepers. At the end of this brief stretch of fencing was the corner of Kinnear Rd and Baltic St. On the opposite corner was a children's swing park which was to provide me with many future pleasures. We turned into Kinnear Rd, a name that for me was to be forever remembered as the imperfect mould that shaped my early years. It ran parallel with the railway for most of its length and ended facing, what all Bridgetonians regarded as the portal of paradise, 'Celtic Park'.

My first impression as we walked was of the bright looking houses on the other side of the road. Unlike the tenements, they were built from grey stone blocks and, excluding the ground floor, were only two storeys high. The ground floor also had a garden girded by an iron fence. We had walked no more than three minutes from our close and yet here was an area that was astonishingly stark in its contrast to the tenements What kind of people lived here I wondered. There then followed an unbroken stretch, which, as you looked along it from my position, seemed to be endless. Suddenly, as if from nowhere, a short distance ahead, I could see the tall slim figure of my dad standing with outstretched arms, his hands beckoning me to run. Needless to say, and with a gentle push from my mum, I took off. As I reached him he grabbed me from a semi-kneeling position and with one unbroken movement he had me off the ground and sitting high on his left arm. I threw my arms round his neck and hugged him, to which he responded with an affectionate tickle. As my excitement ebbed I pulled back and stared at his grinning face. This seemed to make him grin all the more. It was only when he turned that I realised where we were standing.
"Ok, do yae want to see roon' the shop?" He asked.
Getting no response from me, my father paused to let me take it all in. My eyes were darting everywhere. We were standing in front of a tall alcove entrance, which incorporated two steps leading in to the shop. It was flanked on either side by a pair of wooden doors. There were two display windows on either side of the entrance, which gave the shop an illusion of a very large frontage. One of the windows had a lot of glass jars containing small multi-coloured pieces that I

guessed to be sweets. Another window contained fruit and vegetables. The others I had no knowledge of. As I took in the full extent of its frontage I realised that the shop was made of wood and perfectly aligned with the sleeper fencing. It was as if they had removed a piece of the fencing and slotted in the shop. I remember thinking that it was so different from the tenement shops. It was beautiful and my dad owned it.

"Seen enough?" he asked, to which I nodded my head with a grin. He then remarked that I was a ton weight on his arm and put me down. We walked inside the shop. Directly facing us, as we entered, was a large glass display cabinet spreading across nearly half the length of the shop's floor space. It had four distinct cabinets each with their own special food display from bakery items on the one hand to cold sliced cooked items on the other. Stretching from the right end of the cabinet back to the front wall was a partition with a door in the middle, and to the left, also stretching back to the front wall, was the main serving counter.

We went through the partition door into what was the storeroom. The fruit and vegetable display window backed on to it. The walls were fully shelved and stacked with all manners of boxes and parcels. There was a small coal fire at the back of the store and to the left of this was a door leading to a small toilet and wash-up area which dad told me to use as required. Still holding on to his hand he took me along the passage behind the display cabinet where there was a strong smell of candy which I knew mum made and which I was a little partial to. The smell was strongest at the cheese and meat slicing area where there was still evidence of mum's latest effort scattered on the marble cutting slab. Dad prompted me to take one. We then walked round into where the main service counter stood. This was the most spacious part of the shop and it was here that most of the shop's wares were presented. Two of the outside display window backed on to this area and thus made it very bright and cheery. As if to utilise every bit of space the walls were almost wholly covered with shelving - all of them stacked with a multitude of labeled tins and packets that presented a very colourful backdrop. The serving counter had two small glass display cabinets, one at either end, between which there was also a selection of newspapers, magazines, and comics spread along its top.

For a while I was left to explore on my own. I applied myself to tracing the source of smells and helped myself to another candy ball on the way. I rubbed my hands across the labeled tins and playfully manipulated the colourful packaging. My reverie was only briefly disturbed by the departure of dad who was going off on business. A quick glance, however, confirmed mum to be nearby serving a customer. I went on from there to examine every nook and cranny and there were many. Mum eventually interrupted my exploration which, by this time, I felt that there was little else for me to discover. How wrong could I have been? Agnes, who had never been far away from me, took me by the hand with some purpose in mind. Mum then explained that there was another part of the shop that I had not seen yet and that Agnes was going to show me. Following this she was to take me over to meet Granny and Granda, who were expecting us for tea.

Outside, I asked Agnes where we were going. She said that she was going show me around the back of the shop and that she had a surprise for me. We turned right and paused where the railway fencing butted on to the end of the shop. Agnes produced a key and unlocked a padlock hanging from one of the sleepers. She folded back the clasp and pushed on the sleeper, which was bound to the one on its right and cut through some twelve inches from the ground. It swung inwards like a door. Agnes stepped up and into the opening then turned, grabbed both my hands and pulled me up beside her. Almost immediately I was confronted by a dog that gave out a couple of loud barks that startled me. It was tethered by a chain fixed to the ground in front of a wooden kennel. The chain was long enough to allow it to walk around with some freedom but not enough to reach where we were standing. "Don't be frightened, now", Agnes said. "He's our guard dog. His name is Major. He's very friendly when he gets to know you". She demonstrated this by walking straight up and fondling it.

"You're a nice boy, Major, aren't you?" She then took a biscuit from her pocket and held it out to him. He gently took it from her hand and scoffed it. He followed this up with much licking of his mouth and clearly looking for another. She placed another biscuit in my hand.

"Go on, give it to him. He won't bite"

I had never been confronted by a dog before and was more than a bit timorous. But I was greatly assured by Agnes's confident fondling of him and decided to try it. I stepped forward and offered the biscuit to him. He paused for a moment then gently took it from my hand. The next thing I knew he was licking off the few crumbs left behind. My confidence was now high so I stroked his head and fondled him round the neck.

"We hiv another dog." Agnes said. "He's tied up roon the back. Dae yae want to see him?"

I eagerly agreed to this and followed her. Major tried to follow but was restrained by the length of his chain. He sat down and gave a bark as if to show his disappointment. We walked round the back and towards the other end of the shop.

"His names is Kruger," Agnes said as we came up to him. "He's also a lot older than Major"

He was spread out as if enjoying the sun as we came up to him but showed his age his age as he struggled to his feet. He was a dark brown and much larger than Major. He also looked very heavy and docile as if any kind of movement would not be easy for him. Agnes gave him a biscuit, which he took with no great eagerness.

"He's Granda' s favourite. But he says he's gettin' too auld and should be put doon. But daddy's against that. He wants him to go to the kennels."

I had trouble getting the gist of what Agnes meant by the kennels and thought of having her explain more. Instead I gave Kruger a few generous pats on the head whilst he just panted and looked on dolefully.

As we walked back I looked round the surrounding area. Everywhere I looked the ground seemed to be set out in squares formed by railway sleepers lying on their side. There also seemed to

be a variety of vegetation growing in these squares at varying height.
I asked Agnes what they were.

"They're plots" she answered.

"What is a plot?"

"They're pieces of ground where you grow vegetables in, like
carrots, turnips, an' other things."

"And does all this belong to dad as well as the shop?"

"Don't be daft. All this land b'langs to the railway, and the railway
rents the land oot to people as plots for growing their vegetables."
Do the railway rent the land out to dad for his shop?"

"Ah don't know aboot that." she answered "Ah only know aboot
plots. Now let's get yae over to see Granny an' Granda, an' get yer
tea."

By now, I was very taken by Major, who did not seem to mind me
holding one arm round his neck, and fondling his ears with the other.
"Can we take Major with us?" I asked. To which there was an almost
instant no!

The sharpness of her answer resigned me to it as being final. It had
no sooner been said, though, than it was reversed.

"Ok, we'll take him with us." she said.

She unfixed his chain and coiled the end of it round her hand. The
sleeper door was still open so, taking me by the hand, she persuaded
me to jump backwards on to the ground. It was not so difficult and I
enjoyed it. Still holding on his chain Agnes jumped down, followed
by a very eager Major. As we walked past the shop mum spotted us
and came to the door. Spotting my affection for Major, she urged
Agnes to let me share her hold on the chain and promised that I
could take charge of Major when I was a bit older. We were then
told to get ourselves over the road in case Granda' got impatient
waiting for us.

Directly facing the door of the shop was number 40 Kinnear Road.,
with its very tidy looking close. Not far to the left of this was the
next close, which sat directly on the corner of Sorn Street, and on the
opposite corner of Sorn Street, was Granda and Granny's house.
Agnes pointed out these landmarks by way of telling me where we
were going and how near it was. The houses on Granny's side of

Sorn Street were very different from its other side. They were built four to a block with two houses upstairs and two below. The entrance to the Lower House was at the side of the block and, being a corner block, it had it's own garden.

As I later learned, all of the housing in Kinnear Rd. was fairly new and promised to be the new face of Glasgow housing. A promise that was never fulfilled.

Dad - just waiting for the rush

In their best bib and tucker

Chapter II

My New World

The Family

The Shop

Granny and Granda

My New Pals

My first School

My New World - Granny and Granda

In walking over to Granny's house we took the most direct line to the far corner of Sorn St.. This made it appear to me as if we were more walking along the centre of the road than across it. Agnes picked up on me looking backwards by way of checking for oncoming traffic and quickly assured me that Kinnear Road was never noted for its traffic. Except for football supporter buses on a Saturday, only a few horse-drawn vans or carts and the occasional motorised van would stop each day at the shop to deliver fresh bread and other sundries as ordered. To further emphasise her view, she added that there was only one person in the whole of Bridgeton who owned a car and that was Walter McLaughlen, daddy's friend. In her view the quickest thing that moved around here were boys playing football in the street after school hours.

The front gate was lying open. Granny must have seen us coming as she was standing at the door waiting to greet us as we came along the path. She was a small lady but with an ample girth and prominent bosom. She wore a fulsome blouse and wide skirt that clearly had seen better days. They were partly covered, though, by a fresh looking pinny that looked straight out of the wash. Her jovial face and bright eyes were irresistible and made you feel at ease with her.
"Ah see yae've brought Major with yae. He's quite taken wi' yae, isn't he? He's a good dug. Yae look efter 'im"
With that she bent over, not far, and gave me a hug. As she pulled herself up she left me with a strong whiff of alcohol. With a slight gait in her walk she led us into the living room via a narrow lobby.

My first sight of Granda was of him sitting in his armchair by the fireside whilst lighting his pipe with a lit match cupped in his right hand. His mouth emitted puffs of smoke as he sought to bring it alight and it was not until it was fully operational, signalled by a long final puff, that all was well in the world. At which point he stood up and smiled down at me. He was not much bigger than Granny but had muscular looking shoulders that were slightly rounded by the toll of labours past. My abiding memory of him was of this moment in time. He stood there with a floppy cap moulded to his head by years of usage, and an unbuttoned waistcoat, with drooping pockets, that gave shape to an oversized shirt that required arm bands to control the length of its sleeves. Even his pipe had to be different. It was a clay pipe whose stem was broken, not by accident, to half its natural length. This was in order to bring the bowl, held in a down position, closer to the chin. I have always believed that he lifted pipe smoking to an art form. It also appeared to me that it must have been a masochistic pleasure as could be evidenced by the stained blotch on the left side of his chin.

"And how's wee John dae'n", he asked. The referrence to my height was a common term of affection in Glasgow, and not insulting.

"I'm fine, thanks, Granda."

"God, disnae he sound posh, mither?" he said to Granny. "They must hiv taught 'm well in that hospital. Ah see yae've got to know the dug. Take that chain off" he said to Agnes, " an' give'm here."

On being released, Major immediately sidled up to Granda and sat down beside his chair. I remember being greatly pleased at the empathy between them.

"Com'n sit doon an' hiv yer tea ", said Granny, pointing to the table at the window. "You sit here, John, an' yae can see everything that's go'n oan. A've done yae both chopped eggs 'n butter. Is that ok?" To which Agnes and I reassured her. "There's also bananas there if John wants wan. Or, he can hive a piece 'n 'rhubarb jam', if he likes." The latter was to become Granny's speciality.

The view from the window looked diagonally across to the shop and along Kinnear Road towards Baltic St. I was absolutely mesmerized by the vista and the to and fro of people around the shop. My trance was only disturbed by the intermittent bidding of Agnes to eat up, which I did, but slowly. It was finally broken by the sound of the front door being opened and by Major responding with a bark for which he was loudly told to be quiet by Granda.

"It's only Harry", said Granny, struggling to stand up as he entered the room. "You've probably come back fir this", she said to him, brandishing a leather pouch in his face, a gesture that did not seem to please him. I quickly looked at Agnes for reassurance only to find her looking askance at him. On becoming aware of our presence his mood changed and he smiled at me.

"How's it goan, wee man?" he asked.

"Fine, Uncle Harry".

He came forward and gave my hair a ruffle, and that seemed to end his interest in me. I could sense that all was not well but, in the absence of any guidance from Agnes, I tried to ignore it and returned to my window viewing feeling a bit anxious. The exchanges between Harry, Granny, and Granda continued and would, I think, have become quite heated had Agnes and I not been there. There was one incident where Harry tried to move Major aside with his foot and provoked a growl from him. But for an intervening warning from Granda, "touch that dug an' yae'll answer to me", Major may well have received a smack. It did surprise me at this point that Agnes made no effort to have us leave. It later transpired that she was afraid to leave in case it gave offence and further provoked him.

Agnes later expanded on the detail of Uncle Harry's confrontation when she explained the incident to mum and dad, who were not too pleased at my being exposed to it. The gist of it was that Harry had borrowed money from Granny, his mum, to pay an overdue bill to the "Evening Times Newspaper Office" in order to prevent his supply being cut off. He ran a newspaper stand on a busy corner of Dalmarnock Road and he knew that if, for any reason, he missed out on his supply, on any day, there were others who would jump in and take it over. If this were to happen he would lose his livelihood and his neighbourhood standing with the local heavies. And as to the reason for his shortfall. he had been doing a bit of business in his local pub and like all good businessmen he had to be seen to be generous to his friends.

Eventually Harry left with his pouch, the news vendor's sporran, but not before he made one final low-key address to Granny and Granda. He felt affronted at being given a "showing up in his own house" in front of a wean and this offended his pride.

He had no sooner gone than the atmosphere was restored and Granny and Granda continued with their pleasantries towards me and Agnes, but especially me. Eventually, Agnes let it be known that Daddy would be back in the shop, that the schools would be out shortly, and that either she or mum would have to be getting home to receive May from school. As we walked back to the shop we could see the first of the school kids returning from school. They were the early release juniors and mostly of my age or younger.

Agnes with Granda and Granny

Chapter II

My New World

The Family

The Shop

Granny and Granda

My New Pals

My first School

My New World - My New Pals

On returning to the shop we were greeted by Dad who had returned from his business meeting with Walter McLaughlen. Agnes returned Major to his kennel whilst I eagerly rejoined mum and dad. The shop was a little busy with the younger kids returning from school. They were mostly accompanied by their parents, which, with a bit of nagging, gave them a high expectancy of some sweets. As dad said, this was only the calm before the storm, as the elder ones would only be half an hour behind them. From the security of behind the counter I found it all very exciting and also felt a sense of importance. Mum had by now put on her coat and was clearly ready to leave which made me a little disappointed. She then advised me that Agnes was staying on for a while to help dad out with the busy period, and that she was going home to prepare dinner for the family. I had a choice of coming home with her, or following on with Agnes. My first urge was to go with her but I was so excited by all the shop activity and the attention I was getting that I decided to stay on.

Most of the parents were fully aware of who I was and were very warm in their welcoming words and gestures. There were lots of good natured banter, most of which went right over my head, such as "welcome to the land of the living"; "welcome to the real world"; "wait 'till our Tommy gets his hands on you, he'll teach you a thing or two"....... More meaningful to me, though, were those of my age who, mostly urged on by their parents, thrust out their hand and invited me to shake it.....My name's Joe, my name's Jimmy, my name's Annie.....I felt marvellous......These were to be my new pals. Slowly the comings and goings of customers eased and the shop went quiet. This was the promised calm. At Dad's behest Agnes opened a bottle of irn bru and poured us all a glass of 'ginger'. Dad then stood a box on its end, close to the display window and lifted me on to it. There would shortly be a lot of hustle and bustle with the older school children and he thought it would be better if I sat to the side of the main serving area of the counter. Agnes also told me to call out if I spotted anyone trying to steal anything. This made it sound as if the shop was going to be assaulted yet they were both smiling and showing no concern. Looking out of the window I could see the first arrivals; a small group of boys with schoolbags on their back. There was a bit of pushing and shoving between them but they were clearly enjoying themselves. Moments later we had the first arrivals in the shop. Everyone seemed to be talking at the top of their voice. There was a bit of a commotion at the counter as they competed to be served first. Sweets, especially the home made candy balls, and cake had the greatest demand followed by drinks. The fruit machine was also popular with the older boys. It was operated by coins, called checks, which you purchased at the rate of five for a penny. Any winnings or unused checks could only be exchanged for goods in the shop. It all got very lively. But there was only one instance where Dad had to warn two lads for being over physical. Any more of it, he warned, and they would be outside.

The odd question was thrown at dad regarding who I was. By and large, though, they were too engrossed in their own fun to take any notice of me. The excitement of it all was very infectious and I could feel myself being caught up in their fun. It was not to last, though. Just as suddenly as it began, it ended. Having got what they wanted the noise started to move outside. Soon there were only three of them crowded round the fruit machine in the corner. There was a noisy, final pull on the lever, three light thuds as the rings came to a halt, and with a final bang on the machine with a hand to ensure that their feelings were made known, they left.

"Yae enjoyed, that, didnít yae?" said dad, to which I nodded and grinned. "Ok, Agnes, get yerselves off. Yer mither might be needing a haun. I'll see yae later, John, ok?"

I took Agnes's hand and we set off back home. As we left the shop a game of football was getting under way. We paused at the sleeper gate to allow me to have a peek at Major. I called to him and got two loud barks in return.

Lookin' fur someone tae play with

Chapter II

My New World

The Family

The Shop

Granny and Granda

My New Pals

<u>My first School</u>

My New World - My First School

My memory of those early days after leaving Mearnskirk are fairly clear, especially those pointed up by events that were to be milestones in my life. I remember well the constant excitement caused by the freshness of each day and the new experiences it brought. My driving need was to absorb this new knowledge; to understand it and be at one with my brothers and sisters. It was an enormous learning curve from which there seemed to be no escape. It was as if I had crossed over a bridge that took me from one life into another. I remember thinking that I must not forget what went before and that I must not close down this crossing.

I quickly settled into the daily routine of the family. Mornings in particular were always hectic and I was an addition to this routine. To ease the situation it was decided that, just prior to dad leaving to open the shop, I would be wakened and made to take his place in bed. This allowed Dad to close the kumfynite and thus clear the floor in readiness for the rest of the family to do their morning chores. Agnes would always be the first to appear by which time mum had already washed and spruced herself up. After two or three follow up calls to May and Bert they would trek in bleary eyed. Bill, who went to the secondary school, would always be the first to leave. Bert and May, after much persuasion, would eventually get themselves off and Agnes would leave to join dad in the shop. Occasionally I would join her, but mostly I would stay in the company of mum while she pursued her many and varying activities.

A week or so into this daily routine, I was told by mum that I would soon be going to school, just like May and Bert. I was overjoyed at this as it made me feel more at one with them. It also promised to answer my need to know what school was all about. I had seen the daily fun and games and what they got up to on their way home and I wanted to be part of this.

My New World - My First School

Intuitively, mum calmed me down by further telling me that I would not be going to the same school as May and Bert. This did take me aback, and whilst still pleased with the prospect, it was tinged with a feeling of isolation. She quickly sought to restore my excitement by explaining the reason for my going to a different school, and that I would make just as many friends there as anywhere else. The explanation given was that because of my long stay in hospital I had lost three years schooling and hence I needed to go to a special school that would help me to deal with this. The normal starting age for school was four and I was seven.

As an added uplift she told me that we were going to visit the new school that day and that the school was located in Burnside. A very posh area she stressed with a knowing look that was meant to impress me. We had an appointment to meet the headmaster at ten o'clock. He would take us for a tour of the school and would also explain 'things' in more detail. She convinced me that I was going to a very special school and my original excitement returned.

We walked down Nuneaton Street and turned right on to Dalmarnock Road. We made our way to the same tram stop we had alighted from some ten days previous. Soon I could see a tram coming towards us and as it slowly came to a halt Mum prompted me to try and read its destination sign. Relying on the limited reading skill acquired at Mearnskirk, and prompted by the preknowledge of where we were going, I confidently answered her.

"I think it says Burnside"

"Well done" she said as we boarded the tram, "an' remember it'll always be red".

The journey only took some fifteen minutes. But being the first of many to come, my mother thought it important to reassure me that I was on the right tram by pointing out a few landmarks such as crossing over the Dalmarnock bridge with the river Clyde below; and the tram stop at the start of Rutherglen High Street, which was the halfway point of the trip. From there it was straight up Stonelaw Road to the beginning of Burnside High St. where we got off.

On leaving the tram we turned left, away from the High Street, and almost immediately we came on to Greystone Avenue going off to the right. Directly facing and stretching along the Avenue was Burnside School. Its length was fronted by a low wall, topped by railings, and divided in the middle by twin ornate gates. As we walked through the open gates we were confronted by a large building, referred to as the great hall, which sat at the top of a gradient that sloped down towards the gates. The hall was flanked on both sides by five ground level classrooms. All of the classrooms were facing south and fronted by concertina doors that led on to a boardwalk. Being a bright sunny day some of the doors were fully open making the classrooms visible. Fronting the classes to the right of the great hall I could see camp beds spread out on the boardwalk. Shades of Mearnskirk, I thought.

A Nun, who said she was expecting us, met us at the entrance to the hall. I had previous exposure to Nuns in the hospital and was therefore comfortable in her presence. Mum, on the other hand, seemed to behave a little unnaturally and treated her with exaggerated respect. With a friendly smile, that never seemed to leave her face, she introduced herself as Miss Lawson.. She had been appointed to show us round the school and explain its amenities and procedures.

The great hall was the main assembly area for morning prayers and other pronouncements pertaining to the whole school. It also doubled as a dining room at lunchtime and a gymnastic area for PT classes. There were other occasions when it provided extended class space for art and other school affairs. To the back of the hall was the teachers' rest room, the storeroom, and the headmaster's office. She then led us back out of the hall and halfway back to the gates where she turned and proceeded to explain the rest of the school as it fronted on to us.

The area facing on to the classrooms was the playground, which was sectioned into two areas. To the right of the hall was the junior's play ground, and to the left the senior's. To prevent bullying and other unwanted accidents this separation was enforced at playtime. Classes were graded one to ten starting from the far right and ending at the far left. Your position in the school was related to your class. She then turned to face the outer wall and the garden area backing on to it. Great care had to be taken not to intrude on this area, she said forcibly but still smiling. Also, she added, with the exception of pupils in class 10, and those who had been given special permission, it was forbidden for anyone to leave the grounds during school hours. Mum and Miss Lawson then dropped into a conversation that gave scant attention to my presence. I therefore turned away from them and dropped into my own dwam.

I took in the span of the playground. At its widest It had a small circular flower bed surrounded by bench seats. My exaggerated memory was one of great space. My primary interest however was focused on the classrooms laid out side by side in a straight line before me.

One of them had its concertina door fully opened and the pupils sitting at their desks were clearly visible. The teacher with a pointer in her hand could be heard calling out questions to them that resulted in a few hands being

thrust in the air to gain her attention. There was also the
murmuring noise from the other classes that confirmed
their part in this exciting view of tomorrow. My captivation
was disturbed by mum taking me by the hand and guiding me
back towards the hall. We were reminded by Miss Lawson
that we must not be late for our appointment with the
headmaster.

Being still absorbed in my playground musing I paid little
attention to the headmaster as he warmly introduced himself
to Mum. He obviously noticed this and with a well-practiced
manner he brought me to attention with a request for my
impressions of the school. As if to hide any shortcomings
mum answered for me. She assured him that I was very much
looking forward to starting school and prompted me to agree
with her which I duly did.

He then went on to outline his plans for my future schooling.
He stressed that every effort would be made to help me try to
recover those missing years of learning. As he elaborated on
this he made it sound as if it was all going to be very, very
difficult for me. He also emphasised that, whilst hopeful that I
would succeed, at no time would pressure be put on me to do
so. My health and wellbeing, he opined, were more important
to him than academic goals. This seemed to please mum, but
it had a very dulling affect on my previous excitement. It was
further dulled by the contribution of Miss Lawson, who let it
be known that in my first year, as per the Medical Guide
Lines, I would be required to rest for one hour in the course of
the morning. This, she added, was in keeping with my
previous protocol and would aid my concentration. Shortly after
this we took our leave and made our own way home.

On the way mum, in her roundabout way, kept prompting me to

reassure her that I was happy with my new school and that I would work hard. Needless to say I did.

Chapter III

Learning to Cope

The Backcourt

Window on the World

My Gang

Cinemas everywhere

The Shop and Christmas is near

Christmas at Home

Learning to Cope - The Backcourt

My first visit to the Backcourt was on a Saturday (wash day in our house). I had tried on a few occasions to view our courtyard from the back window but it meant me lying across the sink unit with my head barely reaching the window sill and holding on to the window with a clenched fist-like grip. My curiosity could well have been the death of me but for the dire warning of mum that I was never to do this again. I could, of course, see all the other back courts spreading away from me in a diminishing view; each one sectioned off by a brick wall and accessed from two closes - three if it was a corner location. From the rear of our close my first impression of the courtyard was one of dirt and grime everywhere. Yet, in stark contradiction, newly washed sheets, gleaming white, together with an assortment of clothing, hung from ropes tightly strung from metal poles.

The surface of the yard had somewhere in its past been covered by tarmacadam. Usage and weathering over the years, aided by the minimalist approach to maintenance by the Council, had made it heavily potholed and the source of many skinned knees and hands. This was an everyday hazard of Backcourt games and other youthful ventures that provoked many a tear, and many a laugh. It was at its direst, though, when it rained, as the potholes would fill with water and thus disguise the deeper ones that could take you by surprise and bring you down. Also, with lasting periods of rain, some of the puddles would merge to form bigger ones. At such times mysterious colours would also appear in the puddles, generating many idle discussions and questions among us young ones. A more informed reason for this phenomenon was that the rust and other chemicals being washed down the tenement walls from the iron drainpipes and aging lead flashings were introducing these prismatic colours. Only at its worst, accompanied by the direst of warnings from your parents, would you be fully deterred from using the Backcourt in these conditions. Even then, aided and abetted by your 'wellies', it would still be used as a shortcut to bypass the corner.

Our wash house, which prided itself in capturing and dispersing all the most topical gossip in Bridgeton, stood in the far right hand corner of the yard. From the outside it looked much like its surroundings with signs of much needed repair. But inside, especially when in use, it had a warm fresh smell of linen and soap powder. Unlike the Backcourt, though, its floor was made of concrete whose surface had been polished over the years by the to-ing and fro-ing of feet and the frequent use of a soft brush prior to use. Its Spartan washing amenities consisted of a large copper bowl set into a semi rounded brick construction, and double porcelain sink bowls separated by a wooden beam that supported a heavy-duty mangle. Fresh tap water was available only at the sinks and hence had to be transported by the bucket to fill the copper bowl. Heating of the water was by means of a coal or wood fire grate located below the centre of the bowl and guarded on the outside by a small iron door.

Use of the wash house was based on a loosely formed rota between the neighbours and of course each one had to bring their own share of the coal. It also befell the first user to light the fire which, in our case, according to mum, was always carried out by wee Peggy who lived in the close. She revelled in the popularity and status it gave her, which was no small thing. She was not slow, though, in letting her own coterie of neighbours know of the machinations and 'fallings out' that took place between those of other back courts over this very sensitive issue.

Wash day was hard work but for a few its reward came in the deportment of their clothesline. The need to show your neighbours that you kept your family clean was of dire importance. Whilst taking care to play it down, pointing up a selected garment was one of many conversational devices used to promote attention. Noticeably, Mum and Agnes were not above this hurt game. Pride, however, would never acknowledge any offence - none given, none taken. This was the great norm at work, where one always knows their place in life and hence works all the harder to improve it. If a neighbour couldn't handle the exposure then they had the option of taking their wash to the 'steamy' where the gossip was even spicier.

A showpiece in its day, the steamy would provide unlimited supplies of steaming hot water at the end of a tap feeding into large copper cauldrons. Here you could scrub-board your clothes or pole and swish them around with such ease that even the kids accompanying their mothers would take part. In addition to this they provided large bulbous drums in to which you transferred your steaming wash and, at the press of a button, would spin your clothes to extract most of the water and leave them in a moist manageable state. A washerwoman's dream. She could even bring and take it away in the privacy of her own wash basket on wheels, or wrapped up in one of her own sheets and carried on her back. But, like all of life's pleasures not provided by nature, it cost money.

Our back court also shared a degree of status with others around Bridgeton, on the grounds of its suitability for secure 'bookmaking' - three closes that could provide access and exit on to two streets. It allowed the 'Bookie' to post his lookout on the corner and so give himself an early warning of a police raid from either Baltic St., or Nuneaton Street. The legality of street bookmaking in Glasgow was never in doubt, and never questioned. Even the Bookies were more than happy to pay their fines on the few occasions they were caught. What was in doubt though, and what most punters took issue with, was the need for such a law in the first place. Self evidently, Bookies were part of the social order of Backcourt life. They provided a means and hope of overcoming the need for careful money management which at best only provided a modicum of security and a great deal of stress. Who, or what else, could provide the exciting hope and titillating pleasure of a winning double, or better still, a treble, and the orgasmic joy when you pulled it off! On such a day all things were possible. In your mind's eye the Backcourt would become an arena of windows cheering your triumph. Who then were these council nincompoops, these bureaucrats, those dispensers of laws, who would deprive a tenement dweller of these brief moments when all was well in the world? For goodness sake, even your granny would tell you that if you lost, you had only yourself to blame. So why the deprivation?

Our Bookie was a portly little man with a warm smile and a wealth of one liners that went down well with the punters - a classic patter merchant. In quiet spells he would selectively endear himself to the more curvaceous neighbours. Mum and Agnes were always taken by his patter and thought well of him. For myself, I always enjoyed the fun and banter of the Backcourt on a Saturday morning. There were always lots of kids around playing games; climbing walls; having mock fights; laughing at their own jokes. It was a great learning experience.

Learning to Cope - The Backcourt

On that particular morning (my first) I remember the sudden appearance of a mouse scurrying around the court yard trying to escape from the frenzied chase by a few older boys who were kicking and stamping at it with every intention of ending its life. I later learned from experience that mice were not uncommon in the tenements and that the inevitable demise of this poor thing was one less to trouble us. In this case, it was an event that was to be swiftly resolved by the arrival of a neighbour's cat. Soon, it would be just another contribution to the dirt and grime, and the smell of the tenements.

I must admit that I positively detested the little beasts.

Mum on the left earning a few extra pennys

Chapter III

Learning to Cope

Learning to Cope - Window on the World

In my early youth winter evenings were incredibly boring in a tenement dwelling. Bill and Bert, in age, schooling, and experience, always seemed to me much older than their years, and hence we were never close. When not out with their pals, what little conversation we had was mostly intended to remind me of what I was not doing, or should be doing, and nearly always with self interest in mind. May, on the other hand would willingly play with me, but only at such times as when Agnes was not around. Outside of school hours she seldom strayed from Agnes, whom she seemed to hold in awe. In any case she was uncomfortable in my company because, she said, I asked her too many questions. As for Agnes, unless directed otherwise by mum, she would be out and about with her friends most evenings. The word from mum was that she was wynching. When I asked Agnes if it was true that she was wynching and what it meant, a bout of woefully-concealed giggling would ensue together with nonsensical denials that more confused than explained.

Dad was seldom at home before 9 o'clock. He would normally have his dinner brought round to him in the shop. His closing time was flexible but was usually close to 7 o'clock, at which time he would join his friend Walter for a drink in Walter's own bar just round the corner in Nuneaton Street. As mum would say, after all the long hours he worked he deserved his wee drink with his friends. Mum was more than a little partial to a wee drink herself and would often share a 'cerry oot' brought home by dad. Early evenings, though, she would either spend with a neighbour, or by the fireside fondly knitting one of her less than perfect garments while listening to the radio.

Knitting was a great source of pleasure to her despite having no control over the size or shape of the finished garment. I became more than a little familiar with this blind art by her frequently asking me to read out the instructions from a pattern taken from a magazine. No doubt a pair of glasses would have relieved me of this task, but pride and cost would never permit the thought. She would, for example, meticulously count the number of plains and purls on the knitting needle when starting a sleeve yet, the resulting sleeve would randomly vary in width along its length.

Length was also a problem. She would know full well the number
of rows from the pattern but such would be her contentment that
she would knit past it. When finished, her reassurance that all was
well, was to grip both sleeves together by their end, give them a
good stretch, and then visually check that they matched. Yet, when
clearly visible that they did not match in the assembled garment,
she would dismiss the problem with humorous aplomb.
"It wulnae be noticed", she would say. "It's goat a nice shape; an'
jist look at the colours Peggy wull luv it".
To be fair to her, she did get a lot of praise for her skill from the
neighbours, especially those who had supplied the wool.
"Ah really don't know how yae cin dae that, Aggie", they would
say. "A've git nae patience at aw' fur knittin'."
Left to my own thoughts, I would spend my evenings in the front
room looking out of the window searching for anything new or
interesting. I always began by scanning the facing tenement
windows for activity. Most of their lights would be switched on
and, like our own, the curtains were seldom drawn. Hence, apart
from skimpy netting on the lower part of some windows, the inside
of houses at eye level and below were very visible. To avoid being
seen by neighbours, who would also be looking out for anything
new, our light would be left off. The window would also be partly
lifted so that I could hear the window gossip and the noise from the
streets. A few of the street shops would still be open, as would the
bars that never closed till 9 o'clock. There was always a busyness
about the street - like an event waiting to happen.
The corners of Nuneaton St and Mordaunt Street had their regular
corner boys, groups of local youngsters laughing and joking;
pushing and shoving; shouting to make themselves heard. As I was
to quickly learn, the only way to make your point to a corner gang
was first, make your opening statement louder than anyone else,
then talk as quickly as you can to keep their attention. If this verbal
bullying failed to get your point over then a bit of self righteous
pushing and shoving could ensue which usually ended with a push
too far. This of course would be an attack on your dignity and status
which needed to be defended. A few "yeh's", would be followed by
"Go oan! Go oan! Try it. Try it. Yae couldnae bust a paper bag!"
More often than not it would end with one of the more ranking guys

yelling at them to shurrup and deriding them as a couple of bampots.

Occasionally, though, depending on their ranking or just from nothing better to do, the gang would shout them on to have a go, and so their pushing and shoving would extend into posturing with raised fists. Moving around each other they would throw the occasional punch and miss which would elicit a few sarcastic jibes and cause one of the gang to elbow them closer. Eventually, more by luck than intent, one of them would land a hit. Instant retaliation would be a rush and grab to smother any further hits. They would then grapple each other to the ground egged on by the gang. Ultimately, it would either end in stalemate with each grudgingly shaking each other's hand. Occasionally it would go too far and a proper fight would ensue. More often than not, though, it would be noticed from one of the windows above and before it could develop a troop of women would appear causing a quick dispersion. By way of a reminder that fighting would not be tolerated the two assailants would get a verbal lashing and a warning that their parents would hear of it.

Going on 9 o'clock the Bars would start to empty. The forerunners of the final exodus would be typified by the hurried exit of a few people. Some of them would be running with the forlorn aim of making amends for a broken promise to the wife or girl friend - age made no distinction. Then there would the one who knew when he'd had enough. He would always start out with his shoulder close to the wall in the direction of home. Inevitably his shoulder would get too close too the wall quickly causing a diagonal nudge, push, or bounce, appropriate to the impact, towards the outside edge of the pavement. He was clearly practiced in this, for with rapid stamping of his feet and a controlled transfer of his weight directed inwards by his shoulders he would soon find himself heading back in the direction and safety of the wall. Thus, he would weave his way home.

Then there was the chanter. His head would always be upright, his eyes ever searching to make contact and his hand waving to an audience clearly visible in his mind. It was the utter fulfillment of his vocal talents made possible by a wee drink and an immense repertoire of Glasgow's best.

"You name it, an' ah'll sing it!" At such times he knows that he could have made it.

When things went quiet in the streets I would again return to browsing the windows. There was one occasion when I saw a lad, not much younger than me, receiving a right skelping from his father. I remember cringing and felt that I wanted to help him. His screaming, I'm sure, could be heard in the street. But when I looked no one appeared to hear it. I later told mum about it and asked if anything could be done. She said she knew who I was talking about and that she had no doubt that he deserved it. She gave me a hug to assure me and added, "Dinnae fuss yersel' wi such things".

Sometimes, especially at weekends, I would be allowed to stay up later than usual. As a consequence I would often watch people, mostly of my age, strip and prepare themselves for bed. There was one night, though, when the light in the lower room directly facing me was unexpectedly switched on. I had never seen inside this room before and had assumed that I was always asleep at such times. A man and a woman entered the room. He started clutching her and she looked as if she was trying to free herself. They both looked highly excited and hurriedly took off their clothes. He then pushed her backwards on top of the bed. She looked agitated and seemed as if she was going to get back up when he kneeled on the edge of the bed and then lifted himself on top of her. He then started to make all sorts of frantic movements that made me feel as if they were fighting and that he was hurting her. Suddenly, I became aware of mum standing behind me. As my eyes were tuned to the dark I could see that she was smiling. She asked me what I was doing and I told her that I was watching this room and that I thought this man was hurting this woman. No they're not, she said, they're making love. As this meant absolutely nothing to me, I asked her why then was he hurting her. She tried to assure me that she was not being hurt and that she was actually enjoying herself. This answer was even more confusing. How could such physical abuse be enjoyable? As Mum was now insisting that it was past my bedtime I decided to put it aside with all the other things I could not understand. Strangely, though, the curtains on this window were always closed thereafter, as were a couple of other windows.

Chapter III

Learning to Cope

Learning to Cope - My Gang

Life has a pattern, mum used to say, and once you've learnt it, you know where you're going. This always sounded like a bit of nonsense to me. Or maybe it was a pearl analogous to her knitting, I thought. In any case it was too profound for me. Still, a pattern was emerging in my daily routine and I was getting a bit more confident. Walking up and down the tenement stairs and using the lavatory on my own was now an everyday affair. Also, going to and from school no longer required me to be escorted by mum or Agnes. Leaving for school in the morning in the company of Bert and May was a joy. With my schoolbag on my back and my tram fare in my pocket, sometimes with a penny on top, I would walk down Nuneaton Street with great aplomb - the world was going to school and so was I. My return from school was always an hour earlier than the juniors in the local schools in Bridgeton. But here also a pattern was emerging. I would first stop off at home to be rid of my schoolbag. Bread and jam, and sometimes fruit, would be laid out on the table with teacups. Either mum or Agnes would be on hand to pour the tea. This was always much appreciated and hurriedly scoffed, often on my way back out the door. The shop had now become my after-school domain and I could not get there quickly enough. On the way past our sleeper door I would call out to Major, or, if the door was open, I would go in and untie him and take him into the shop with me. We had become good friends and he would now readily sit at my bidding. Dad was always glad to see me. I was now his go-getter when he got busy. "Go get me a bottle of irn bru; go get me a tin of this; go get me a packet of that." I very quickly learned about everything that we sold and where it was displayed and stored. Dad was quite proud of me, especially as I was always at my post before the school rush. My reward, I think, was that occasional penny I got on top of my school tram fare. Not that I needed any reward for my enthusiasm knew no bounds.
The first time I met James Hargreave was on one such occasion. He came in to do some shopping for his mum shortly after the school rush. He was a bit older than I was but we took an instant liking to each other. While dad attended to his written list he introduced himself. Compared to most other schoolboys he sounded quite polite. He was curious as to why we had never met before. I explained that I had been in hospital for a while and that I was now

attending Burnside school instead of the local Sacred Heart which, he told me, was his school. He asked me to meet up across the road at number 40 after he had his tea, to which I readily agreed. "See you later John", he said, and went off with his bag of messages. "Yae've made a pal there, son", said dad, "he's very popular aroon here."

"Do you know him well, dad?" I asked.

"Yes, he's the son of one of ma best customers, Mrs. Hargreave." The shop went quiet, as was usual after the school rush, and I found myself checking the clock and counting down the minutes to my meeting with Frank. Dad was aware of my impatience, and by way of passing the time, he told me to take Major back to his Kennel and tie him up. On my return he gave me a small bag of candy balls and told me to share them with James. I thanked him and went and stood outside the shop door and gazed across at the close hoping not to be disappointed. Almost immediately I spotted him hurrying down the stairs at the back of the close. He didn't stop and came straight across and joined me.

"Whit dae yae wantae dae?" He asked. "Wantae play a game, or sh'll we go tae the swings?"

I told him I did not know any games and that we should maybe go to the swings, which he agreed. I told dad where we were going which was ok by him, but he stipulated that I must be back in time for dinner or mum would be out looking for me.

I shared out the candy balls as we walked down to the playground. The swings were fairly quiet so we were able to choose two swings side by side. This was my first time on a swing and my timidity showed.

"We'll hiv tae git yae up tae speed before the other guys get to yae, or yer in fur a bad time."

He got behind me and started to push - slowly at first, then, checking that I was ok, he increased it till I reached a comfortable height. He then mounted his own swing and from there he showed me how to control it myself. At the top of the back swing, he said, you stretch out your legs, lean backwards and then swoosh down. After a couple of tries I got the hang of it and got really excited by my success. I flattered myself that I was getting up to James's height when suddenly someone grabbed me on the way back and pulled me to a halt. It was Agnes, and she was not pleased with me.

"Daddy told yae tae be back on time fur dinner and now I've hid tae find yae an' take yae hame", she said.

I felt guilty and said that I would go now. I said goodbye to James and passed on the remainder of the candy balls to him. He was overly grateful and promised to meet up the following day at the same time. He would teach me to play jauries and moshie, he said, and introduce me to his brothers. I then followed a very sullen Agnes home.

In the following weeks James and I became very close. He even invited me upstairs to meet his family. His mum was a very friendly woman and asked me to stay for tea. I was a bit wary of this after my previous run in with Agnes. But Mrs. Hargreave reassured me by saying that she would go over to the shop and let dad know where I was. I sat down with James and his two younger brothers, Frank and Joe. In the course of our chatter, and with the help of Mrs. Hargreave, we established that James was ten months older than I was and that Frank was three months younger. As for Joe, well, he was only five. I was very much at one with the family and especially liked Mrs. Hargreave who made me feel so comfortable.

After tea we reassembled ourselves at the front of the close where we met Charlie Gillan. He lived in one of the two ground level houses whose entry doors were in the close. Dad appeared at the shop door and waved over to me. James glanced at me then the others and, for whatever reason I will never know, we all moved as one across the road to the shop. Each one politely said hello to dad, which he acknowledged with a grin. "Yae don't mind us hangin' aroon here, Mr. McBarron?" James asked.

"So long as yae don't obstruct the customers from comin' intae the shop", he jokingly replied.

At that moment, I think, the gang was formed. Soon, others who wanted to know what was happening and why we were hanging around the shop, joined us. I had come to know everyone of them by sight, but I still had little knowledge of them personally, nor did I know their names. It was a similar situation for them and hence, I became the centre of attention as they tried to get to know me.

Learning to Cope - My Gang

One of them, Archie Gemmil, was from Lilly Street. All the others, the Cloherty brothers, Mungo and Jackie, Joe O'Donnoll, John Lipton, and Charley Clark, were all from Sorn Street. We were all of a similar age group except John Lipton who stood out from the rest by his over confident manner and I guessed that he was much older than James. When he introduced himself he made a big play about us both being named John.

"Ah think that we'll nickname yae Barney. We canae hiv two of us named John", he added.

"But I don't want to be called Barney", I protested. "My name is John - after my dad."

Sensing I was being bullied, James intervened. "John disnae waant tae be called Barney, so why don't yae back off Lipton."

Mungo and Archie mockingly jeered at this on the grounds that Barney was an ok name. Pointing his finger at them James stared them down.

"You pair stay out of this", he said.

"C'mon, James, it's only a bit of fun", said Lipton. Everyone went quiet at this, which made me feel very isolated and wishing that I had not objected. But, in the weeks to come, mostly down to prompting jibes by Archie and Mungo, Barney it became.

As I came to know my new friends (my gang) a whole new world started to emerge. I found myself becoming competent in most street games such as peevers, jauries, moshie, rounders, and football. As each game was learned and practiced so it became compulsive and for periods would dominate my life. They each took on their own importance in accordance with the time of year, the weather, fashion, and who knows what. Competition could be fierce at times and could bring to the surface many unseen facets of our personalities. Even the placid James could get quite heated at times and, as for Frank, he always had to be the winner. Being smaller than the others I was never a natural competitor and so, by way of compensation, I tried to master he technical side of the games with a varying degree of success.

My early years in the gang taught me many lessons. Not least of these were that not one of us was alike. We had many common bonds and shared many common pursuits and pleasures but still we

differed. Strangely enough everyone seemed to take this for granted yet for me it was always a problem; I did not want to be different.
As the gang developed so likewise did the personalities; the talkers and the listeners; the clever and the dull; the strong and the weak; the leaders and the followers. From this, a gang ethic also emerged. The gist of it was that all things pleasurable were right and just, and all who disagreed were boring and stupid. Police and parents must be respected but, when intrusive, or ignorant of your rights, they should be ignored. Strength in numbers, a big family stronger than a small one. An early example of this was when Archie Gemmil asked me if I was a Billy or a Dan, or an aul' tin can? I don't understand I replied.
Lipton then shouted. "Ur yae a Proddy, or a Pape?" Followed by another. 'Ur you a Gers or a Celt? Although they were bullying me I think I was more bewildered than afraid. Besides, I felt the security of James close by.
"He's a catholic", James said. Then, looking at Lipton, he closed the subject with his own question. "You're a Proddy, like Archie, is thur any problem in that? Ok, so now yae know."

Chapter III

Learning to Cope

Learning to Cope - Cinemas everywhere

My first winter at home was now in full flow and another aspect of home life was about to unfold. With no longer having the diversion of school, owing to the seasonal closedown, daytime assumed a different pattern. Days no longer merged into night; they were now distinct entities. By day I found myself spending most of the morning in the shop trying to be a help to dad. There was always a buzz in the early morning shopping as the locals purchased their needs for the day. As dad pointed out morning shopping always started a little bit later when the schools were in recess. As the morning moved on and things quieted down James and Frank would usually show up and so as long it was ok by dad we would stand around blethering and sorting out our hopes and maybes for the afternoon. As others turned up we would move across the road to the close head. The shop was becoming a focal point and my new friends were beginning to expand..

However, as the light faded, so I had to be at home. It was now November and darkness was all-pervasive by 5 o'clock. By solstice it would be 4 o'clock. Given my age and experience this conjured up the prospect of many long evenings confined to home. Although I could have no true understanding of the causes, I was already aware of the discomfort of living in a tenement house when the whole family were present, such as dinnertime on Saturday and Sunday. Conflicts and frictions were now beginning to appear that previously had not been noticed. Also the license and protection that had been provided by my parents were now beginning to slip as I increasingly took control of my day to day activities. I was now expected to fend for myself in many areas and many emotional bumps and bruises from Bill, Bert, and Agnes were beginning to appear. The lack of space was the biggest problem. There were now fewer occasions when I was on my own. Even my window browsing in the front room was no longer practical owing to its increased usage by the rest of the family. Playing the odd game with May could be fun but such was her attachment to Agnes and mum that she preferred to seek and languish in their attention.
The beginnings of a wondrous solution to this malady were near at hand and I was about to have my first indulgence of it. Shortly after dinner one day I was sat pondering what to do. I repetitively scanned

through the newspaper in search of an interest and was now browsing through mum's magazine. She picked up on my boredom and sympathetically asked if I had nothing to do to which I dolefully nodded. She then looked over to Agnes, who was washing up the aftermath of dinner. "What picture's showin' at the Plaza today?" she asked.

"I'm not sure, but ah think it's a Gene Autrey fillum." Agnes replied.

"Ah think ah might jist take masel' roon there", Mum said.

"But ah thought yae didnae like cowboy fillums?" Agnes said with a smirk.

"That's true, but ah wis thinking of takin' someone who will", she said nodding over to me. "How wid yae like to go to the pictures, John?" she asked.

I stood up with obvious excitement. "You mean the Plaza?"to which she nodded with a big smile.

"Whit time is the furst hoose?" she asked Agnes.

"The back o' seven", she replied.

"Ok, John, we've got twenty minutes to get oorselves doon there. Give yer face a quick wash an' we'll be oan oor way"

We walked down Nuneaton Street with a hurried step. The Plaza, which was formerly known as the Dalmarnock, was a bit mystical to me. I passed it every day to and from school but on the other side of the road, and whilst I had heard others talk about the latest pictures being shown there, I always assumed that this was an adult pursuit and would therefore be of no real interest to me. Its colourful frontage, though, always fascinated me, and I always knew that one-day my curiosity would be satisfied - but not this soon. There was a small queue leading from the street upstairs to the ticket kiosk. This allowed me to look around and take in more closely the brightly coloured billboards and the framed pictures of extracts from the main film.

The ticket kiosk was flanked on either side by doors leading into the hall. As we walked through into the hall two usherettes met us with torchlights that were meant to illuminate your passage but, as the film had not yet started, the hall was fully lit. I stared down the long passage that flanked rows and rows of seats. This carried my eyes down to the bottom where a raised stage with drawn curtains at both ends. Filling the back of the stage was this enormous white screen bordered with a black band.

Thoughtful of my lack of height mum found us a seat just a short way back from the front row thus allowing me to look upwards at the screen and also prevented my view being obstructed by someone sitting in front of me. I was still gazing round this enormous hall when suddenly the screen lit up and the lights slowly dimmed and went out. There then appeared a series of meaningless images on the screen that made me think that it was breaking down. The screen stabilized and the film title appeared. After some other captions the film finally got under way.

I sat there absolutely entranced. Before that moment I had only seen images of cowboys in comics but now it was real. Gene Autrey was there, and I was following his every footstep, and living his every action. He was so athletic, full of verve and confidence; and so intelligent. His mind was always ahead of the intents and thoughts of the baddie; and justice would always be done and celebrated with a song. His voice had few equals in those memorable days. I was so immersed in the magic of it all that even the tub of ice cream given to me by mum was an intrusion on my reverie, though gleefully accepted. The film lasted for over an hour. There then followed another film which I later learnt was the "B" film, and always followed the main feature. This ran for not nearly as long as the Gene Autrey film but was almost as good - it was called "The Lone Ranger and Tonto". A black eyemask to shield his identity and his close Indian friend whose wisdom and talents made him stand above others. As it came to an end I partly stood up expecting to leave, but mum bade me to hold on and see the coming attractions. This turned out to be yet another form of excitement. They were excerpts from the films that were going to be shown in the Plaza over the coming weeks with emphasis on the one to be shown in the next three days. They really carried you along and left you with not the slightest doubt that you would be here next week to see it. As the lights came on everyone stood up and proceeded to push and shove their way to the exits.

"Haud own a bit an' we'll let them get clear", mum said.

My head was birling with a multitude of images many of which were unique and all of them exciting. This clearly shone from me as we

walked out on to Nuneaton Street. Mum looked at me with a self-satisfied smile on her face. "We'll do that again next week, ok?"
 I just beamed back and squeezed her hand. This was the beginning of many great pleasures in my life. Not least of them, and not long after my introduction to Gene Autrey and the world of cowboys and Indians, was to be my first pantomime, 'Dick Whittington and his Cat'. This was proposed by dad, who, on seeing and hearing of my great pleasure that evening, suggested it as one of his own great pleasures in early life.

I woke up late the following morning in a bed of dreams; I could not have been happier. I was still in a dreamlike state as I sat down to my tea and toast. Normally, I would have been helping dad in the shop by now but, like all good excuses, there must always be a time when the pleasure of dreams forcefully oppose the attractions of the day. I noticed Agnes coming in and whispering in mum's ear. Mum then came over and sat down facing me. She held a group of tickets in her hand, which she fanned out and slid them over the table to me. "I don't know how he's done it", she said, "but yer dad's managed to get four tickets fur the Pantomime at the Queen's Theatre on Saturday afternoon".
I was absolutely thrilled at the prospect of yet another adventure. "Who's going with us?" I asked.
"Yer dad 'n May", she replied.
This was fantastic. I sat there perusing every word on the ticket trying to extract every bit of meaning from it. The following few days were long days but Saturday did arrive.

We took the tram to Glasgow Cross, which I well remembered, from my coming home trip. Being a Saturday afternoon, the cross was hugely busy and with great care my parents escorted us across to the Gallowgate where the Queen's Theatre stood. Merged in with the shop fronts it looked surprisingly small. It was incredibly colourful, though, with its name above the entrance marked with large brightly-lit bulbs that, despite the daylight, made the fronting pavement glow. On either side of the entrance were glass-fronted pictures of scenes from the show. At this point, May and I were told by mum to hold each other's hand as we looked in wonder at the pictures. We were given some moments to take it all in before presenting ourselves at the entrance where the doorman checked the validity of the tickets presented by dad.

May and I just stood there absolutely aghast at what we saw. Before us lay this cavernous staircase that rose steeply from very little floor space. May and I had to crane our necks to see the top. As we started up May sought the greater security of mum's hand whilst I proceeded on my own in front of dad. At the top was the ticket office fronted with a placard showing that it was fully booked. On either side of the ticket office, just like the Plaza, were double swing doors leading into the theatre - the stalls. In addition to the doors there was also an open staircase leading to the balcony seats. We entered the theatre, which was fully lit, and were greeted by an usherette. She checked our tickets and led us half way down the passage where she directed us to our seats with her torchlight.

There was band music being played, which I quickly identified as coming from the front of the stage. In answer to my question dad pointed out the band sitting in front of the stage slightly below floor level and separated from the audience by a wooden balustrade. Dad said this was the orchestra pit. I gazed round the full width of the theatre. As I turned round and looked up I could see the rounded ornate frontage of the balcony just above us. The shapes and colours in the main hall were opulent. Balcony boxes protruded from the walls with two in particular looking directly down onto the stage. The colours were cream, gracefully contrasted with flashes of green, yellow and red, and generously gilded with gold. The stage curtains, as were those backing the balcony boxes, were lush red velvet. The whole thing was a visual joy.

The band stopped playing, and an atmosphere of hushed expectancy enveloped the hall. Suddenly, with loud upbeat tones the band launched itself with great gusto. Almost simultaneously the lights quickly dimmed and went out, the curtains slowly opened to reveal the cast in full regalia, shouting, and tumbling, singing, and dancing. The show had begun. What followed was an unforgettable experience of music and fun, combining to tell the enthralling story of Dick and his cat. But there was one magical excerpt that will always live with me; a mystery that I will never try to resolve. It was a scene where Dick got separated from his cat by some malicious intent of a conspirator. The pathos of his words expressing the loss of his beloved cat was instantly forgettable, but, the reunion with his cat, or rather the means of that reunion, was something else. Whilst delivering his grief stricken words his cat suddenly appeared through one of the exit doors close to the stage its every move tracked by a beam of light from somewhere in the roof. With incredible agility it jumped on the end of the stage close to the curtains. It stood back on its hind legs, gazed round the entranced audience with luminous eyes, and gave out a very audible 'I'm home again' purr. It then dropped back on all fours, turned, and sprang up the lower reaches of the curtain. Everyone started shouting with glee to Dick that his cat was back. Then, to the massive screeching of everyone, it ran straight up the curtain to the top, hung there, looked back at the audience and purred. We all screamed at Dick to notice. Then very slowly, as if hearing calls from afar he responded and started calling out to his cat, "where are you, where are you?" In response the cat started to crawl down the curtain. It was some two thirds of the way down when it paused, took one last look at the audience, and jumped on to the stage with gleeful applause from the audience. As it landed, however, it rolled over seeming to be hurt from a bad landing. This resulted in an audience silenced by concern. Dick of course was now beside his favourite cat but fearful that the landing was fatal. But with much stroking and tearful words the cat regained consciousness to great applause. To this day I still don't know how the cat climbed those curtains, let alone get down. What I do know, however, is that I cannot forget the excitement.

After the Gene Autrey experience I had, of course, shared my growing worldliness with James. To my astonishment he had not only been to the Plaza, he had been to many others which, he claimed, were not too far away from where we lived. For example, he said, there was the Strathclyde cinema which was far bigger than the Plaza. He and Frank often went there and it was only a five minute walk from where we stood in front of the shop. Seeing the disbelief on my face he insisted on walking me there to prove it. Look, he said, you can either walk to the top of Lilly St., or the top of Sorn St., and from there you cross the Springfield Rd, first right and your there. Come, I'll show you. I checked with dad that it was ok and we set off.

We chose to walk up Lilly St., as James said it was a wee bit closer. This again was a new adventure for me as I had never been to the top. Sure enough, though we had not walked for any length of time and we were there; and he was right, it was bigger. Its frontage was covered in light blue tiles with lots of glass fronted pictures of scenes from the current film being shown. James also said it had a gigantic balcony. I was absolutely enthralled by it all and on the way back I could not stop asking James questions. In response to this he launched into a glorious inventory of cinemas. In Bridgeton alone he said, we had the Plaza, the Strathclyde, and the Olympia at Bridgeton Cross. In addition to this we had the Arcadia in London Rd., and the Dan Doyle (The Royal) in Main St. Also, if you took the tram to Rutherglen High Street, (I passed it on the way to school), you had the Odeon, the Rio, and the Orient. James sounded so worldly, compared to me. "Glasgow must hiv hunners of cinemas", he concluded.

Later confiding to dad what James had said, he not only confirmed the number of local cinemas but also amply expanded on the 'hunners'. A whole new world was now open to me. But it took a few more years to fully appreciate the scope of it all. Never, I later thought, had so much pleasure, so many dreams, and so much hope, been made available to so many deserving of it.

Chapter III

Learning to Cope

Learning to Cope - The Shop and Christmas is near

In those early years the shop was the centre of my universe. It was a wonderfully ephemeral period in which I felt advantaged and protected from a closer awareness of the shortcomings around me. The shop had an atmosphere and charisma that identified with its surroundings and the people it served. Every requirement seemed to be stocked, and everything that was not stocked could be obtained, according to mum and dad. An extensive assortment of food, confectionery, magazines and newspapers, were the mainstays of the shop. This would be topped up, though, by seasonal demands for such as sporting casuals and footwear. Driven by the motivating influence of Celtic Park at the top of the road, street football was high on the activity list of most school kids hence, at the height of the summer, the 'Tanner Ball' was much in demand. Sannies and Baseball boots were always popular throughout the summer.

We were into late November now and the mood and feel of Christmas was everywhere. Candles, tinsel, and fairy lights were beginning to appear in the tenement windows of Baltic Street and those in Kinnear Road. I got great fun helping mum to decorate the shop display windows. She said I had a talent for it, which flattered me. Two of the shop windows were dedicated to Christmas, with wine, fruit, cake, and caps on display in one window, and toys and stocking fillers in the other. In addition to this, the baker's board suspended from the roof over our main display cabinet, which normally displayed the morning bread and rolls, (demoted to shelves under the cabinet), was reutilised as a further display for various other Christmas items. It was an irresistible attraction to our customers. Some of them would repeatedly visit over the day with no other reason than to browse, evaluate and to have a gossip with mum or dad. I was absolutely fascinated and even excited at the comings and goings of people whom I thought of as our neighbours. More, they were the parents of my growing gang of friends. This made me incredibly pleased, and proud, that mum and dad were providing so much pleasure for them. Initially I was content to dwell in the reflected glory of it all, especially when James or Frank turned up. On such occasions when they did, it was noticeable that dad would humorously persuade us to stand outside. It had to be, I thought, that he did not want them to know what the neighbours

Learning to Cope - The Shop and Christmas is near

were buying for their kids, especially the parents of my friends. Strange to say, though, it seemed never to occur to James or Frank to ask such a question. I think it was because of this fact that my thoughts on the matter began to widen.

As we moved closer to Christmas my awareness of our customers heightened. More and more they would browse through the displays and price them. Choosing their moment they would then draw the attention of mum or dad and together they would discuss various items and their cost as they had done many times before. This was now being taken a lot further though, as choices were now being made and written down in a book. Occasionally it would be pointed out that the chosen item was the last one in the shop and would therefore be immediately withdrawn from the display and placed underneath the cabinet. Having not noticed before, I now learned that there were open boxes under the main cabinet and most of them had a customer name written on it. I instantly realised that these were customer shopping boxes. As they ordered a Christmas item they were either written down in the order book for subsequent packaging, or stored in the order box if it were the last one in stock.

The more I understood what was going on the more incredibly clever I thought my parents were. Feeling pleased with my insight, and reviewing it all again in my mind, it struck me that there was something missing from this clever system. Never once, I thought, had I seen a customer paying for what they ordered. Yet surely my parents had to pay for all these goods in the first place. Maybe they paid for it when they collected their order. They would have to be very rich though. My parents would also have to be very rich to pay for all these Christmas goods. After much pondering, I concluded that none of these solutions could be true. I therefore decided to put the question to mum or dad.

Dad opted to answer. They pay into a Christmas menage, he said, and before I could ask the obvious he went on to explain that a menoge was a kind of savings account. They paid into the menoge as much or as little as they could afford, and as often or as seldom as they choose. Most customers, dad said, would pay in something at the same time as they did their weekly shopping. This all gets recorded in the ledger, he added, proudly pointing to a heavily bound book which lay on a shelf just below the cash till. He lifted it from its shelf and placed it down behind the raised display in the outer display window.

The ledger is very, very private and must never be opened on the counter, he said in a studied tone. It is hidden from view here, he said, gesturing to where he had now placed it. At this point he was drawn back to the counter to serve a customer. In all innocence I opened the book and proceeded to turn over the pages. At the head of each right hand facing page was, I surmised, the name of a customer. This was confirmed by the names of some of my friends. It was more than confirmed when I hit on the name of Mrs. Hargreave, James's Mum. Laid out beneath the name, as were the others, was a triple group of columns each group being delineated by a bold red line. I was trying to understand what it all meant, when suddenly mum appeared from behind. She bent over and closed the book; then picked it up and replaced it on the shelf under the till.
"You really shoudn't hiv bin lookin' at that", she said.
With the tone of her voice and the severe look in her eyes I knew that I had done something horribly wrong and immediately burst into tears and said I was sorry.
"It's no' your fault it's yur dad's. He shouldn't hiv allowed it"
Dad freed himself from the customer and joined us.
"Ah'm sorry Aggie", he said to mum. "It's no' the boy's fault, it's mine. I wis startin' to explain things tae him when a customer drew me away."
"Ok, she said, let's forget the whole thing. C'mon, dry your eyes."
Even as she spoke I could sense that she was still angry with dad. Later that evening mum explained the importance of the ledger to the shop accounts and that the ledger must always be kept private. She also made me promise I must never divulge anything that I had read. This I could easily promise as, apart from the names in the book, I understood nothing else. In the meantime my face was wiped; a sweet put in my mouth; and everything quickly returned to normal. As if to reinforce this, Granda turned up looking for his

regular portion of his black twist tobacco. He took his small tin
tobacco box from his waistcoat; removed the lid and placed it on the
counter.

"A'll hiv ma usual, Aggie", he said to mum.

As if to reassure me that all was well again Mum prompted me to
serve him, which was promotion indeed. I pulled open one of the
drawers suspended underneath the main serving counter, which I
knew to contain the tobacco. Black twist was his favourite. In the
drawer it looked like a coil of twisted black rope. I took the end of it
and dragged it up on to the counter where we had an embedded
brass ruler held by two screws. This lay along the edge of the
counter and was used specifically to measure the tobacco in relation
to its weight. Granda always had an ounce, which was equal to three
inches. I laid the tobacco along the ruler and dug my thumbnail in,
just as dad had shown me, to mark the point where it had to be cut.
Having done that I took the small sharp knife from the drawer, and
to the accompaniment of dire warnings to be careful, I sort of slowly
got the knife to cut its way through. I replaced the knife in the
drawer and handed the tobacco to Granda. As I knew from previous
experience, no payment was required. His tobacco was one of a few
items that were always to be free. He grinned at me as he enclosed it
in his tin and restored it to his waistcoat pocket.

"Yer a clever wee boy, aren't yae?" He said. "An' yur still a wee bit
posh win yae speak. Ah like that; you haud oan to it. Don't let the
eejits aroon' here tell yae itherwise. Noo, whit's Santa Claus gettin'
yae fur yur Christmas?"

I was a bit taken aback by this and did not answer. "Then whit wid
yae like fir yer Christmas?" he went on.

I looked at mum and dad for support but they just grinned back at
me.

It was not that I did not know what I would like, for I certainly did.
Maybe it was over exposure, but the toys in the shop had no
personal appeal to me. Ideally I would like something much more
outgoing such as a bike. Not a two wheeler; that would be too scary
for me. But a three wheeler; now that was something else. I had seen
a brammer in a bike shop in Dalmarnock Road, but the price was in
pounds, so I gave it no further thought. But Granda was obviously

enjoying my embarrassment and kept pressing me for an answer.
With no support from mum and dad, and just to be free of the
pressure, I blurted it out.

"I would like a three wheel bike. But I know it would be too
expensive. So, honestly, I don't care what I get".

Judging by the reaction of mum and dad to my outburst the cost of a
bike was obviously well out of reach. Their reaction did not
disappoint me, though, as my thoughts of a bike had been more
imaginary than real.

"Gimae five checks fur the fruit machine", said Granda, laying a
penny down on the counter. "Am gonae try ma luck".

With that he picked up his checks and sauntered over to the
machine. He had no sooner pulled his first check than Granny
turned up to remind him that his dinner was ready.

"Ok, wummin, a'll be over in a meenit".

With her usual cheery grin on her face she ignored him and
immediately fell in to conversation with mum.

Suddenly, without warning, Granda loudly banged the face of the
machine with his hand.

"Bloody thing, it never pays oot", he shouted. "C'mon wummin, let's
go".

"Don't b' sae crabbit", she responded. As she made to pass him on
the way out he sniffed her.

"Wait a minute, hiv' you bin drinkin' again? Ah swear tae yae
wummin, if ah find where yer plankin' the stuff a'll put an end tae it
wance 'n fur all".

Again, granny just ignored him, her composure undisturbed, and
that cheeky grin still to the fore. As for mum and dad they also
grinned and shook their head; they had seen and heard it all before.

The shop was particularly busy that morning which I enjoyed. The
customers were now familiar with me and would always
compliment me for working so hard. A few would even ask me to
serve them, which was flattering, but mum or dad would always
take care of the charging and changing of money. Getting on to mid-
day mum said she would make us some dinner in the back shop. In
no time I was called into the back of the shop where laid out on a
turned over wooden box were three mugs of tea and a plate of ham

sandwiches. Mum and I sat down on upturned boxes whilst dad stood where he could keep an eye on the front of the shop which had now gone quiet. On finishing my dinner I returned to what was now referred to as my customer lookout post which was the display window at the end of the counter which looked out on to the road. It was from here that I spotted Uncle Harry crossing the road towards the shop. Mum and dad seemed to get a little bit tense when I called this out to them. Their smile also looked a bit forced as they greeted him.

"How's it gon', Aggie? Ok, John?", he said in a mannered sort of way.

"An' how's the wee man goin', Ok?" he called over to me in a more friendly tone, to which I politely responded.

He was unshaven, and looked as if he had just got out of bed. Even the twist in his nose looked more pronounced.

He turned back to mum and dad.

"Ah take it, there's no Geordie, yet?" he asked.

Even as he asked, Uncle Geordie arrived. He had his working overalls on and must therefore, I thought, be on his dinner break. (He worked in the iron foundry in Dalmarnock Rd.).

"Sorry if am late, but it's a bit tight gettin' here in the dinner break", he said.

He then looked over at me. "Ok, John? Gimae five woodbine over, wid yae. Is that ok, Aggie? Am a bit skint at the moment".

I looked over to mum, who nodded her head without saying anything. I gave him his cigarettes, in response to which he grinned and ruffled my hair. Dad then turned to me and told me that they were going through the back for a discussion and that I was to call him if a customer came in. Their discussion did not last too long. On reappearing they all seemed to be in agreement with each other as betokened by their smiles. They both waved goodbye to me and left, with Uncle Geordie seeming to be very much in a hurry to get back to his work.

What they discussed that day I will never know.

Agnes in charge

Chapter III

Learning to Cope

The Backcourt

Window on the World

My Gang

Cinemas everywhere

The Shop and Christmas is near

Christmas at Home

Learning to Cope - Christmas at Home

My first Christmas at home was a strange and wonderful experience. It was made strange by the many conflicting events that were to be the source of much awakening and wonder, which was mostly due to the generosity and spirit of goodwill that abounded everywhere, but in particular, among the neighbours. Despite the shortcomings; the self-evident lack of resources; you just knew that money would be spent. From somewhere it would be found and that for this brief blessed period of time none of their kith or kin would be without; great or small, gifts would be provided.

In such a spirit was our Christmas tree given to Dad as a gift from the fruit and vegetable vendor who provisioned the shop. Given the freedom to choose, mum and Agnes had selected a tall and well-proportioned tree. Its lower girth nearly filled the expanse of the front window and its height nearly reached the top. They spent many fun hours decorating it, and were quite begrudging in allowing us to help. Its crowning glory, though, were the fairy lights. As was the norm, great efforts were made to reutilise the lights from previous years. However, after many abortive efforts by dad, supported by one of the neighbours, it was agreed they had run their course and would have to be replaced. As it happened they were a Christmas stock item in the shop and hence the tree was to be proudly adorned with new lights. They were multi-coloured and shaped like miniature bulbs. I was told that they were a great improvement on the old ones. I was quite proud of them and, so much so, that I frequently had a look at the growing window displays across the street for comparison. There was no way I could confirm the comparison but I was sure that our window had to be at least as good as theirs.

The morning of Christmas Eve arrived, and although I awoke early it was still too late to catch dad before he left to open the shop. It had been my hope that I could begin the day with him, and thus savour every moment, but the persuasive early morning coorie-in had won out. Despite my disappointment I was now up and about and nothing was going to dampen my feeling of great expectations. Mum and Agnes seemed to share my feeling as they busied themselves about the house. I quickly washed and dressed and was ready to go, even without my morning tea and sandwich, when mum bade me sit down, have my tea, and listen.

Today, she said, was going to be very, very hectic for everyone and that we all had to play our part. The shop was going to have its busiest day of the year. Christmas orders had to be packed in readiness for customers to pick up, and, as might be required, some would have to be delivered. In addition to this there was still shopping to be done at the butchers to keep us over the holiday. Also, the house had to be cleaned from top to bottom and made ready to receive visitors - the neighbours no doubt.
"Now the arrangements ur this", she said firmly. "Agnes is gonnae to take care of the hoose and get it ready fur the evening. Bill and Bert will do the shoppin' and anything else that Agnes might need - and she's not tae stand any nonsense from either of yae. As fur you an' I, we'll take oorselves roon the shop an' help dad. An' don't you go thinkin' this is gonnae be easy", she warned, whilst trying not to smile.

Dad was more than glad to see us arriving. He was rushed off his feet, he said. Sure enough there was a steady stream of customers with a few waiting to be served. In addition to the normal early morning purchases of bread, rolls, and newspapers, they were ordering other additional items such as sliced ham, corn beef, dumpling, and cake. As the morning rush eased off mum applied herself to the checking and packing of Christmas orders. My contribution was to bring the boxes from under the display cabinet through to the back shop where she would check the content against the order list. Any item that was short, I would then fetch from those on display and wrap it in coloured tissue paper. The box would then be sealed and returned to its shelf location. Around mid-day all was completed and ready to 'ship out' as dad put it.

As was usual at this time, the shop had gone quiet. This relaxed feeling was countered by mum with the familiar comment that it was only the 'calm before the storm'. She then told dad to cut a couple of slices of ham and corn' beef and for me to take it over to Granda and Granny and have my tea with them.

"An' while yae'r are at it", she said to me, ah waant yae tae take these two presents over to them. This one is for yur Granda, and this one for yur Granny. Tell them that these are thur presents from us an' the family, and that they musn't open them before Christmas. When yae get back yae cin take Major for a walk."

I was quite proud of myself as I walked up to the front door. As was not unusual one of them must have spotted me walking across the road and left the door open.

"It's only me, Granny!" I called (imitating Agnes's cry) as I walked in and bumped the door closed with my backside. She was sitting at the table in front of the window as I entered the room.

"Where's Granda?" I asked on seeing his chair empty.

"Ah think he's gone fur a walk, John, he usually dis at this time".

"These are your Christmas presents, Granny, from mum and dad, and all of us. And she said you were not to open them before Christmas.

"Sure, ah widnae dae that, son. Thank yer mither an' faither fur me". With that she bent over and kissed me on the cheek.

Learning to Cope - Christmas at Home

As usual I got a whiff of alcohol which I was now becoming quite familiar with as an aroma not entirely unique to Granny. "Ah suppose yae wid like some tea. Which of these wid yae like?" she asked, taking the ham and corn' beef from me. I don't mind, Granny, corn' beef will do me fine. But I'll also take a piece with your home made jam - she made great rhubarb jam.

I took her seat at the window and observed the frequent passage of customers in and out of the shop. I also saw dad leave and head towards Baltic Street. No doubt, as I had come to know, he was off to meet up with his friend Walter in his pub where they would exchange a daily dram. There was also a sighting of a few of the gang messing around. Granny interrupted my browsing by placing a mug of tea and sandwiches in front of me. "Now, get that down yae", she said and sauntered back to the kitchen.

I scoffed my sandwich and took a drink of my tea to wash it down when I discovered it had no sugar in it. Yuck, I thought and took the mug through to the kitchen. I was about to make my presence heard when I saw Granny, who had her back to me, take a brief drink from a small bottle of whisky. Knowing how dismissively she denied drinking alcohol to Granda, and not wishing to be thought of as spying on her, I tried to quietly withdraw, only for her to turn round and, still oblivious to my presence, she slid the bottle deep down her cleavage.

I stood there absolutely shocked with embarrassment, as she became aware of my presence. We both stood like forever, waiting for one of us to speak. My embarrassment grew even more as the thought crystalised in my head that I knew her plank. What was I to do?
The brief silence was broken by Granny.

"Yae wulnae tell yer Granda... Tell mi that yae wulnae tell yer Granda.... It'll be oor secret...Promise me".

I felt horribly guilty, and would have done absolutely anything not to see the fear on Granny's face.

"I promise you Granny. I really, really promise you that I will never tell anyone, not even mum or dad".

It was lovely to see the relief come over her face, and her smile return. I was still transfixed with the mug of tea in my hand. She took the mug and placed it on the worktop.

"Yur a very honest boy, John, an' a' thank yae fur it. Now wit's wrong wae this tea?"

"It has no sugar in it Granny."

"Go an' sit doon an' a'll fix it fur yae".

The moment was gone; all was well again; and to this day I have never told anyone. I had just finished my tea when Granda returned.

"How's wee John do'n?" he asked.

"Fine", I replied. "I brought over a Christmas present from mum and dad. Mum said you musn't open it before Christmas."

"That was very kind of them. And where's yur dug the day?"

"In his kennel, but I'll be taking him for a walk when I get back." Granda had a great affection for Major and always asked after him.

"Hiv yae any tea left in the pot?" he asked Granny.

"There's plenty", she replied. "Sit doon an ah'll go n' get yae some".

With that I said cheerio to Granda and followed Granny out. As I made to leave, she tapped me on the shoulder and, with an upright finger pointing at her mouth, she whispered, "Remember. Oor secret".

I replied by likewise putting my finger across my lips, and nodding. For me it was all very serious - but for Granny? Well she knew she could trust me.

Learning to Cope - Christmas at Home

As I made my way back to the shop dad was returning from his break. I got him to unlock the sleeper door and got an excited couple of barks from Major, as I uncoupled his chain. My usual route was up the length of Lilly St, take a left at the top then back down Sorn St. With Christmas being near, and everyone being on holiday, Lilly St. was unusually lively with people of all ages hanging around the closes. Normally I would hope to run in to a few of the guys and stop and chat, but today this was never going to be a problem. I first of all ran into Archie Gemmil, who lived up the first close in Lilly Street. For some reason he was always a bit fearful of Major and quickly put himself on the other side of where he was walking. He wanted to know what I was getting for Christmas, which I'm sure he was ready to top. I made it easy for him by telling him that I did not know. As we sauntered on we could see James and Frank coming from the direction of Springfield Rd., each carrying a message bag. They had been picking up their Christmas order from the butcher, they said. After a few more queries on Christmas expectations they carried on home with their load. At this point Archie also decided that he had walked far enough and left with them.

People wanting to stroke and fondle Major would frequently stop me on the way, and in doing so, neighbours would call out and ask how mum and dad were faring. Coming down Sorn Street I met up with Mungo Cloherty and Frank Mc Quillan. Going on from there I saw one of my favourite friends, Joe O Donnell. He was Irish and spoke with a nice accent. I always got on well with Joe, mostly because he could be so humble and humorous with it. When I asked him what he thought he was getting for Christmas, he said he was hoping for something great, but expected less. As we stood blethering I spotted Granda in his garden across the road beckoning me over. I said cheerio to Joe and agreed to meet him later.

"Sorry t' pull yae away from yer friend, John, but this dug's not gettin' enough walking.", Granda said. "So, why don't yae leave him wae me fur a while. Ah'll take'm fur a walk roon the plots an'll chain him up later. Ok? Jist let yer faither an' mither know whit's happening".
This was more than ok for me, as Granda often took him for a walk. I gave Major a final stroke and a pat, and left them to it.

On returning to the shop Mum and Dad seemed to be rushed off their feet. Even Agnes had now joined them. She was primarily wrapping up whilst Mum and Dad served the customers. We must also have taken a fresh delivery of ginger as the back shop was now stacked with fresh boxes of irn bru and cream soda which were our best selling drinks. They were so busy that I could not intrude. I therefore just made myself visible to them and eagerly waited to react to their beck and call. This went on for some time, but eventually it started to slacken off.

Everyone was leg-weary by then, including me, and I had not been nearly as active as them. Unnoticed, Agnes had taken time out and made mum and dad a cup of tea, following which, she and I indulged ourselves with a large glass of irn bru. Great fun. I loved it. Dad probably picked up on this for, with the rush now reduced to the odd customer, he told mum and Agnes to take themselves off and sort out the dinner for everyone. He asked me to hang on and help him out for a little while longer. You can send Bill or Bert round to get me when the dinner was ready, he added.
"Is that ok by you, John?" he asked.
Needless to say, I agreed. This was one of the great mannerisms of dad that made him liked by so many. Whenever he wanted to do something or, have you do something, he would always make it sound like he needed your approval. It always made you feel one on one with him,

like he was your friend. His generosity was also well renowned, especially among his customers. He would seldom refuse credit unless he had good reason. Even then his anguish would make him struggle for words. Both aspects had been in evidence over the last few hours much to the annoyance of mum. Not that she was ungenerous herself, but she just felt that he was too soft.

Customers continued to filter through the shop at intervals. In the course of this, dad explained to me his plans for the coming evening. He and mum, he said, always celebrated Christmas Eve with a small party for the family, friends, and neighbours. This of course would mean that they could not open my bed until after the party, as it would take up too much floor space. To overcome this problem he and Mum had decided that it might be best if I slept in their bed, at least until the party was over. Did I have any problems with this, he asked.

"Can I sit up in bed and watch?"

"Of course you can", he replied, "and when you get bored you can go to sleep and dream of Santa Claus coming down the chimney in the front room. Is that Ok by you?" It sounded great to me I replied.

It was dark when Bill turned up to take me home. Dinner was ready, he said, and we had to leave immediately. We said cheerio to dad and set off. As we turned in to Baltic St. I asked Bill if we could walk on the other side of the road so that I could see how our Christmas tree looked in the dark. He had not seen it himself and was only too pleased to do it. We stood facing our own close and looked up. It was absolutely stunning. From where we stood it looked like it reached to the roof. Its branches, draped with glitter and outlined by the lights, spanned nearly the whole of the double window.

"It's fantastic, isn't, John?"

Learning to Cope - Christmas at Home

My eyes browsed the full extent of the tenement windows, three up, and stretching as far I could see. For both of us, it was truly Christmas. We walked over to our close and turned round to take in the windows on the other side. They were equally stunning. Oh! you haven't seen Nuneaton Street yet, have you? With that he grabbed my hand and we both ran to the corner. The view all the way down to the brightly illuminated Plaza was by far the best yet. I stood there mesmerised by it all. Bill grabbed my hand again... "C'mon, we're late. Mum'll kill me. I wis supposed tae bring yae straight hame."

When we arrived mum made a mock attempt at sermonising us as she laid out our dinner. It was steak pie, my favourite. Bert, May, and Agnes had already finished theirs and, as Bill and I were a bit hungry, dinner was over and done with in no time.

In a brief summary of what dad had told me, mum let everyone know what the early evening held for us. She wanted a quick clearance, a wash-up, and the table re-spread with the party offerings. Extra chairs on loan from the neighbour had to be fetched by Bill and Bert. She concluded her presentation with a dire warning to everyone that they could all be seen, but certainly not heard, after the guests arrived. Bill and Bert let it be known that they would be going out after they fetched the chairs, and that they would go straight to bed when they returned. As for May, she joined me in the front room where she pestered me on and off with what she wanted for Christmas. As I had absolutely no idea on what anyone was getting she eventually tired of my lack of cooperation and rejoined Agnes. By the time our first guest had arrived I had already, more from boredom, stripped off, got my jammies on, and climbed into mum and dad's bed.

Learning to Cope - Christmas at Home

May had fallen asleep in the front room and had also been put to bed.

The first arrivals were our two neighbours from the close, who were referred to by everyone as wee Peggy and Sconey. Peggy was small, not much bigger than me, and had bandy (rickety) legs. She was well known to have a heart of gold, and would do anything for anybody, mum said. Sconey, nobody knew where he got the name from, always seemed to have a permanent grin on his face and, like Peggy, was well-liked for being helpful. Next to arrive was Uncle Geordie and his wife Rachel who had a very noticeable black eye despite the makeup on it. She seemed none the worse for it, though, as she greeted mum.

When asked, she said that a clothes pole had slipped and clouted her on the eye. A right keeker, right enough, I thought.

As for Geordie, smiling as always, he made little of Auntie Rachel's little accident and seemed impatient to have his first drink. Agnes was making him wait for it while she gave priority to Auntie Rachel. Dad arrived shortly after in the company of his friends Walter McLaughlen and George Daily. A few more neighbours came in. And finally, Uncle Harry arrived in the company of a girl who had to be no older than Agnes. She was quite a pretty girl whom he introduced as Bridget. A strange quietness came over mum and dad as Harry introduced her. There was also a similar discomfort displayed by dad's friends.

Harry, who had obviously had a few before he arrived, was aware of the reaction he was causing and, with a newly filled glass in his hand, he boastfully flaunted her.

"She's the daughter ah niver hid, aren't yae, Bridget? A'm gonnae make'r a star, aren't ah hen. She's goat talent, jist yae wait'n see. "

He was now the centre of attraction and his excitement was rising. Bridget was also beginning to look a bit forlorn and confused by all the attention she was getting and clung closely to his arm. He was now ordering everyone to drink up and get the party going. This did not get the eager reaction that he was looking for and there was now an aggressive tone in his voice as he tried to whip up some enthusiasm. Dad was clearly discomforted by it all and, behind Harry's back, he made a knowing gesture with his head to mum. As if it were the signal she was waiting for mum, with great aplomb, imposed herself on the situation.

"Look Harry, yer gless is full, so sit yersel' doon an' gee us a song...Ah'll look efter Bridget... You sit doon, hen, beside Harry, an' tell us whit yae wantae drink.... Agnes, you see tae Bridget...Now, whit aboot that song, Harry?...Give us yer favourite, 'Sonny Boy'."

A bit more contented with himself, Harry launched into his rendition with a fair larrup of pathos. It was a great success and mum demanded that he give us another one. This seemed to restore his self-confidence to the extent that he dismissed mum's request and demanded that she sing the next song. As was her wont, she did not need much encouragement.

"This wan's fur ma mither, everywan's favourite granny...'Aul' Scot's mither mine'."

She had everyone in her hand, now, and went on to move the singing around the company without once failing to get a response. She would also, at frequent intervals, aided by Agnes, douse everyone's glass with a generous top up. It was only a matter of time though, for the singing order to come back to her. "C'mon, Aggie, it's yur turn, again."...

She was now in full flow as she took over the centre of the floor. It was fascinating to watch their joy develop as the evening progressed... Harry was now showing distinct signs of falling from his chair. Unnoticed by Auntie Rachel, Geordie was now canoodling with Bridget... Dad was in deep conversation with his friends... Sconey was waiting for something to eat whilst Agnes, to try and satisfy him, was making more sandwiches.... As for Mum, she was still singing to a group of neighbours... I never did see the end of it all... I vaguely remember me being lifted and laid on my own bed. I also remember the tall figure of dad pulling on a red cloak and white bearded mask. He then picked up a bag full of goods and left the room. I had seen Santa Claus. Whilst worthy of the myth, the reality was more pleasing.

****

When I woke up I had the immediate sense that I had slept late. My first thought was that it was Christmas, and I was fearful that I had missed it. This thought was instantly dismissed as I spotted a net stocking full of assorted sweets hanging from the bottom panel of the kumfynite. But it was so quiet. I quickly got up and looked around. To my amazement all trace of the previous evening had disappeared and everything was back to normal. Even mum and dad's bed had been made up with a brightly coloured new top sheet. I could hear muffled sounds coming from the front room and my excitement rose. I quickly pulled on my shirt (it was freshly ironed), and my trousers, and slowly made my way through to the front room, whose door was closed.

It had gone very quiet as I turned the handle and slowly opened the door. Suddenly, from the inside, it was pulled fully open to a loud scream of... "Merry Christmas, John!!" With mum and dad to the fore it was hugs all round. May, dressed up as a nurse, was excitedly calling for me to open my presents from under the tree. Sure enough, lying there, as the last present to be opened was a fairly large box wrapped in coloured paper. I dropped down and dragged it in to the centre of the floor. Surrounded by the others, who were just as keen to see the contents, as I was, I ripped the paper off to reveal a large multi coloured label with the words, "Gene Autrey. The Singing Cowboy".

Now, I was really excited, and could not stop saying, "this is great...this is great!", as I opened the box. It contained his hat, his neck scarf, and a book of his songs. But when these were removed from the box, it revealed the best thing of all. His gun belt, complete with holster and gun. It looked so real. I strapped on the belt and put the gun in its holster. I then, by way of a practice, slowly withdrew the gun, pointed it at the Christmas tree and pulled the trigger. I jumped with shock as it gave off a loud cracking noise. What I had not noticed was that the gun was loaded with a roll of caps. Straight away Bill, and Bert, wanted a shot at it, which I agreed to while I more carefully examined the hat and the neck scarf. They finally handed the gun back to me and I returned it to its holster. I tied on the neck scarf, just like Gene, and pulled on the hat. In my imagination I was there as I slowly strutted around the room. At this everyone seemed to go very quiet and I blushed at the thought that I was showing off, which seemed to be confirmed by dad grinning and staring at me.

"Ur yae not going tae open yer other present?", he asked.

"Where is it?" I asked looking at the empty space beneath the tree.

"Look behind the tree", he said. I did, but could only see a large heap of coloured paper, which I thought were the remnants from the others unpacking their presents.

"Pull the paper away", he said.

With the first grip of the paper I knew there was something big there. I peeled away a few more pieces to reveal the handlebars of a bike. I stepped back a couple of steps in fright.

"What's the matter?" dad asked. "Don't yae like it?"

"Is that mine?" I asked in disbelief.

"Of course it is", he said with a reassuring grin.

Learning to Cope - Christmas at Home

I looked round at the others for their reactions. First Bill, then Bert, then Agnes. To my great joy, they were all smiling and nodding their heads in approval. I was fearfully looking for signs of jealousy, and there were none.

By now mum had stripped all of its wrapping way and pulled it in the middle of the room. I was still in shock and it was only with the persuasion of mum that I finally mounted it - my first three wheeler bike. It was built of chunky tubular metal painted in an enameled brown with the maker's name printed in yellow. It also had mudguards back and front and chunky rubber grips on the handlebars. It was stunning, and it was mine. Bill and Bert promised to carry it downstairs and bring it back up if I promised to let them have a shot.
"That wont be necessary", said Mum. She explained that dad had arranged with Sconey for it to be stored downstairs in the unlet shop beside the close. There was an access door in the close and Sconey had been given a key by the factor in return for keeping it clean.
"Ok, John, let's go", said Bill, "Bert and I will carry it down stairs for you. We'll look after yae while yae learn to ride it".

The next few hours were to be among the best moments of my life. As for Christmas, it has never yet been surpassed.

Chapter IV

The Growing Years

Fitting in

The Games of my Youth

The Gangs

Still Catching Up

Family Matters

The Growing Years - Fitting in

The weeks following that Christmas had to be the most joyous period of my early years. The pleasure of my three wheeler bike had now replaced those of the shop. Each morning could not come soon enough; no more lazy morning slumber. When I woke it seemed as if my mind was energised with one thought, and that all else was an intrusion. Only the restraining directives of mum, or Agnes, to wash properly, and have my breakfast, prevented me from dressing and going straight downstairs to retrieve my bike from Sconie's store. But, properly washed and prepared for the day, I would be knocking on his door no later than eight thirty each morning. Curiously enough, it was never Sconie who opened the door but Peggy. She understood me well, and to remove any doubt, she assured me that the key would always be available, and that should there be a problem with this arrangement, then I would be allowed to take the key home. She was so helpful.

Bill and Bert had taught me well, and as each day passed I became more self assured and daring in my manoeuvres. In a matter of weeks I was traversing up and down Baltic St from our close to Springfield Road, which, being a main road, I would never dare cross. I was not quite ready for that. Nuneaton Street, was my next big challenge as there was always some traffic to contend with, though most of it was horse drawn carts. Mastering its length was tricky, as I often had to slow down to a crawl in order to maneuver my way round parked carts and the odd van. This was fun, though, as it brought me into contact with the shopkeepers who were now familiar with my tripping up and down the street. I would often see George Daily, dad's friend, as he washed the front window of his bar. This was a daily routine for him and he would always give me a wave as I passed.

Soon, I was ready to take on the rest of Baltic Street. It started from the corner of Nuneaton St. and ended at Heron St., just beyond Mary Street. where, I was told, Walter McLaughlen had his shop. Looking down its length I could not see its end, and therefore decided to tackle it in stages. The first stage would be to cycle to the next street

up from Nuneaton, take stock of my bearings, and cycle back. This turned out to be not that far away and I was back in no time. Not only that but from where I turned, I could now clearly see the end of Baltic St.. This gave me the confidence to dispense with the repeat trips and to go straight to the next stage. This time I cycled past Dunn St. to the next street, stopped, and looked back towards Nuneaton St.. It was still visible so I carried on to the next street, at which point I confidently deemed that I had come half way and turned back. It was all too easy, I thought, and went on to repeat the halfway trip three times, always quickening my pedal stroke on the return trip. I was now ready, I thought, to take on its full length.
I pedalled up to the halfway mark, which was Ruby Street, fairly quickly, then stopped to have a brief look back. All was well so I decided to go for it all the way. My pace was very slow, as I wanted to identify each street as I passed through. But, there was to be no other street before I reached Mary Street, which was where Walter had his shop. Mary St. was very short and I could easily take it all into my view. There were few shops on the side that first came into view and the first of them looked like a newsagent, cum sweetie shop, and it had Walter's name displayed as part of its sign above the window. I had never seen Walter's shop before so I sat there for a little while just taking it all in. It seemed to sell most of the things that we sold, but it was a tenement shop and it was much smaller. I would have liked to have gone in and viewed it more closely but I was much too shy to brave it. Maybe next time, I thought, and turned to make my way back.

The following morning I repeated the trip twice. On the second trip I was turning into Mary St., when Walter emerged from the shop and spotted me and beckoned me over. He fussed over me and praised the quality of my bike, which he seemed to know a lot about. He also complimented me on my courage for having cycled this far. He wanted me to come into the shop and look around but I said no on the grounds that I really had to get back. The truth was that I was afraid to leave my bike unattended outside the shop. In compensation, I thought, he gave me a small bag of sweets and I set off back along Baltic Street. In the ensuing days I not only repeated my trips along Baltic St., but also explored the streets running off it.

The most fascinating of these was Ruby St., which had a tram depot where the trams parked at the end of the day. The street also housed the only automatic washhouse in Bridgeton, and was referred to by everyone as the 'Steamie'. On two occasions I had been inside with mum and Agnes, and as I sat there on my bike watching the steam gushing from open windows the now familiar smell of carbolic soap was everywhere. I would always associate this smell with the much-used phrase in the Backcourt on Saturday washday - 'It scrubbed up well...'

Bridgeton was now my domain. There was no street, no nook or cranny, that was not known to my bike and me. I felt hugely proud of my achievement, as were mum and mad, who would patiently provide an audience for me to recount my daily exploits. There now remained one final challenge that had to be met, which I had knowingly avoided since day one. I had deliberately avoided cycling in Kinnear Road. Partly based on warnings that Bill and Bert had given me, I was fearful of mixing with my pals until such time as I was fully practised. Also I would have needed to have fended off demands by them to have a shot, and I was fearful of it being prematurely damaged before I had fully savoured it.

My main fear, though, was that a few of them would be openly jealous of it. I had already received scornful remarks about my dad having a shop, and that I was not any different from them. I dreaded this most of all and had tried very hard not to be seen as such. But my bike could not be hidden, and I was proud of it. So, there was no way out; I had to face them. I chose to do it around mid-day when I knew that James and Frank were usually hanging out at the close. As I turned into Kinnear Road, I could see I was not to be disappointed. They saw me coming and came forward to meet me as I cycled up to the close.

"Where've ye been fur the last few weeks?" said James. "An' this is the new bike", added Frank, fondling the handlebars.

"Can ah hiv a shot?" he asked.

"Ok, but just to the corner an' back", I reluctantly responded. Surprisingly, Frank, who could be a bit aggressive, did not take advantage. He did go beyond the corner, but then turned in a wide circle and slowly pedalled back to me.

"It's a brahmer!" he said as he dismounted. "Yer a lucky wee guy, John. But good on yae." he added.

"Would you like a shot?" I asked James.

He was pleased at my asking and set off. He went a good bit further than Frank, but I trusted him to quickly return, which he did.

By now we were joined by Charlie Gillan, and Davie Smith, who both lived in the close. I wanted to offer a shot to Charlie but this meant that Davie would want one too, and there was no way I would let him near it. He was a lot older and taller than us and had his own two wheeler bike on which he was a bit of a trickster. This of course drew a sarcastic remark from him which he was prevented from expanding on by James telling him to shut up, backed up by Frank. Before long Archie Gemmel and others turned up and added to the circle that had formed around me. I was beginning to feel uncomfortable with all this attention when suddenly I heard dad's voice calling me from the shop doorway.

"Come'n git yer tea, John!".

I said cheerio to James and Frank, and with a nod to Charlie and the others I mounted and cycled across the road. Dad lifted the bike into the shop and I followed him in.

My first meet up with the lads had not been as bad as I expected, but I was still uncomfortable with the situation. After tea and a few reassuring words from dad I felt that the day had gone reasonably well and decided to make my way back home and get the bike into the safety of Sconie's storage. Dad carried the bike out and put it down at the edge of the kerb. Across the road most of the guys had dispersed. But there were still a few hanging around that I knew came from the top of Lilly Street, headed up by Archie Gemmel. Dad told me to get off home and he would stand there until I got past Lilly Street in case one of them tried to get funny. With an assured nod to dad, I set off. I glanced over at the guys as I passed and made a friendly wave to Archie. I had barely got to the corner of Baltic Street, when suddenly, just like Bill and Bert had warned me to be on the lookout for, someone jumped on to the back axle frame and grabbed me by the shoulders for support.

"Hi Ho, Silver! Up, up, n' away!" he screamed.

I knew immediately from the voice that it was Archie. Holding on tightly with one hand I swung the other one back at him to try and dislodge him. I felt him pull away to avoid me but as he was still holding on to my shoulders the result was catastrophic. The front of the bike came up, he jumped clear, and I went over backwards pulling the bike into the air. I heard the whack as the back of my head hit the road leaving me unable to prevent the bike crashing down on top of me. Lying still, and looking up at the sky there was the strong sensation that this experience was not new, there had been another time. I could hear dad in the background shouting abuse at someone. I was then aware of him trying to slip his arm under my neck by way of making me feel comfortable.

"Don't touch me, Dad! Don't touch me!" My calls to him emerged as a whisper. As in a previous time, I thought of Jean and went to sleep.

I woke up in hospital with the family sitting round the bed. Even Granny and Granda were there.

"So yae've decided tae rejoin us", Granda said with a feigned grumpy smile. C'mon, Granny, tell'm whit a tough wee man he his." Putting her finger on her lips and then patting me on the cheek, she responded..."Ah don't think he needs anywan to tell'm that."

Mum and dad sat on either side of the bed with Agnes, Bill, Bert and May at the bottom. I felt great. But as I tried to sit up I felt a wee bit soreness in my head which I now realised was bandaged.

"Yur goin' tae be ok", said mum. She went on to tell me that I had suffered a slight concussion from my head hitting the ground and that it should right itself in a couple of days. They had also been very concerned about my spine, which had taken some of the impact, but the doctor had said that my straight jacket took the brunt of it and that no harm had been done. Becoming self-conscious with all this attention I felt relieved when a nurse came up to the bed with a tray in her hand. She gave me a glass of water and two tablets, which I was to swallow.

"I'm sorry everyone", she said, "but I'm gonae hiv' tae ask yae all to leave as John needs tae get more sleep. It's the best cure in the world fur him". With drawn out good-byes, they all took their leave.

****

I was kept in hospital for two days observation.. My coming home was reminiscent of previous fuss and attention with all its do's and don'ts, and all with the best possible intent. It had to be suffered and it took another couple of days before it receded into the background. In the course of all this my thoughts dwelled on much more important things such as - what did the future hold for my bike? Now that I was aware of its dangers, would I ever cycle again? I immediately convinced myself that the fear of falling off would not deter me.

But, there were other more important fears such as always having to look over your shoulder when any of the lads were around. But no, it went further than that, I thought. Deep down I knew there to be another fear that I could not come to terms with. Eventually it crystallised. But not in words, I was not that clever, but in a feeling for what had to be done. To be one of the lads was essential; to be otherwise was not a consideration. This was my world and I wanted to be part of it. If this meant certain things could not be, then so be it. For a brief period after this all was clear, then self-doubt set in and I was back to where I started - with needs and conflicts.

When asked by dad about the bike, I told him I would give it a rest for a while and for the moment I would prefer to help him in the shop. Nothing more was said about it and I soon settled back into the routine of helping dad in the shop and hanging out with my pals at the close. The lads, of course, headed up by James and Frank, made quite a fuss about the absence of the bike and the reasons for me not riding it any more. They did not buy into my 'giving it a rest for a while', and insisted that Archie Gemmel was the cause of it all and needed a good 'hiding' for it. Despite my efforts to play it down as an accident they would have none of it and made even more threatening promises for when Archie next turned up. Fortunately, by intent or otherwise, he did not show his face for some while by which time the matter was history.

For my part, I revelled in the surprising affection that the lads seemed to have for me, especially James.
Some weeks later I was setting out for the shop. As I made my way down the stairs the thought (that had never been too far away) came to the front of my mind. I still had not decided on the bike. Was I afraid of it? No, I could not admit to that. Did I want to keep it? I was not sure. What did I want to do? I did not know. I got to the bottom of the stairs and paused outside Sconie and Peggy's door. Maybe if I looked at it again It would make my mind up. Without further thought I knocked on the door. It was immediately opened by Peggy who, as usual, started to fuss over me.
"Could I have the key, Peggy?"
She went quiet at this and seemed unable to answer me. None the less she unhooked the key and handed it to me. I went back and unlocked the door. Pushing it open I looked to where it normally stood but it was not there. Taking a couple steps forward I looked around the dimly lit area of the store. It was gone. I closed and locked the door behind me. As I turned round Peggy was there before me.
"Where is my bike", I dolefully asked.
"Yur faither took it away jist after yae hid yer accident. Ah don' know whit he's dun wi it".

I was near to tears as I walked very slowly round to the shop. Dad took one look at me when I arrived and instinctively knew the reason for my sadness.

"C'mere", he said and took me round the back. "It's about yer bike, Isn't it? ...It wis fur the best, son.... Ah jist couldnae bear it if yae wur tae hiv anither accident...Try tae understand.... Ah promise yae that yae'll hiv anither bike, an' it wul be a two wheeler...but no right noo, eh? We'll leave it fur a wee while...Whit dae yae say?"

I agreed with maybe a restrained tear in my eye. My problem had been solved, and somewhere ahead there was to be a two wheeler. But as dad said, "Maybe no' the noo."

Chapter IV

The Growing Years

Fitting in

The Games of my Youth

The Gangs

Still Catching Up

Family Matters

The Growing Years - The Games of my Youth

My first winter had settled in. Gloves, balaclava, thick socks, and a warm jacket, their quality not always of the highest, were now the order of the day. With much prompting from mum, Bill and Bert offered to teach me how to ice skate. I gleefully accepted and thereafter was often taken by them to Crossmyloof ice rink. It was good fun and eventually I became reasonably practised at it. Among the other winter games available to us, street sliding was the most popular and it cost nothing. A good slide was difficult to create, I was told, and could be the cause of many nasty tumbles before it was finished.

A prerequisite for a good slide was a night of heavy frost settling on smooth sections of the road. In this respect Baltic Street offered the best surface. The gang, however, preferred Kinnear Road where you had to be more selective owing to its gravelly surface. To get the slide started it was a big help if you were reasonably heavy. For this reason we always looked to one of the older lads which in our case was Davie Smith. He was not especially heavy but he was tall and very agile. In Kinnear Road, the two most popular spots were on the railway side of the road facing Sorn St., and Lilly St., but we normally favoured Sorn Street.

Davie, as usual, was the self-appointed expert and would walk around for quite a while looking, as he said, for the most slippery spot to start. He would test for this by alternately rubbing the sole of his boots on the selected surface. If he found little resistance he would quicken his movement until a shine started to appear. Clearly pleased with himself he would grin at us and wave an erect thumb up and down. He just loved showing off when he had an audience. There would be shouts for him to stop the posing and get on with it. Concentrating on the chosen spot, he would take a few steps backwards, pause, then, with brisk forward steps, he would launch himself side on and legs apart on to the selected surface. There would be just a suggestion of a slide before he came to a staggering halt on the rough stony ground. He would repeat this many times, with each effort taking him that little bit further. In no time at all he had extended it to quite a few yards. He paused to preen himself and to admire his handiwork..

"Noo, remember the rule. Any moron who's not wearing leather boots or shoes is not gettin' on. Ok, let's go!", he shouted, beckoning everyone to follow. "Let's streech it further".

With that everyone gingerly made their maiden run. As confidence built up so likewise did the pace of the run up, and, in no time, the slide was stretched out to a respectable length. Credit to Dave, though, he was very agile and showed great flair on the slide but did he really need to milk it that much? Frank, who was more than keen to pull him down a peg, called on him to show us a few tricks in the hope that he would bugger it up.
"Dae yer arse slide, Davie...The same as yae did last year", yelled Frank, with mischief written all over his face.
Davie, now high as a kite on conceit and never one to back down on any athletic challenge, yelled back, "Ok, Frank, watch this!"

Without any hesitation he ran at the slide in a lowered body position and as he arrived he kicked both feet out in front and made a faultless forward landing on his bum and took off. By now the slide was so slippery that there was no doubt that Davie was going to reach the end at some pace, and by his screaming antics of holding both legs and arms in the air, there was equally no doubt that he would not disappoint anyone. As expected, he came off the end of the slide at a terrific pace and carried on for quite some distance on the graveled hardness of unmade road. He continued screaming on this part of the journey but this time in pain.

As everyone rushed forward to help, he rose slowly to his feet. The back of his trousers was shredded and his exposed buttocks were red raw with gravel rash. Near to tears, he was not a sight for sore eyes as Frank sympathetically patted him on the back.
"Yae did well, Davie...It wis even better than last year... But its given yae a fer sore arse, hisn't it?"

The Growing Years - The Games of my Youth

The slide could last for weeks providing there was no rain; and it attracted a few early morning users to top up its polish and keep its pace. Occasionally, though, it would be vandalised with a bag of salt by someone not attuned to our winter fun - usually by someone who had come on to it by accident, or was vengeful for someone who did. In such a situation we would again call on the services of Davie - but not that year, as it was a good winter and the slide held its ground.

Winter was over and you could feel it. A bit early, maybe, but for us it meant the start of summer. In our youthful innocence it was an adult quibble to talk of seasons. Spring and autumnal equinoxes had no meaning for us. Summer began when the ice and snow disappeared and your pieces of clothing got fewer and lighter. There might be recourse to the calf-chafing wellies and other rain protecting garments, but the important thing was that it was getting warmer, and the evenings were getting longer.

This meant that a greater range of street games would become available, with most of them being new to me. Games, such as Peavers, Peerie, Bools, Moshie, and, of course, football, I had still to learn. Peavers was primarily the domain of girls, but boys, usually by way of showing off, would join in. To play you first had to chalk a series of contiguous squares (beds) on the ground, usually numbered 1 to 9. Their layout could vary, but the most common one was laid out in the sequence one bed, two beds, repeated three times. The most desirable Peaver was a polished piece of marble the size of you palm, but the norm was an empty polish tin filled with mud to give it weight and resealed. In play you would move the Peaver through the beds with a skip and nudge action with the outside of your foot.

There were many variations with its own rules, which I learnt from Charlie Gillan's sister, Annie. She was around the same age as sister May, and like me was very shy. In an instance we both recognised each other's frailty and with an instinctive honesty we accepted it. Consequently, I found it easy to talk to her.

The Peerie, on the other hand, was more of an individual game, and easier to learn than Peavers. It was nothing more than a wooden spinning top that was controlled by a whip made from a piece of string tied onto a small length of cane. If you were to be really skillful you had to improve on the whip to get better control. Instead of the coarse string that came with the Peerie, you needed to replace it with strong smooth twine. It also helped if you had a heavier piece of cane or wood. To spin the Peerie you wrapped the twine tightly round its rebated ridge; then, with the Peerie in one hand, and the whip in the other, you threw the Peerie forward to the ground and, with a simultaneous action, you pulled the whip in the opposite direction.

The real skill and pleasure was in keeping it spinning. To achieve this you flicked the whip at the Peerie with a sharp movement of the wrist. This sent a ripple down the string to its tip causing it to flick at the Peerie in a clockwise direction. Once you became really skilled at this you could drive the Peerie in any direction. When playing with your pals your aim was to knock over their Peeries and so force them to restart it. You were also expected to personalise your Peerie by chalking multi-coloured circles, or any other design, on its top. The position and shade of the colours could make each one stunningly different.

Other great pastimes were marbles and Moshie. The marbles sometime referred to as Bools, or jauries were primarily made of glass and by design or accident, their random mix of colours could make some of them massively attractive at our age. Their size was generally constant. Larger ones were available and were regarded as superior, and of greater value based on an agreed exchange rate. There was also the steely, or the plunker, that would start its life as a ball bearing in the local steel works only to be nicked by someone's dad and passed on into the fray of competition. It too had an increased value over the common marble.

The Growing Years - The Games of my Youth

At source, marbles had to be purchased and hence, they had an intrinsic value. Consequently, as marbles were exchange at the end of each game, it was accepted as a form of gambling, which also meant that it was fiercely competitive. Even the simplest of games, such as Ringy, could be very tense. Frank for instance, who was one of the best would challenge any one to a game. He would scrape a circle in the dirt close to a railway sleeper and place a single bool in the middle. He would then walk back three steps and draw a line.
"Anywan wantae hiv a go?" he challenged.
Charly Gillan took him on and placed a bool beside Frank's."Make it four steps, an' a'll go furst", said Charly.
"Yae're on. But remember the bools must clear the ring - touchers cannae count", responded Frank.
Charly toed the line with his shooter, his special bool, gripped by thumb and two fingers. He moved his hand back and forward along his line of aim and let go. He clipped one of the bools but failed to move it outside the ring. Frank then toed the line and with a similar aiming style to Charly, he released his shooter at great pace. He hit one of the bools well clear of the circle and such was the impact that he got a lucky bounce on to the second bool which also skited out of the circle.
"Yae're too good fur me, Frank. Nae mare. But ah'll gee yae a gem of moshie, if yae like".
Frank turned this down as a few more of the crowd arrived, including James, Mungo, and Davie. As usual, to the fore, Davie Smith bustled his way in looking for attention. Frank proceeded to do James for three bools and Mungo for three plus a plunker worth another two. By now I was excited and wanted to have a go, even though I knew he was too good for me. But I had little chance to get lucky as Davie Smith stuck a large gleaming white and gold plunker under Frank's nose.
"This, against six" he challenged.
"Yae've goat tae be kid'n"...Ah'll gee yae five", responded Frank.
"Ok, yer oan, but nae usin' steelies unless yae go back tae the edge of the pavement. Ah don't wantae damage ma plunker".
Frank agreed to this, even though he knew, that because of the extra distance and the weight of the steelie, he could not use his normal

throwing action. This meant that the shooter had to be rolled or thrown underhand. After some further argy bargy it was agreed that Davie would go first but that Frank would be allowed to arrange the bools in the ring. We quickly got the gist that Frank had some tactic in mind as he placed Davie's plunker forward of center of the ring. He then placed his own five bools in two rows behind the plunker; one row of two touching the plunker, and a row of three tightly behind. Davie had quite a reputation at the game and was said to have won a couple of 'Big yins' around Bridgeton. He took up his position and, true to character, his strutting around as he weighed things up drew a sherricking from James.

"Cut oot the palaver, Davie, an' git oan wi' it".

Davie got a bit riled at having his style put down.

"It's ma bools", he shouted back, "an' ah'll play any bliddy way ah wantae, aw'rite!"

James just shook his head and Mungo called for some wheesh. Davie, by way of justifying his previous preparations strutted around even more. Eventually, he slowly bent low to the ground, pulled his arm back, and with a forward step, released his shooter with an under throw that caused it to skip twice, and with great pace, it smacked the plunker in the ring dead center. To everyone's astonishment, the plunker hardly moved from its spot, and only two of the back row left the ring, with a third one fairly close. Dave stormed up to the ring shouting his disbelief. Deserving of sympathy, he pleaded with everyone and got none. As for James, he stared back in contempt, and called for Frank to get on and finish it.

Frank took his position; steelie primed in his fingers. His style was more traditional than Davie's. Low to the ground, he swung his arm backwards and forwards a couple of times, in line with the target, and released his shooter at a slower pace than Davie's. The steelie hit the soft ground with a thud and shot along the ground. It hit Davie's plunker clean out of the ring and ran on to nudge another bool over as well. Frank, who had followed though on his shoot, quickly picked up the plunker and brandished it in his fist. He had got what he had wanted; he was not interested in who won the other bools. Davie angrily ranted that he had been cheated and that he wanted his plunker back. He claimed that Frank had arranged the bools in such a way they could not be moved with a direct hit. Frank would have none of it and told him to "go hame'n cry oan yer mammies shooder".

Finally, James got fed up with all the "moanin' an' groanin' " and stepped up to Davie, with finger raised. You always knew when James got really angry as he would always raise his finger and partly point it towards who, or whatever, was annoying him. With out turning his eye away from Davie, he held his hand out to Frank. "Gees a len o' that plunker, a minute, Frank".

Knowing that he was not to be denied. Frank handed it over.

"Ok, big man...are yae gonae renege on yer bet?"

"He cheated, an' ah waant it back"

"Yae cannae talk aboot cheatin'!. Ah've heard some o' the stories aboot yae play'n wi' kids from Patna Street an' cheatin' them. So yae've goat two choices. Yae kin say nae mer aboot this; quit yer bliddy moanin'; an' niver again accuse ma brither of cheatin'. Or, if yae still waant this plunker, then Frank an' I ur' gonnae stick it up yer arse; an' yer face wull no' bi shoin' aroon here any mer. So whits it tae be? Ur yae gonnae shake hauns wi' Frank?"

As he grudgingly held out his hand, Davie knew, there and then, that he would never again confront the Hargreaves. There was a lesson to be learnt here..

It was a great summer that year. You just could not get home quickly enough from school so that you could meet up with your pals and carry on where you left off the previous evening. You would stop off at home just long enough to get rid of your schoolbag, and grab a double slice of bread spread with margarine and jam. Then it was straight round Kinnear Road, a quick hello to dad in the shop, and then over to the close to meet up with the guys. It was even better when the school holidays came round; the six weeks seemed to fly by. Even the shop had now dropped a little in stature. It was now regarded as a reference base for replenishing our needs.

Our games would come and go, with no discernible reason as to why one would start in preference to others. Each, at their peak, would be pursued with great passion before seamlessly passing on to the next. Certain games, such as marbles, would continue well past their usage peak and still be pursued on an impromptu basis. Others would be called upon depending on the time of day and weather. A popular one in the evenings would be a form of hide and seek, called K.C.R.F - Kick Can, Run Fast. An empty can, usually retrieved from the Backcourt midden, would be placed upright on the pavement in front of the close. One of us would then run at it and kick it as far we could. The unfortunate seeker would then have to retrieve the can and replace it on its spot before he (or she) could begin the seek. On finding someone there would be a loud shout that the game was a bogey and everyone else would reassemble for the start of the next game.

There would be many occasions, especially in the evenings when, for whatever reason, we would run out of ideas on what to do and, out of sheer boredom, we would just hang out at the close and talk about this, that, everything, and nothing. Sometimes there would also be bouts of good-natured pushing and shoving - little trials of strength, with a wary eye on it not going too far. At such times we could also be very mischievous and play tricks on the neighbours - no harm meant, of course. On one occasion it was suggested that we tie the two facing doors in the close close together with a piece of string; then knock on it loudly and watch the fun.

It was agreed that we could not do it in our own close as Charlie Gillan and Davie Smith lived there. It was therefore decided that we would volunteer Joe O'Donnel's door in Sorn Street as a penalty for turning up late that day. Also under their direction, I got a long length of string from the shop and met up with them at Joe's close. We waited till we thought it was suitably quiet then Charlie and Mungo took the string and tied the doors together. It was now down to who would knock on the door. Under a heavy dare from Mungo and Charlie, Joe backed down and agreed to do the dirty. He tip-toed up the close and we followed. When he reached his door he stood there petrified. The final cutting thrust of a knife was being made from a small forced opening and as the door flew open there stood

an irate Mr. O'Donnel. With knife in one hand, he grabbed Joe by
the hair with the other.

"Yae wid be waantin' tae play a trick oan yer family, wid yae. Then
let mi show you, a trick or two".

With that he gave Joe a resounding smack on the back of the neck;
pushed him inside, and kicked the door shut behind him. We all
fearfully took off in case he decided to come out looking for us.

Another trick that we believed we invented was the invisible
window knocker. You would get a bobbin of thread; again, this
would be my job. You would then get a small button and pass a
length of the thread through it at which point you would tie a knot to
fix the button. The idea was to pin the start of the thread on to the
top of the window and have the button hanging close to the glass.
With the bobbin in your hand you could now make the button rise
and fall against the window to make a small clicking noise. If you
then climbed up on the dyke, (the roof of the midden enclosure), and
unwrapped sufficient thread for your needs, you could then hide out
of sight and make mystery clicks on the window. If anyone came to
investigate you simply pulled the button above the line of the
window.

On a pretext of revenge against Davie Smith for doing something to
him, Mungo volunteered to try it out on Mrs. Smith, Davie's mother.
With the help of Frank, Mungo set it up. He climbed up on the dyke
and Frank threw the bobbin up to him. He then reeled in the thread
on the bobbin to take up the slack. While we stood around the back
of the close, just out of sight of the window, he tried it out. The
clicking sound was low but distinctly audible. It was not long before
Mungo was pulling in the thread to raise it out of sight. Mrs. Smith
came to the window and had a good look around; but she could now
neither see nor hear anything and moved away. Mungo repeated the
operation and was nearly caught as an irate Mrs. Smith stormed back
and fully raised the window.

"Whit 'r yae up tae yae buggers? Ah know yae're there. If ma Dave
catches yae, he'll give yae a right seein' tae."

The Growing Years - The Games of my Youth

At this point Dave did arrive and he knew immediately what was going on. We all took off amidst a lot of swearing and loud threats. Mungo was not so lucky. As he jumped down from the dyke Davie was waiting for him. There was a flaying of clenched fists, which ended up with Mungo running off holding his nose.
"You ever try that again wi ma mither!" an excited Davie, shouted at the fleeing Mungo. By now a few of the neighbours had come to the window to witness Davie's triumph.

Whilst our games were many and varied the one that was to dominate our summer, and be the major anticipation of those to come, was football - street football. Celtic Park (The Football Club) stood in all its glory at the top of Kinnear Road, and we were still not aware of it yet. It all began one day in early summer. Someone suggested that we have a game of football and. in response to the obvious question, he produced a well-worn, baldy, tennis ball.

As it happened, and still verifiable today, there were two lampposts that stood some forty yards equidistant on either side of the shop. We had seen Mungo kicking a ball around as if he enjoyed it and it was rumoured (probably by him) that Davie Smith was fairly good - after all he was older than we were. It was therefore decided that Mungo and Davie would pick sides. There were eight of us with Mungo, James, Charlie Gillan, and myself on one side; and Davie, Frank, Joe O'Donnel, and Archie Gemmel, on the other side. The game lasted for most of the afternoon; and we were swamped, as I recall, 28 - 22. It was the first examination of our skills, and it has to be said that a few of us, myself included, had a lot to learn.

Only Mungo, Davie, and possibly Archie rose above the unremarkable. Mungo showed some natural skill when gathering and running with the ball. Dave showed athleticism and had that extra strength in keeping with his extra years. Archie was a willowy kind of runner, and on a couple of occasions showed the beginnings of a deceptive swerve. All in all it was brilliant and each day could not come soon enough. Before long other lads from the top of Lilly Street and Sorn Street were joining us. With the odd grumpy exception, and that included Granda, there was now an acceptance by the neighbours of us playing in the street. Some would even warn us of any sighting of the 'polis' as it was illegal, but nobody cared. It now dominated our lives and would be played at every opportunity. Sunday became our big day, where seven a side became the norm. Before that first summer was out we came to recognise the importance of having Celtic Park on our doorstep. We now watched the reserve team, every second Saturday, when the first team was playing away from home. And because of our age we were allowed in free through the 'Junior's gate'. Another great privilege we had as local kids was that the groundsmen, on certain days, would allow us in to watch the team train. And, if we were not too cheeky, we could pick up an autograph from one of the first team. For some of us, dreams were beginning to form. This was the beginning of a very fulfilling time for all of us.

1937-38

LEAGUE CHAMPIONS

Back row: C. Geatons, R. Hogg, J. Morrison, J. Kennaway,
G. Paterson, J. Carruth, and J. Divers
Front row: W. Maley, Manager; J. Delaney, M. McDonald, W. Lyon,
J. Crum, F. Murphy, and J. McMenemy (Trainer)

Chapter IV

The Growing Years

Fitting in

The Games of my Youth

The Gangs

Still Catching Up

Family Matters

The Growing Years - The Gangs

Bridgeton was the heart of the East End of Glasgow. Like its close neighbourhood, the Gorbals, its throbbing beat was to be heard in every nook and cranny of its tenement slums. People did not so much live there as survived there. Not that they sought pity for their condition. How could they, when their awareness was dampened by the acceptance that everyone shared it? Ambition and hope were plentiful but their aims were modest. Youth was still a joy; and that which lay ahead was still to be lived. Pleasure was to be sought and taken as opportunity presented.

Religion, despite its evil use as a divisive tool by sectarian ignorance, was not only a redemptive hope for the many, it was an identity, and very often an essential one. Inequality was primarily measured in the warmth of your clothing and the quantity of your food; the quality of both being a remnant of good fortune. Social structure, as represented by the professional classes, was of another order, to which access was only by blind respect and humility.

It was into this culture that the gangs of the 20s and 30s were borne. But to say that they were borne out of this culture as a cause, would be to insult the thousands of families who lived out their hopes and dreams in the tenement slums; who survived with their humour, their memories, and their learning, and made their own contribution to the culture of Glasgow.

Gangs are born of other needs, more vainglorious and unappeasable than those of tenement families. They are borne from the pubescent drive for identity, for self-importance, and meaning. Emotions that are common to us all. But, when driven by the energy of youth, they can be fearsome in their demands. It is an energy that rises above the poverty of the ghetto and replaces it with the pleasures of mindless violence sourced by boastful bravado and envy.

Provocation is ever present, and the seeking of insult, when none is offered, is de rigueur. This can grow to an evil understanding of the power of fear and its mindless application.

Fortunately it is a pursuit of the few. Appeased by the pleasure of female companionship; the warmth of the family; and access to a modicum of the common pleasures of the day, our emotions are harnessed and redirected.

The Growing Years - The Gangs

I must have been going on nine years old when I had my first real acquaintance with a gang. It was a fairly common subject with the guys, but with little meaning for us at that time. Our parents would have us believe they were a thing of the past. Still, we were regularly updated on the hearsay exploits of the gangs around Bridgeton and the nearby areas, and could also list them by rote. There were the Billy (protestant) Boys and the Fenian (Catholic) Boys, the only two with religious associations. Then there was the Cumbie, the Sticket, the Baltic Fleet, and the Nunie Boys. Living just off the corner of Baltic Street, and Nuneaton Street, as I did, these two gangs could not have been more local. Yet none of their rumoured exploits had been local in my two years to date.

On meeting up with the guys one day the main topic of gangs was to the fore. Mungo Cloherty said that that he had heard from a guy in Nuneaton Street that the Nunie Boys were going to be paid a visit by the Sticket, whose base was the far end of Dalmarnock Road. The story goes, said Mungo, that a group of the Nunie Boys had gone to a local dance hall, just off Bridgeton Cross. Their leader had taken a fancy to one of the girls and was chatting her up when he was approached by a guy who claimed to be the leader of the Sticket. He told him that he was chatting up his girl, and that he had to beat it now, or else! She denied being his girl and insisted that she had broken it off with him some time ago.
In support of his conquest, his proud response to the warning was to tell the Nunie leader "go an' jump in the fucking Clyde, or dae somethin' aboot it".
Knowing that he was under scrutiny by the 'dance-hall bouncers' the Sticket leader with a pointing finger angrily retorted, that he had been warned, and that he would be 'seen to' in the near future.
The word on the street, according to Mungo, was that the near-future day had arrived for the Nunie leader, and that the Sticket were coming for him the following day.

The following morning the area was buzzing, but especially so in Nuneaton Street. Women in wrapped shawls gathered at the closeheads, deep in conversation. There was an air of expectancy everywhere and "you could cut the atmosphere with a knife". Mum warned all of us that we must be indoors at the first sign of trouble. In particular May and I were not to leave her sight all day. I remember being none too pleased at being tied to the house all day. To cap it all, mum had prearranged a get-together with a group of neighbours who were heavily into knitting. A more lifeless day I could not imagine.

The only consolation was that she had borrowed a tea urn from somewhere to save her constantly boiling kettles of water. Around mid-day it was put in position on the fire grate. It looked like a huge tin can with a spout at the bottom. But its presence meant that there would be lots of tea and cake all day.

The afternoon passed with predictable boredom, and out in the street, it looked like it was going to be a huge non-event. It was now getting into late afternoon and our visiting neighbours were preparing to leave. Needless to say, knitting had not been the main topic of conversation. Instead, they had angrily disected the expected battle. True to their emotions, the women reviewed it with utter contempt and, with the constant nodding of her head, mum affirmed her support for all that was said.
"They're brainless heed cases", was their main summation. "Take their weapons away from them, an' they're nuthin...An' its us who hiv tae pick up the pieces an' listen to thur self pity when its over. It's niver them that's in the 'rang. Ah'll tell yae Aggie...If ah knew the time they wir cumin' the day, ah'd go an' get the polis to thim, masel'...They're bliddy heed cases, ev'ry wan o' them...An' ah'll tell yae, somethin' else...men're only good fur wan bliddy thing... wan bliddy thing!"

As the neighbours made their way out on to the landing mum let it be known that she wanted me and May to get ourselves ready for an early bed. We knew by her tone that there was to be no leeway in this requirement and dutifully obeyed. On her return we were told that we could join her and Agnes at the front room window. But, she added, if any gang fight starts we were not going be allowed to see it. We were to get ourselves in to her bed and stay there until it was over. Mum and Agnes ensconced themselves at the windows with myself and May securely positioned beside them. Dad called in to say that he had closed the shop early; and was joining George, who was doing likewise, for a few drinks. As for Bill and Bert, dad let it be known that they were hanging around the close with Sconie and Peggy. He confirmed this, when he went down stairs, by having them wave up to us. Dad then gave a final wave and took himself round the corner to join George.

By now May had decided that she was bored and took herself back to bed. With mum holding her arm round my waist I pushed myself as far out of the window as she would allow. I was scanning intently along the length of Baltic Street. I was excited, and expected the gang to arrive any moment. The pavements were milling with people, but it was the street that I scanned. I expected to see a well-organised troop of guys, brandishing their weapons, just like a platoon of soldiers. Suddenly mum's arm tightened around me. "Oh my God!. They've arrived", she shouted in a fearful tone accompanied by a shriek from Agnes. She hurriedly pushed me away, and without turning, shouted loudly at me to get to bed and for me not to come back until it was all over. I hurriedly took a step backwards, trembling slightly with excitement. But, realising that they had lost all awareness of me, I quietly stood up on a chair close to the wall from where I had a clear view, over Agnes's shoulder, of the corners of Nuneaton Street.

The gang was gathering in the middle of the street. They had arrived by stealth, mingling with the crowd on the pavements. Their number must have been more than thirty. They were mostly brandishing pick- and axe-handles, supported by bayonets and various sizes of knives carried by those to the fore. The smaller knives, I later learned were razors. They were now shouting themselves into frenzy, with calls for the Nunie to give up their leader. With a final escalating roar, weapons raised in the air, and accompanied by the screams of women hanging out of every visible window, they set off running down Nuneaton Street. As they disappeared from sight we were still left with the fearsome screams and clattering sounds. Suddenly, they were back at the corner and regrouping, very much the worse, it would seem from their combat. They were not done, though. With adrenaline coursing with blind rage and pride, they generated another fearsome roar and took off again into the fray.

As Bill and Bert later filled us in, their first attack had been met with similar numbers and weapons and much blood had been spilled. Both sides, though, had no defences against a common enemy from above. As they clashed halfway down the street they were showered by an avalanche of water poured from buckets and basins of water. In their next attack they not only had to contend with the water; this time, after releasing the water the basins and buckets, and many other household objects were thrown down on their heads. This had the desired effect as many of the Nunie Boys ran for cover in the nearby closes whilst their attackers had had enough and fled. A few of them were chased back up the street and came back in to our view. There were now a few one-on-one fights going. Suddenly Agnes let out a scream.

"He's been bayoneted...Look at the blood...Where?" shouted mum.

"There, there...He's crawlin' intae that close", she screeched.

At that point the sound of sirens signaled the arrival of black marias filled with police. They hit the ground running as they emptied from the marias and in no time it was all over.

The sirens stopped and the street below went quiet. Maybe, by way of respite, or for some other reason, mum turned away from the window and immediately spotted me. I did not wait for the inevitable response and took off, with her hurriedly following. I had to get into bed in a hurry and get under the bedclothes for fear of a smack for defying her.

As I ran into the back room I immediately spotted the fireside armchair and thought I would be clever. My intent was to bound on to the armchair and with one continuous movement bound into the bed - I had done it before. This time, however, I hit the chair too fast and it started to topple. To steady myself I grabbed the handle of the tea urn. I heard the agonising screams of mum as the scalding tea poured down me. I was numb with pain as I heard mum screaming at

Agnes to get the oil and flour. Just before I passed out I could feel the cooling balm of the oil and flour.

The next thing I remember was lying on a trolley gazing up at passing lights as I was hurriedly pushed along a corridor (in the Royal Infirmary). My awareness was returning, but with only minimal feeling. I was wheeled into a room, which was warm, and smelt strongly of liniment. They positioned a lifting apparatus beside the trolley. It had four hanging straps with loops that connected to each corner of where I lay. I then felt myself being raised as if lying on a stretcher. I was lowered into a bathtub of what felt like lukewarm water. As I slowly submerged I became aware of the massive blisters that seem to cover all of my left side. Two nurses equipped with scissors then proceeded to clip into the blisters. As they did so I could see the fluid oozing out into the surrounding water. They then cut away the superfluous skin exposing the bright pink underlayer. When all the skin had been removed I was partly raised from the tub and repositioned on my right side. Holding me in this position they wheeled the apparatus to the side of a specially prepared bed. From there they lifted me on to the bed and placed cushions on either side to hold me in position.

By now I was beginning to feel the throbbing ache of the exposed wound all the way down my left side. My left arm, which was supported, clear of my side, also throbbed. The doctor was aware of my soreness and assured me that it would not be for much longer. Two nurses approached carrying a brush in one hand and a jar of yellow coloured substance in the other. They proceeded to very gently paint the substance directly on to the wound. It felt cold and smooth and with each stroke the throbbing subsided. As they applied it the doctor held my attention by chatting away to me. He told me that he expected me to fully recover without any scarring; that the treatment I was receiving was a very new development and that, had my accident happened earlier, I would probably have been severely scarred.

The whole of my left side now felt very cold, but very comfortable. The nurses, still with brush in hand, kept standing back to review their work, and returning to brush on more medication. It was absolutely essential, they had been told that every single spot on the damaged area had to be sealed. They were eventually satisfied with their efforts, at which point they lifted a tent like structure made of wire, and placed over the top of me on the bed. This in turn was covered by a neatly spread sheet.

I woke early the following morning, having been disturbed by the removal of my tent by two nurses. As I became fully aware that the burn wound stretching down my left arm was completely encased by a hard scab. Lifting my head slightly I could see and feel my left side to be the same. Whilst one of the nurses tidied and corrected the cushions that prevented me from rolling from my right side position, the other nurse looked down at me with a grin and a feigned apologetic appearance.

"Now, it's like this, John", she said with a soft accent and pointing to the other nurse. "Her name is Janice...and she is the nice girl...My name is Margo, and I'm the one you're not going to like". She quickly calmed my concern at this and quickly got me to smile. She went on to explain the reason why it scabbed all over. It was meant to seal the wound, and to protect the new skin growing underneath. Eventually, she said, when the new skin had fully grown, the scab would fall off. But, until then, it must remain intact. She then pointed to the scab on the back of my hand, which had a small crack that was leaking fluid. This, she said, would have to be sealed otherwise the doctor would not be happy. She then produced a small bottle of liquid that reminded me of the dreaded Iodine, and gave it a good shake. She then tore open a sealed paper bag to reveal a small slim brush.

"Now this is going to be a bit nippy", she said with a feigned grimace. "Promise me that you will not move your hand while I paint over the crack. I nodded, and lay there watching her.

She dipped the brush and removed the excess on the edge of the bottle. As she slowly dragged the brush down the crack I could feel the nip - it was just like Iodine.

"One more time?" she asked, to which I murmured ok.

To my relief there was no pain at all from the second stroke. There were a few more minor cracks on my arm, and down my side, which I hardly noticed.

This treatment continued for some four weeks with my hand taking the brunt of it. Margo said that the instinctive movement of my fingers probably caused it. Curiously, it was the outer edge of my palm that was most prone to cracking, and also the most painful to seal. Because of this I cheated a couple of times by obscuring it from Margo's keen eyes. After about three weeks the sealant was discontinued. There were still cracks appearing, and Margo still monitored them, but they did not leak, which meant, that the new skin must be taking over, As the weeks went by, pieces of the scab scaled and broke off.

Finally, one day Margo appeared in the company of the doctor. After some banter with me he looked at my leg which was still encased. He placed his hands and gently moved it with his fingers. To my astonishment most of it came away in his hand revealing lovely new pink skin underneath. Excellent, he murmured, and proceeded to examine the rest, including my arm, with similar results. The final piece was on the back of my hand which, for a moment, looked like it was going to resist his efforts. He persisted, though, and it came away in small pieces. He then turned my hand over and looked at the palm.

"Oh dear", he said, rubbing his finger down the outer edge, "We seemed to have missed a bit, .but I think we can live with that, John. Don't you?" I smiled back and then looked at the gnarled tissue on the outer edge of my palm.

Over the years I have occasionally looked at the scar with amusement.

"If only I had been more brave."

Chapter IV

The Growing Years

The Growing Years - Still Catching Up

My early years at Burnside School were fraught with difficulty. Miss Lawson, the friendly nun who first welcomed me to the school, had more than borne out the warning from the headmaster, that it might be difficult for me to catch up on the lost years in Mearnskirk. Not that I had difficulty in learning; on the contrary, it was stimulating and I enjoyed it - when I was allowed to do it. But this was of no concern to Miss Lawson. She seemed filled with the best of intentions for me to be more well in body, than in mind; and that this could be best achieved by lots of rest, and lots of 'fresh air'. There was blindness to the fact that I was no longer ill and with no small amount of compelling energy. What enthused her more in this excessive good will was that she had taken a liking to me.

In addition to her welfare work, she was also responsible for religious instruction in catholic prayer and catechism. Both were mostly taught by rote, with little intrinsic meaning. Between the latter, and my requirement to rest and to take in lots of 'fresh air', my mornings at school were fully occupied without any danger of it ever taxing my mind. As a consequence of this recurring morning boredom, I relished the afternoons all the more, with its emphasis on reading, writing, and arithmetic. Here again though, there was a problem. The level at which the subjects were taught assumed me to be an infant, with no prior learning. It took no account, or chose to ignore that I had received a modicum of teaching over my three years at Mearnskirk Hospital. Consequently, I learned little that was new to me in my first year. Nonetheless, it did consolidate my early learning, and gave me a lot of confidence in my work.

Inevitably, it could not last. I started to become more and more aware of the difference between Burnside School and Sacred Heart School, where most of my friends went, and I knew that I was dropping further behind them. In truth, I did not feel inferior to them, but my fear was that I could be made to feel so if the difference continued. Towards the end of my first year I spoke to my parents, and asked if something could be done about it. Having assured them that I was still happy at Burnside, they agreed to go and see the headmaster.

True to their word, and with no delay, all three of us met with him.

The Growing Years - Still Catching Up

He recapped on his earlier warning that this could be a difficulty for me. He went on to compliment me on my work to date, and, on the basis of this he was prepared to move me to the next class ahead of my year. I was effectively jumping ahead one year, which excited me no end. I was to be monitored in this class and, depending on how I progressed, he was prepared to move me again. Much to the regret of Miss Lawson, I quickly progressed beyond her well-meaning morning directives. Whilst her religious instruction still remained a requirement, it was now a tolerable item in my expanded curriculum.

Time passed quickly and I was soon into my second year. I was now in the first of the five classes on the left wing of the school. To get to the final class would take me two years based on half term promotion. At the end of the first year I was in class four; ahead of schedule. Exams were not far off when I was called in to see the headmaster. He was impressed by the speed of my progress, he said. So much so, that he was convinced that I could take the class five exam instead of class four, and asked if I would like to give it a go. I was flattered, and instantly agreed. I was now nine years old, and knew the exams to be still quite junior.

When I got the news that I had passed I was absolutely ecstatic. It was like I had opened the door to freedom and a new world of learning. Nevertheless, I still have pleasant memories of those early years in Burnside. The times when we broke out of school for fun - our great escape. We would go down to the main gates and hang around till we felt that no one was paying attention. We would then slip behind the shrubs that fronted the playground. In a crouched position we would run to the end of the shrubs where there was a slim iron gate, referred to as the janitor's gate. Still blinded by the shrubs we quickly raced over to the main street and its shops. Our target was nearly always the 'City Bakers', where, for a penny, you could get two cream cookies.

We would then hang around looking at shop windows and licking and munching our cookies. We were never once caught, though we did run in to the janitor a few times. He was a good guy, though, and we knew he would never give us away. This was borne out by occasionally meeting him on other adventures - so we thought. In particular, though, I have very fond memories of Miss Lawson who, despite her foreboding presence, dealt kindly on me. As for the headmaster, whose name I cannot remember, his contribution to my early confidence by advancing my learning, was immense.

****

I joined Sacred Heart School in early 1938 at the age of 9, going on ten. My first day was filled with great enthusiasm and pride as I walked to school in the company of James and Frank. Their learning grade was some years ahead of me - James was three years ahead and Frank was two. But this had no bearing on our personal standing, as they knew that this was a circumstance of accident. Mum was also present on that first day to help me through the induction procedure. We met up with my new classmates, for whom it was also their first primary day, in the main school hall. We were greeted by the headmaster who introduced us to our first year teachers. As the formalities progressed I became aware of the stark difference between my classmates and me; they were all two years younger than I was. As I took this in I decided there and then that this would never become a problem for me - after all I was more mature and had to demonstrate it.

The difference between the new culture and that of Burnside was fairly stark. The caring attitude that went hand in hand with the teaching at Burnside was replaced by a more structured regime, where discipline and rules would be strictly enforced. Led by Miss Payne, most of that first morning was taken up by instruction on the school rules, and the associated punishment for certain infringements. Showing concern for our age group, and first year primary status, it was stressed that we had nothing to fear, but any infringement would still receive a 'Talking to'. There would be a 15-minute milk break at ten o'clock, and an hour dinner break at twelve.
At the dinner break I met up with James and Frank in the playground. After we had our sandwiches, they showed me round

the rest of the school. They genned me up on the do's and don'ts of the playground and which teachers to be on the lookout for. Old Wainwright, for example, hates football; and when he's around you donít even think football. You kick anything against a wall, said Frank, and he will put you on report. Then there are the priests; with one in particular, Father Butler, needing a special eye. There he is now, said James, pointing him out with a partly raised hand. Look at the strap he has hooked on to his belt. Step out of line with him and he will whack you on the spot - he'll never put anyone on report if he can avoid it. "It's a waste of good teaching time." he would say. Then there's Miss Payne, head of religious instruction. Anyone that swears has got to stay well away from her.

We walked to the far end of the playground, which butted on the chapel. Here stood the entrance to the youth club, which was sponsored by the chapel and run by the priests. We were allowed to use it in the dinner break to buy sweets and ginger. James led us in for a quick saunter round. It was fairly extensive and, in addition to its shop, it sported three full-length snooker cum billiard tables and two others for table tennis. There were other areas laid out with table and chairs for the members. My brother Bill, James and Frank, and their older brother, Jake, were members. They had let it be known that it was a bit of a gambling den at the weekends with some heavy card schools on the go. The priests, they said, turned a blind eye to it on the grounds that it kept crime off the streets - 'if they were not doing this they would be doing something else'. The other side of the story was that all winners had to make a generous donation to the priest's collection box.

Slipping into the routine of the school was easy, and with the odd exception, a joy. Maybe my two years made me a little bit wiser, or just a bit more experienced, whatever the reason learning came easily to me and I enjoyed it. The catholic emphasis and traditions, heavily pushed by mum, were also enveloping me. Sunday mass was now compulsory and processional ceremonies were now familiar to me. It was as if they were a preparation for the grandest of them all - The Eucharist, and my First Holy Communion. Leading up to it, and by way of consolidating previous instruction, the class received extra catechising by Miss Payne and Mr. Butler.

For tenement families this was a huge occasion each year. And especially so for the parents, whose children were being confirmed. In the case of mum it was doubly so, as sister May was also to be presented. Specially tailored clothes had to be bought or made for us. They also had to conform to the traditional design. In my case it meant a white satin blouse, topped with a broad scarlet band of ribbon, draped diagonally from your left shoulder to the right side of your waist. Short, or long, trousers could be worn, but always with a pronounced crease. New grey stockings with highly polished boots completed your turnout. The girls would be dressed in white satin dresses whose style could vary according to their height, shape, or fashion. Most of them, like May's dress, would be frilly. They would also be girded with a broad scarlet sash. White socks and black patent shoes would complete their outfit.

On the morning of the big day, Sunday, everyone gathered in the school playground. Our parents ringed the perimeter as the priests and nuns, headed up by Miss Payne and Father Butler, assembled us into a formal column of pairs of boy and girl. When all was ready, and on the follow signal from Father Butler, he would lead us through the gates and on to the middle of the street. He would then turn and walk backwards by way of checking that we were walking in an orderly line. Satisfied, he would resume his disposition at our head with a dignity and pride that radiated down to all of us.

As the parade got under way we tried to maintain our forward-looking posture as instructed. Nevertheless we could not suppress the smile of wellbeing at the respectful applause from the pavements and closeheads as we passed by. It was as if we were being exalted. The parade followed a predetermined route that took it through the streets surrounding the chapel. Although it was a fairly extensive walk it seemed like so little time had passed when we were being led through the main door of the chapel. The gentle sound of organ music was all pervasive as we walked down the central aisle towards the altar. Still directed by Father Butler, we each of us curtsied in front of the altar and proceeded from there to take up a position in the front two rows on either side of the aisle. When we were all in position Father Butler gestured with his hands for us all to sit down. At this point he and Miss Payne positioned themselves at the far end of each row facing on to us. The service began.

As instructed, we waited for their signal, which duly arrived. With an upward gesture of his hand we all stood to attention. We were then beckoned to walk in a file and take up a kneeling position facing the altar. On completion of their ceremonial blessing both priests turned to face us, each with a chalice poised in his hands. Starting at either end they proceed to bless and dispense the bread. As he moved up the line and my turn came closer I could feel myself getting very nervous.

There was an aura of mystery and expectation that excited me. Suddenly he was there in front of me. I raised my bowed head towards him and proffered my tongue. From the chalice he picked up the bread in his fingers. I shivered slightly, as he blessed me, and placed the gleaming white object on my tongue. It was round like a very small biscuit, but dry and tasteless. As I closed my mouth, I remembered the instruction not to bite on it. I stood up, with clasped hands in front of me, and returned to my seat. I was still very nervous and my mouth had become very dry. I looked sideways at May, by way of seeing how she had coped. She looked back with the slight suggestion of a grin on her face. From her contentment, I concluded that she must have swallowed it.

The mystery of the occasion was now being replaced with guilt as I struggled with the reality of my discomfort. It seemed like an eternity, but as we came to the end of the service I could feel the moisture returning to my mouth. Soon after I was able to swallow. I was now a confirmed Catholic, fully ensconced in a catholic school. The future looked bright.

Chapter IV

The Growing Years

Fitting in

The Games of my Youth

The Gangs

Still Catching Up

Family Matters

I first met Jimmy Miller shortly after I came home from
Mearnskirk. I usually dropped in after school to check on the
dogs and play around with Major. On one occasion I was
surprised to find Jimmy there feeding them and showing great
familiarity. He introduced himself as a friend of dad's and
clearly knew a lot about me. He loved the dogs and as a
favour to dad he always ensured that they were fed and
regularly walked each day around the plots.

Thereafter I met Jimmy on an almost daily basis. In response
to my surprise at the amount of time he spent on this, and
other jobs, for my dad he told me that he worked night shift at
the Dalmarnock Iron works and this gave him a lot of spare
time each day. He was a fascinating man, and very talented.
He it was who did all the odd jobs around the shop. He had
his own little plot of ground at the back of the shop on which
he had built a small hut that acted as his workshop and store.
He could put his hand to almost anything but his specialty
was woodwork. It was he who laid the basis of many skills I
developed in later life. He would positively encourage me to
use his saw, his chisels, and wood drill, which I found
incredibly trusting. He was also full of little sayings. If I got
something wrong he would typically dismiss it with; "Niver
be afraid tae try"; or "Niver be afraid tae make a mistake".
But what if I damage the wood? - I would ask.
"Yae cin replace it, or repair it. Yur confidence is mer
important than a bit of wid."
In terms of skill the one achievement that stands out in those
early years was when he tried to repair the shop's lavatory
seat. One of its hinges had broken away from the wood owing
to a damp spot. He said he would saw off the affected area
and glue and screw a new piece on to it. I watched him
closely and the repair seemed to be going to plan. He was
screwing the hinges back on to the seat when suddenly, to my

astonishment and shock, the seat split in two. "What do 'we' do now?" I asked.

He looked and grinned at my shocked expression.

"We'll make a new wan", he replied.

"Can you do that?"

"Wi' your help, ah can", he confidently said.

He went to his hut and returned with a thick piece of wood, which he laid on the ground. He then placed the broken seat on top and patiently maneuvered the broken pieces together. I was then asked to kneel down and place both hands on the broken seat and press down firmly. My job, he said was to ensure that it did not move while he drew a pencil line round its outside and inside contours. When he had done this I removed the pieces of the old seat to reveal a perfect tracing of its shape on the new wood. He then explained how he would remove most of the outer wood with a handsaw, then, using a fret saw, he would cut round the outer line to produce the shape of the old seat. The wood inside the internal line would be removed by similar means. He would then round the outer and inner edges with chisel and mallet. Finally, the new seat would be sandpapered till it was completely smooth to the touch. Two days later it would be a work of art.

My contribution to Jimmy's creation was a lot of patient sandpapering. He was so pleased with my efforts that he accorded me the pleasure of applying its first coat of varnish. When it was finally fixed to its lavatory bowl Jimmy called out to dad to come and give his opinion. All three of us stood looking at its glossy brown image through the lavatory door. I think its fit for a king to sit on, said dad. What do you think, John? At this point Mum appeared with a tray containing two glasses of beer and two glasses of ginger. I propose a toast, she said. "To all who sit on it! May the outcome be restful!"

****

Unemployment, sub-standard housing and poor levels of health had a dramatic effect on the national character of Scotland in the early 1900s. The commercial glories of the 19th century had been replaced with the great depression, and Glasgow, with its depleted industry, took the brunt of it in the 1930s. Widespread poverty and deprivation was at its worst in the tenement slums of Bridgeton and the nearby Gorbals.

Outwith my knowledge and memories my parents had worked and slaved for every penny in those early days to bring up their family. Jobs were few and hard to come by. Every device that could earn a penny was tried and tested. My father would walk far and wide to do any job that would pay a pittance, whilst mother would pool her skills with the neighbours to make a little food go far. It was this willingness of my father to walk any distance to find work that inspired mother with the idea of getting him a hand cart that he could stock with cheap low margin goods which he could sell across the city. This great idea was foundering on its cost when it was salvaged by his friend Jimmy Miller, who offered to help him to build one. All they need do was find a couple of old wheels down the Barras, the rest he would pick up on the by. In addition to this Jimmy allowed him to store the cart on his railway plot in Kinnear Road (the future site of the shop).

As it turned out it this was an even more backbreaking job for a very small income. But spurred on by mother he eventually built up a regular round of spots (outlets) where his income became more regular and rewarding. It was his friend Walter McLaughlen, a salesman at that time, who suggested that he specialise in fruit. He told him that he could buy fresh fruit by the box very cheaply from the Glasgow Fruit and Vegetable market in Bell Street, just up from Glasgow Cross. Because of its cheapness it was always a highly saleable commodity, especially to the kids.

This proved to be a successful venture and allowed him to vary his wares in line with the seasons. The summer would be primarily fruit with his sales outlets being the many parks across Glasgow. At other times the emphasis would be on vegetables which he sold in Kinnear Road, where there were no shops, and the streets running off to Springfield Road. The absence of shops in the Kinnear Road area and the modicum of success he had in selling there was the pointer to his next venture. After discussion with mother and ably supported by the helpful advice of Jimmy Miller, he successfully applied to the Railway for a small plot of land facing on to 40 Kinnear Road.

By now the family were living on a regular and stable income. But despite this improved standard of living (food was no longer a problem) they still could not afford to progress their ambition. In the meantime their plot would cost them a shilling a week. Eventually, through the initiative of mother, they visited the office of Laidlaw Limited, who were joiners and builders to trade and well known in the Bridgeton area. They outlined their plan to build a small shop in Kinnear Road and asked how much it was likely to cost. Based on their approximate dimensions it was estimated that it would cost around fifty pounds to build.

As this kind of sum was totally out of their reach, that should have been the end of it. Fortunately for them, James Laidlaw, the senior member of the company and well versed in the local economy, recognised the business potential of their proposal and made them an offer. On the condition that they make an advance payment of 10 pounds, he would not only build the shop, but would allow them to pay the balance over a maximum period of 2 years. And so the deal was done. Three months later, built entirely of wood , the shop was up and running. Such was its success that they not only paid off the debt to Laidlaw inside the set period; they also had him extend the shop to twice its size. Up until it was demolished in 1990, the wooden strap that ran down the centre of the shop to disguise the join was still visible.

****

As a consequence of my accident with the tea urn it was decided that the time had come to modernise the house. A priority of this was to rid ourselves of the fire range and its demands on time and effort to kindle and maintain its heat, and the burden of keeping it clean. The lobby was also to be renovated and customised to support our cooking needs. Prior to this decision, though, there had been another option which I later learnt from Bill. It had been proposed by mum that we could buy a plot of land in Burnside and build a small bungalow. This would provide us with the comforts and freedom that were just not possible in the tenement. Dad, who was quite keen on the idea, obtained an estimated cost from the local builder, James Laidlaw Limited, who had built the shop for him some 7 years earlier.

Bill told me that Laidlaw offered to build it for 350 pounds, which was considered to be good value for money at that time. But it was not to be. Memories and friends; hard times and good times; a way of life all at risk by a leap into the unknown. When faced with the choice they rationalised that for a fraction of the cost needed to build the bungalow they could convert their tenement room and kitchen into a very comfortable house. This would suffice in the short term and give them more time to plan the future. In later years Bill remembered it as a lost opportunity. But looking back at this decision I am convinced that it was influenced by the outcome of an even bigger leap in the dark when the decision was taken to build the shop.

It was no surprise to me when Jimmy Miller turned up early one Saturday morning carrying his toolbox. Jimmy was like my dad in many ways - tall, slim, and always with a ready smile as if he enjoyed life. After a bit of banter with me, he sat down at the table with mum and discussed her plans for renovating the house. She wanted the grate stripped out and replaced with a modern low line, fully-tiled fireplace. The lobby had to be stripped clean and painted. A modern gas cooker was to be installed and flanked with work tops and storage shelves. All wood around the sink, the jawbox, was to be replaced, as were all facing boards around the alcove beds and doors.

I sat there in awe as she outlined her plans and tried to visualise the outcome. Could Jimmy do all of this? My admiration for him was growing. Can you handle all of this, she asked? I think so, he replied. He rose from the table and started to rub the palm of his hand across the wallpaper.

"We could hiv a problem here, Aggie. Dae yae mind if ah strip a bit off to show you?"

"Ah waant the whole bliddy lot off, anyway...the quicker the better", she laughingly retorted.

It seemed as if Jimmy was trying to prepare her for a surprise. He took a penknife from his pocket, opened it, and made a small incision in the paper. As he did so a powdery dust came out and ran down the wall. Jimmy explained that the wall surface beneath was crumbling. He inserted the knife behind the incision and peeled back a piece of the wallpaper to reveal an even more startling problem. The exposed crumbling wall had insects crawling over it. I hurriedly took a step back in horror.

"What's that?" I called out.

Jimmy tried to assure me that they were harmless.

"They're caused by not strippin' off the auld wallpaper before hanging the new. All tenement hooses hiv this problem." He said. "Ah've done walls that hid ten layers oan it. People are jist scared of the cost of havin' to replaster if they strip off an' find the auld wall is damaged. You'll also hiv a similar problem wi' yur woodwork, Aggie, especially the facing boards. Look it the layers of paint on them. They've got to be at least 20 years auld"

Taking a chisel from his toolbox he knocked it behind the facing board of the alcove with the butt of his hand. He prised it back to reveal the underlying wood that the facing board was nailed to.

"Look, it's infested wae wood lice. They love dry rot."

I ventured a look at it and immediately turned away in horror. To think that I had been sleeping close to this vermine for nearly three years. Mum picked up on my fear and told me not to worry. She said that, as of today, she had arranged for me to live with Granny and Granda for the next two-to-three weeks. Similar arrangements had been made with neighbours for the rest of the family.

"It'll be a new hoose by the ti me yae git back" she said.

I looked at Jimmy, by way of getting further reassurance.

"Trust mi, John...By the time a've finished, yae wulnae know the place... It'll be a hame fit fur a king."

I trusted Jimmy, and thought no more about it.

****

Living in Granny and Granda's house was always a pleasure. For a start, they had an indoor lavatory and bathroom. In addition to this they had a proper kitchen with a grate that comprised an oven and a gas ring. But the greatest luxury of all was that they could have hot running water. It only required the living room fire to be burning which, outside of summer, seemed to always be. Then again, all the grey stone houses in Kinnear Road, and stretching back to Springfield Road, had the same comforts. I never understood this gulf in quality. My bed was made up in a corner of the living room. It was a collapsible camp bed made of tubular rods and canvas, which could be folded and put way when not in use. Granny said that dad had bought it as a standby. It took up very little room and I was more than comfortable in it.

Granny and Granda were always a joy to me. In her fulsome body she radiated comfort and security. I never knew her to be irritated except in the presence of Harry, or Geordie - her boys. Her cooking was great, and much better than mum's, I thought. And her rhubarb jam was superb, I can still taste it. Made from fresh rhubarb taken from Granda's plot at the back of the shop, it always came out sweetly flavoured. It only had one failing - try as she may, she could not get it to gel. But this was of no consequence. Your bread might be a bit wet but this was a small price to pay for the taste. Then, of course, there was her wee frailty, and our big secret. From her past, a well-deserved comfort of a wee dram had grown into a needy support for the present. Deep down in the hollow space of her ample canvass brassiere there would always be the remains of a quarter bottle of Teachers, her favourite tipple. Pschycology had no place in understanding Granny. Just witness the outer edge of her lips tweak upwards as she took her infrequent sip - just the one. Watch her eyes; I'm sure they twinkle - just the once.

As for Granda, although his shoulders now had a slight stoop. He still had the profile of his muscular past. A proud man who had salvaged some of his strength and pride from the ravages of a working life down the pits. Many, including his sons, referred to him as a cantankerous, grumpy, old bugger. I could never see him in that light. Sure he could be grumpy and cantankerous with Granny, but I never once saw her react with other than a smile. But with certain people, including his sons, Harry and Geordie, his reputation could be said to be justified. Again, as if from the past, aggression in others would provoke him in kind. He had no truck or patience with the 'flymen'; even less when they indulged in self-pity. Bloody cowards, the lot of them, he would often say. And be it on your head if you tried to cheat him of a penny. Conversely, he was not above indulging the generosity of mum or dad. Then, paternity must have some rights.

In the time I spent living with them I had a few insights into other facets of his life, not least of them being this medical condition, and the pain and suffering he hid from others. I woke up early one morning and in the dim light coming through the window I saw him sitting by a newly lit fire with only his simmet and trousers on. Granny appeared with two cups of tea. They were unaware of my awakening and but for what followed I would probably have gone back to sleep. They were having their tea when suddenly Granda gripped his side and gave a subdued moan.
"Turn the light oan, Jessie, ah cannae take this any mer...You've got tae hiv a look"
Granny turned the light on and looked down at me. With concern, I asked her what was wrong with Granda.
"Go back tae sleep, John", she said and turned her attention to Granda, who was now unfastening his simmet.
"Stand up Bill", she said.
She then took the unbuttoned simmet by the neck and very gently eased it down his arms to reveal the white skin of his upper body. As she did so she turned him facing into the living room and thus fully exposed his other side for her attention.
"It looks like it's infected again; an' it's also leaking", she said.

"Git the methylated spirit, wumman, and clean it up", he said with restrained pain in his voice. "Ah'll go an' see the doecter later, an' let him hiv a look at it."

"Ok, while I'm gettin' the spirit, strip yersel' so wi can check oot yer bottle."

I was now sat up in bed watching every painful movement as Granda stripped off. A brown tube was protruded from his lower stomach and was connected at the other end to a rubber pouch strapped to his leg. He stood there totally naked, his white body highlighting the inflamed area that surrounded the protruding tube.

I was absolutely aghast at the contained pain of Granda, as Granny gently wiped the skin above and around the inflamed area with the strong smelling spirit. She also cleansed the area of his leg where the pouch was strapped.

"That's aw ah cin dae fur yi, Bill. Dae yae feel any better?"

"It's easin' aff a wee bit", he replied.

"Let mi help yae git dressed", Granny said.

"A'll manage, wumman...dinnae fuss", he said.

As I watched him slowly dress himself, I knew he was aware of me. With his simmet and trousers back on and fully buttoned, his braces back in place, he sat down and pulled on his boots.

"Can I tie your laces Granda?" I humbly asked, whilst fearing a gruff dismissal.

"Yae're a gentle wee man, John.... Thur's much o' yer dad in yi...An' yes, ah wid be thankful if yae wid tie ma laces."

"Are you still sore, Granda?"

"Naw, am aw right noo", he replied. "But whit aboot you?...Ah hope ah didnae scare yae wi ma groanin? "

Borrowing a phrase from my dad, I told him no' to be daft, which brought a grin to his face.

"Now look, ah don't waant yae tae tell anywan aboot whit yae've seen an' heard this mornin'...Nae body, except yer mammy, knows aboot ma problem, an' ah want it tae stay that way...Ok?"

"It's ok, Granda, I promise. No one will ever know from me."

Granny winked at me when I said this.

"Don't worry Bill, yur secret's well safe wi' John".

****

In all, I lived with Granny and Granda for three weeks. It was the summer school break, but it felt like I was on a real holiday. No tenement stairs; no cold smelly lavvy; my everyday pleasures just outside the front door. It was a great time, spoiled only by the daily obtrusion of Uncle Harry and the occasional visit from uncle Geordie. Not that it caused any problems for me, but it did seem to irritate Granny and Granda. Uncle Geordie's visits were always short and usually on his way home from his work in the Dalmarnock foundry. As a consequence he was always unwashed and wearing his work overalls. This would irritate Granny, who would warn him to stay away from the soft furnishings and sit on the wooden seat at the window. Equally, Granda was never fond of his visits and usually gave him a grumpy reception.

To get to Granny's from his work meant a slight detour, which I thought strange, considering the reception he always got. Then one day, out of sight of Granda, I saw her take money from her purse and hand it to him. Granda must have had some knowledge of this as I heard him on occasion warning Granny not to lend him any money. No one seemed to know why uncle Geordie was always skint. Even mum and dad were occasional providers as I had witnessed. There was always something about him that I could not relate to. Seldom without a smile, he was always eager to please with a ready word that was often left unsaid. He seemed more of an irritance than a bother to Granny and Granda.

Uncle Harry on the other hand was a definite bother to them. He would turn up each morning at ten o'clock with his unsold morning newspapers and his money pouch. Granny would always prepare his breakfast of tea and hot sandwiches while he counted his morning takings. Granda would always try to ignore him. He would take one of the unsold papers and sit himself down by the fireside with his mug of tea. This scene would sometimes be repeated at six o'clock with the only difference that there would be more unsold papers and money involved. This was owing to him only selling one title in the morning, the Daily Record, and two in the evening, the Citizen and the Times.

In the football season Saturday was always a big day for him. He would have two men working for him. They would man the Dalmarnock railway station and the corner of Baltic Street and Springfield Road. He himself would man the corner of Springfield and Dalmarnock Road, which was referred to as the pub pitch. From this corner he would have a clear sight of the other two whom he would service from his main stack. He had an agreement with the pub that he could use their corner door to protect his paper stack from the weather.

On a Saturday, when I got back from Celtic Park, dad would usually have me go round to his pitch and collect a few dozen papers for the shop. I always enjoyed the buzz of Saturday afternoon in 'Spring'y Road'. The shops were at their busiest and the sound of Uncle Harry's pervasive calls to "Get yur piiiipur here! Ceetiziiiin! an' Teiimes!!!" To achieve his bellowing call his lips took on a distorted pout. This, added to his broken nose and scarred cheeks, gave him a frightful facial image. Yet, when his face relaxed into a grin, as when he paused to sell a paper, he looked no more fearsome than the many other characters that breezed around the Spring'y Road.

He was very well known in the Dalmarnock area of Bridgeton and, in my naievity, I suppose that by association it gave me a degree of self-importance. But this had to be balanced against Granda's belligerent opinión that he was a flyman, and a crook, and that he would not trust him as far as he could throw him. This posed a quandary for me. Granda, I respected and trusted, but Uncle Harry, in my presence, did little to support Granda's opinions. Maybe, at my age, ignorance was a blessing.

****

In the course of my stay at Granny and Granda's, I saw very little of Bill and Bert, and even less of May. As Agnes helped out in the shop I would see her every day. Whilst I soon began to miss them it was also a welcome break from the many small frictions that would arise from time to time because of the confinement of our house. It was therefore a surprise when Bert dropped in one day to see how I was getting on. He said he was going round to the Sacred Heart youth club for a game of snooker and wanted to know if I wanted to join him. Knowing nothing about snooker or billiards, he offered to teach me. We dropped into the shop to let mum know where we were going. On the way out James and Frank, who had spotted us going into the shop, came up to us as we left and offered to join us.

The club was fairly quiet when we arrived and so we had no problem in getting on a table. Bert suggested that he would take me on one table and James and Frank would take another, This would allow him to teach me the basic rules and show me how to hold and use the cue. I picked up on the basics fairly quickly and soon Bert and I were playing James and Frank in a foursome. Although I was a beginner it was soon clear that the skill level of the others were not that high either. As a consequence there was quite a bit of skylarking and much trying to hit the cue ball as hard as we could in our attempt to pot a colour.

This soon brought us under the watchful gaze of Father Butler who stood there with a cue in his hand.
"Would you like to join us, Father?" Frank cheekily asked.
"Yes, if only but to teach you all some etiquette. And you, young man, some manners", gently smacking Frank on the buttocks with his cue.
"Rule number one." he said whilst chalking his cue. "In the presence of clergy you will always show a mannerly respect."
He now walked forward and, holding the cue erect on the table, he continued.
"Number two. When you address a priest, you will not presume to a familiarity that confuses politeness with insolence!"
With that he brought the cue down flat on the table with a startling noise.

The point was made, and we all stood in awe of him. With that aura of knowledge and certainty, which we fearfully respect in the priesthood, he looked at each of us in turn. Suddenly, a large cheery smile transformed his image.
"Set them up Frank, and I will demonstrate a few shots for you."
A remorseful Frank hurriedly obeyed. His remorse soon disappeared, though, as Father Butler put on a show of potting and trick shots that left us all aghast. So much so, that when he put down the cue the four of us spontaneously applauded.
"You are much too kind, lads", he said impishly, and went off.

Thereafter all we wanted to talk about was snooker. Bert told us that our brother Bill was a helluva good player, and that he played for the team in the Bridgeton Public Halls. James and Frank were astounded at this; if true, this was celebrity status we were talking about.

"Yae're kiddin' us!" James said.

"Ah'm kiddin' yae not", retorted Bert. "He also plays fur money in the Hampden hall."

"Where's that?" asked Frank.

"It's up the lane facing Dalmarnock station. Ah'l show yae tonight if yae waant. Ah'n if ah see Bill, ah'll try an' get him tae come doon."

"Haud own, said James, we're too young. We'll no' be allowed in."

"Ah'll see if Bill can wangle it", said Bert. "He's done it fur me before. Failin' that ah'll try an' get Bill to take us in tae the Bridgeton Public Halls, when he's playing".

We were all pretty excited about this. So much so that I glued myself to Bert until we met up with Bill on his return from work. Bill was so flattered by the build up that Bert had given him that he immediately agreed to try for the Hampden that night.

After dinner we all met up in the shop around six o'clock. Dad, who never closed up before seven, gave Bill a good talking to before we left. He warned him that if Wullie did let us in that none of us four were to touch a cue; that Bill was to play one game, and one game only, and that we had to leave after it. Finally, if we were not back by the time he closed the shop he would come looking for us.

It was only a five-minute walk from the shop to the Hampden Snooker Hall. We went down Mordaunt Street; turned left at the bottom; under the Railway Bridge; then left again into the lane. On the left side were the opposite ends of the railway arches that stretched back into Mordaunt Street. The fourth archway down was home to the Hampden Snooker Hall. Bill told us to stand outside while he had a word with Wullie. He was only gone a couple of minutes when he returned and beckoned us in. As we filed in Bill introduced us to Wullie who let it be known that he owned the place, and that he was letting us in for a look around, but only as a favour to Bill, who was one of his best players, he added.

It was early evening and the hall was quiet. The first thing that struck you about the place was its huge cavernous shape whose upper reaches were lit by a line of naked bulbs hanging from the roof. There was also a pervasive smell of dankness not dissimilar to that of a tenement backcourt on a wet day. As we looked around the dimly lit area we could see two lines of tables stretching back into the arch, making twelve in all. Bill gave Wullie a tanner and said he would take a table for half an hour to give the lads a flavour of the game.
"Ok", Wullie replied, "but ah waant them oot soon as the light goes". With that he went into his office and switched on the nearest table light.
The green cloth of the table glowed under the intense light. Bill racked up the red balls as they were retrieved from the six table pockets by Bert. He then explained which of the other colours went on which spot. Placing the white ball in the Dee area he then broke the reds with a resounding crack. To score he now had to pot a red ball he said. Having done so you can then attempt to pot one of the other colours, whose score value range from two to seven. I was incredibly proud of Bill as he proceeded to pot balls with great skill. He could even make the white ball spin backwards or sideways from the ball it hit. This allowed him, he said, to position the white ball for his next shot.

Bert, who knew how to play, helped Bill by retrieving and respotting each non red ball that was potted. He also let it be known at the end of one bout of potting that Bill had made a scoring break of fifty. After all the balls had been cleared, he went on to show us how to swerve the ball round another ball, and a few other tricks. Then, without warning the table light was switched off. Instinctively we all looked back at the office only to see Wullie pointing to the clock. Our half-hour was up; it was time to go. On leaving the hall we could not stop talking about snooker and brother Bill's talent. It was agreed that his overall display of skill was well ahead of that given by Father Butler. Bill left us on a high and with the promise that he would meet us again down at the Sacred Heart club where we were allowed to play, and that he would show us how to improve our cue action.

****

My stay with Granny and Granda was over. It had lasted the full three weeks but it felt like half that time. Mum and dad told me on the Friday that Jimmy expected to finish his work the following morning and that I could come home anytime on Saturday. The following morning around ten o'clock I said goodbye to Granny and Granda and made my way over to the shop. Saturday morning was usually busy and Agnes was there helping dad out behind the counter. She told me mum was back home helping Jimmy in a final tidy up. I asked her how the house had turned out, but she teased me by telling me to get round and see for myself. I stopped in to have a few playful moments with Major, then made my way home.

As I turned into the close I was met by Jimmy who was depositing a bag of debris at the back of the close. With a fond ruffle of my hair he put his arm round my shoulder and steered me upstairs. "C'mon, let's see whit yae think o' yer new hoose", he said. As we came on to the landing mum was stacking boxes just outside the door.

"These hiv all tae go", she said to Jimmy.

With a smile on her face she took me by the arm.

"C'mon, ah think yae're in fur a wee surprise."

We paused at the open door so that I could see the lobby, which had been totally transformed into a kitchen. A new cooker, its enameled surface gleaming white, was flanked on either side by new worktops. Above the cooker, just as mum had instructed, were new storage shelves, which were painted white and already partly filled with pots and pans. The background to this was newly plastered walls painted with a warm orange colour.

"What do you think", Mum asked? Marvellous. I replied.

We walked in and paused for me to have a good all round look. The doors and facings leading to both rooms had been replaced and painted white. We slowly walked into the back room, our main living room and former kitchen. This brought on a huge wowee! The fire grate, that huge monstrosity, had gone. In its place was a low line, all tiled fireplace and integrated hearth. Beige in colour, it was square to the wall but had a raised half round in which sat a small coal grate. Its smallness made the surrounding wall look massive. It had been replastered and re-papered with a flowery lemon colour pattern. Everything looked so bright and spacious.

Turning to the windows, every piece of woodwork had been replaced and painted. A white porcelain sink bowl had replaced the old iron sink basin. It looked so refreshingly clean. Taking in the rest of the room the alcove bed also looked bigger and brighter. Its wood facings had been removed and not replaced. Instead it had all been replastered with a sharp delineating edge. It was no longer papered, but painted with a light green pastel colour. New, white painted skirting boards vividly contrasted with the new beige coloured linoleum that covered the floor. To complete the decor there were three scatter rugs. There were other improvements that I saw but could not take in at this point. "It's fantastic, mum, it's fantastic", I called out. "Did you do all of this, Jimmy?" I asked.

"Yeh...ah suppose", he answered.

"You really are clever, Jimmy. This is beautiful."

I was then directed into the front room where the only difference in our newfound quality and comfort was the colours. On that day, I do believe, was borne my ever-lasting admiration for the trade skills of people like Jimmy Miller. Yet, amazingly, he was never a qualified tradesman; he was better than that.

Chapter V

Reality Kicks in

A Taste of the Real World

War Declared

The Black Market

Uncle Harry

My Final Year at School

Reality Kicks in - A Taste of the Real World

On the Saturday morning following my return home from living with Granny and Granda, I was lounging in front of our new fire when there was a knock on the door. It's probably one of the neighbours wanting to have another nosy at the house, mum said. Opening the door she was taken aback by the portly presence of our Backcourt bookie, Neil McAteer.

"Neil...Whit brings you upstairs? Hiv yae cum fur a look at ma new hoose? C'min, c'min", she said.

"Naw, it wisnae that, Aggie...But ah must say yae've done a smashin' job of it", he said, looking around in admiration.

"Naw, ah'm lookin' fur yer brither, Geordie", he went on. "He's nowhere to be found at the moment".

"Whit's he done noo?" mum asked..."He prob'ly owes yae money...Disn't he?"

"Aye, he dis that, Aggie."

"How much is it, this time", she asked....

"Fifty quid", he said.

"Yae've got tae be bliddy kiddin'...Where wid he find that kin' of money?"....

"He's bin runnin' on the slate fur some time, noo, Aggie"

"An' you let him!" she retorted. "Mer the bliddy fool, you!"....

"The only reason ah let him, Aggie, wis that he said that you wid be good fur it"...

"Did he noo. Well yae certinly goat that bliddy wrong, Neil...Because ah'll tell yae this, noo...there's no bliddy way that yer gonnae git a penny oot o' me...an' certainly not fifty quid...Dae you know how hard me an' John hiv goat to work to earn that kin' of money? Naw, naw, naw...You find Geordie, an' you sort yer problim oot wi him."

"Ok, Aggie, ah hear whit yer sayin'...But a debt is a debt, an' there's no way it's gonnae go away. If Geordie reneges on this, an' you don't back'm up, then he's gonnae be a very sorry man."

"Yer no threatenin' me, are yae Neil? Like am to be responsible fur Geordie's problems?"

"Naw, Aggie, ah widnae dae that. But fur Geordie's sake, ah wid ask yae tae tell him tae come an' see me - an' soon. We can always sort something oot."

"Ok, Neil, ah'll tell him, if ah see him. Now, if yae don't mind", said mum, opening the door for him.

"Sorry to hiv troubled yae, Aggie." said Neil as he left.

She unhooked her coat from behind the door and pulled it on. From habit she then dipped her hand in her pocket and checked that she had her door keys. She spoke to me with impatience in her voice "Look, Ah've got to go roon an' talk tae yer faither aboot this. If yae go oot, don't furget to lock the front door.", she said.

As I wanted to know the outcome of her agitation I decided to leave then and there and follow her round to the shop. Being Saturday morning, Agnes was behind the counter as usual. As mum walked into the shop she gestured with her hand to dad that she wanted him to come to the back of the shop. In doing so she told Agnes to look after things, as she wanted a few words with dad. She took no notice of me as I went round the back and sat myself down in a corner.

"Ah've jist hid Neil, the bookie, up to see me. Yae wulnae believe whit Geordie's gon an' done. He's jist run up fifty quid in gambling debts on the slate wi' him!"

"Whit in hell's name did he let 'im do that fur." responded dad. There's nae way he can ever afford that kin' o' money. An' he calls 'imsel a bookie! He's a bliddy fool."

"That's whit ah told him. Bit wait 'till yae hear this...He said Geordie told him that we wid be good fur it."

"Yur kiddin'...Ah'll tell yae noo, Aggie, there's no way we're gonnae gee 'im a penny, of oor hard earned money, towards his gambling debts...An' that go's fur yer other brither, Harry...They've both hid enough from us. We've got tae stand up to them, Aggie...Ah might take a beatin' from the likes o' Harry...Bit if that's whit it takes, they're still no' gettin' anither bliddy penny from me. You've bin too soft wi' them in the past, an' this is whit it comes doon to in the en'...So, cin we agree on this; nae mer?"

Mum nodded her head in agreement, but you could see that she was not entirely convinced. You sensed that something was being left unsaid.

****

The following day, Sunday, we were having our now regular game of football. I was running with the ball towards the Sorn Street end when I heard a shout from Charlie Gillan. At first I thought he was shouting for a pass, and paused to look back for him. He had caught up with me and was pointing towards Granny's house.

"Look at yur uncle Geordie...He looks like he's hid a good kickin'."

I looked with shock at the state of him. His face was heavily swollen with black and red weals, some of them still leaking blood. He was being supported underarm by Uncle Harry. They passed by closely and took no notice of me. As they did you could see the pain in his face. He also had his arm stretched across his chest; his hand clutching his ribs. Uncle Harry also had an angry fearful look on his face and was clearly leading Geordie towards the shop. Looking back I could see Granny and Granda standing in their doorway staring after them. At this point I ran ahead to the shop to warn mum and dad of their coming. As they entered mum let out a scream at the sight of Geordie.

"Whit in hell's name's happened tae 'im?" she shouted.

"You should bliddy know!.. It wis you that did this tae 'im!" shouted Harry. "Yae widnae bliddy help 'im oot wae a bit o' debt. Yae're a couple o' bastards, the pair o' yi... Yae're rollin' in the stuff, and yae cannae help yur brither oot."

"You haud own, Harry. Geordie knew full well whit he wis gettin' intae...He's done this time an' time again, and we've bailed 'im oot...An' it's goat tae stop...We're no standin' fur any mer o' this." retorted dad.

At this Harry flew in to a fury and grabbed dad by the neck of his shirt, which he screwed up in his clenched hand.

"You shut yur fuckin mooth, big man, or a'll gee yae a taste o' whit he goat."

In total agitation, mum threw her arms around his shoulders in an effort to pull him off.

"Leave 'im alone", she screamed.

It took a flailing arm to the head before she let him go. At which point he turned on her with even more fury. His fist was raised to strike when he looked down at me holding on to her waist, and crying fearfully for all I was worth. Breathing heavily with anger, he dropped his militant stance and stood back. As he did so, dad, his eyes wide with fury, stepped between him and mum.

"You take the boy through the back, Aggie, and calm 'im doon", he said.

"Ok, Harry, this is get'n us nae where...This is between you an' me...Let's try an' soart somethin oot...Noo, bye the look o' Geordie, he's mer than paid his debt."

"Haud own", intruded Harry, with contempt. Yae stull don't know whit's happenin' here, dae yae? He's paid nuthin' of his fuckin' debt...Noo, Neil McAteer might be an arse-hole, but when yae renege on a debt wae a bookie like him, he'll sell it oan to a couple o' hard-men fur half the debt an' then wash 'is haunds wi it. Noo Geordie owes them the money an' he's goat a week to pay it. Noo, it's not gonnae go way!.. An' the kickin he's taken changes nothin'...That's only a doon-payment on whit he wull get if the money they're owed isnae piyed in full by the end o' the week."

At this point mum rejoined them.

"Pay 'im the money, John", she said.

Dad looked long and hard at her before he responded.

"Ok, Harry, ah'll see to it. Ah don't hiv that kin' money oan me, but ah'll git it tae yae by tae morrow...But ah've wan final thing tae say on aw o' this...As yae well know, ah'm no a fightin' man...But if that's whit it takes, then aw this stops here. As fur yur brither Geordie, he's hid 'is last penny frum me an' Aggie; an' ah don't care whit the reason is."

"We'll see, John", retorted Harry. "Don't get too faur ahead o' yursel'."

He turned to Geordie, who throughout all of this had stood cowering in the corner, still holding his ribs.

"Let's get yae hame."

"Thanks, John; thanks Aggie", mumbled Geordie as he left.

When envy raised its ugly head,
Revengeful wrath did follow

Chapter V

Reality Kicks in

A Taste of the Real World

War Declared

The Black Market

Uncle Harry

My Final Year at School

Reality Kicks in - War Declared

Throughout the later months of 1938 the main topic of conversation was of impending war with Germany. Newspapers and cinema newsreels tracked and reported the movements of Hitler's armies across Europe. There was a sense of excitement about our lives even though we did not fully understand why. When we met after school at the close-head James, Frank, and the rest of the guys would only refer to it when any aspect, or detail, affected us directly. We could sense the importance of it all from our parents, but it was all still a bit unreal to us. Who was Hitler, anyway? In the cinema newsreels he came over as someone bigger than life, who led his country into war against others. Exciting as it was, he came over as just another film baddie wreaking harm, who would always get what he deserved in the end.

Some of its reality, though, started to filter through in early 1939. I was now eleven years old and there was an increasing awareness that war was imminent. The matter was now sufficiently serious for us to have our schoolteachers lecture us on the preparations that were now taking place, and how this would affect us. The primary fear was that Glasgow, because of its extensive shipbuilding facilities on the Clyde, and its manufacturing capability, was certain to be attacked from the air. There was also the fear of lethal gasses being released in these attacks. A.R.P. committees were now in place all over the city. They had been around for some years, but in very small numbers, and as unpaid volunteers. Now their presence was to be seen on every street. In their distinctive A.R.P armband they would preen themselves with pride when stopped and asked for advice on the rules and guidelines that had now been distributed to every household.

To combat the fear of gas attacks, gas masks were now being issued to everyone starting with those of school age. When not being worn they were stored in a small brown cardboard box, which had a looped piece of string for hanging it on your shoulder. When first issued we would meet up at the closehead with them hanging over our shoulder. For a while they were the source of fun. It was an ugly thing made of rubber; with a wide view window over your eyes, and a lower piece that looked like the bottom end of a tin can with holes in it for breathing. It did stink of rubber when you pulled it on.

It was smart alick, Archie, who called it into question, one day.

"Whit ur these gasses, that this mask is suppose' tae protect yae frum?"

We don't know, we dismissively replied.

"Then how dae yae know it works?"

For his cheek we gave him peltars across the head, and made him wear the mask for the rest of the day while in our company.

There were also plans in place at this time for the evacuation of children from the cities to the towns and villages in selected areas of Scotland. This was already underway at the time of the gas mask issue. It was a huge operation. The reported estimate was that Glasgow would require to evacuate 237,523 individuals. These comprised school children, their teachers, and in certain instances, their mothers. Also, to move this huge number it was reported that it would require 338 trains and 23 trips by Clyde steamers. Many families protested and refused to leave their homes. In the event, only 118,833 choose to go. Among them was my sister May, brother Bert, and cousin Thistle. Mum refused to let me go on the grounds of my medical condition. At the time I was none too happy with this statement, as I had no awareness of having any medical condition other than my need to wear a straightjacket. I was later assuaged in this by the knowledge that James, Frank, and the rest of the crowd were not going either. It still rankled though, and was the basis for thoughts that would grow.

It was around this time that Agnes stunned me, and a few others, by announcing that she was going to get married. I knew that she was 'seeing' someone, or wynching, as they called it; and I had often been witness to her blushes when jocularly challenged on the matter. It was not the notion that she was getting married that troubled me; I could even be pleased on the grounds that she was pleased. No, it was much more important than this. I was stunned only by the thought that it meant she would be leaving us to live somewhere else. For me, Agnes was the stalwart of the house; she was the leader in all things; she was the organiser; she got things done.

She could be irritating; she could be a bully; she could even provoke, but she was only these thing because she had to get her own way. And she knew, and we knew, that this got things done. For example, none of us liked to get out of bed in the morning, unless driven by necessity. So her favourite ploy was to set all the clocks in the house to fifteen minutes ahead of time. And then the morning call would come; be it for Bill at 7 o'clock to get up for work; or for us at 8 o'clock, to get up for school. This was the gist of how Agnes kept us disciplined. You would get angry when you found out that you were up too early, and of course, you would correct the clock. But, unless you were last into bed that night and that you always corrected the clock before doing so, there was no way you could beat her. Inevitably, to avoid the hassle, you would go along with her wiles in the hope that you could mentally adjust the clock in the morning. But no chance! The mind does not work at that time in the morning.

She had many such tricks and ploys. But, the thought of her not being there in the morning to calm the moans and the groans; and to get our world on its way for the day, was, for me at any rate, a big problem. The reality of living in the confined space of a tenement house was very different from the naive tolerance, which I had accepted it in the preceding years. It could be, and usually was, a noisy, brimful environment, with more than a little friction thrown in to stimulate the emotions. Mum had one way of dealing with it, and Agnes had another, and it was blissful when they were in union.

Yes, I was stunned by her announcement, but it was partly cushioned by her follow-up that she and her husband to be, Mick Doyle, would be moving into the vacant single-end across the landing from us. More elation when she let it be known that Mick was a soldier.

Reality Kicks in - War Declared

He had been conscripted into the army, and had been in service for six months. I found the idea of having a soldier in the family quite exciting in the current atmosphere of pending war. That all of this had been planned for some time was quickly confirmed by Agnes announcing that Mick had been given special leave, and that they would be getting married next week.

The days that followed were a constant frenzy for mum and Agnes. So much so, that I found myself helping out in the shop even more. Fortunately, it was the spring school holiday. The wedding went off exceptionally well, with tables laden with food and drink on the landing as well as in our house. The neighbours, who were all welcome, praised and talked about it for weeks to come. For my part, I got to see and handle Mick's gun, which was very heavy. He even showed me how to load, and unload it - without bullets of course. I thought Mick was a great guy. We got on well together, and I was a bit sad when he left to go back to his barracks. As for Agnes; she looked lovely and I was very proud of her. Her only complaint, which she later made to mum, was that she thought that there had been too much whisky. She hated excessive drinking; and still does to this day.

The news of war continued unabated, as did the preparations of the A.R.P. It was now deemed essential that air raid shelters be built all over the city. The exceptions to this were the tenement buildings which, in the wisdom of certain A.R.P. dignitaries, were deemed to have strong enough closes to withstand the expected weight of bombing. There were two main types of shelter built. The Anderson shelter, which was made of corrugated metal and dug some four feet into the ground and then covered with earth. This type could shelter two families and were usually used in low-level houses such as bungalows, or maisonettes such as granny and granda lived in. The other type was brick built with a flat concrete roof. These were quite spacious and gave protection for up to a hundred people. This type was built in the Backcourt of the grey stone buildings and were much in evidence in Kinnear Road. In particular, one was built in the Backcourt of number 40, facing the shop. The shelter building program spread very quickly over the city. They were now in such numbers that they soon became part of the street culture with kids using them as play areas. To keep you alert, though, practice air raid warnings would be periodically carried out in daylight by the wardens. It would consist of a two minute signal from a siren whose high pitched warble would rise and fall to indicate an imminent attack. The end of the attack, the all clear signal, would sound out at a constant pitch.

Despite all the building going on in the city; the constant efforts of the A.R.P. wardens to raise our awareness that we were on a war footing, the middle part of 1939 was becoming an anticlimax. Even the radio news, which we listened to most mornings, was beginning to lose its urgency.

The news now was that the Prime Minister, Mr. Chamberlain, was negotiating a peace deal with "Adolf", and that maybe all our fears and preparations would be in vain. The cinema newsreels continued to sensationalise the exploits of Hitler across Europe. But it was now beginning to sound and look even further away. So much so that the former buzz on the street had now dropped low key to the point where wardens were now being treated as a nuisance. There were now occasions when their self-importance was no longer being tolerated. They were seen to be lecturing people, which, in Glasgow, could earn you a smack. But, it was early days, and incidents were few and far between.

At home the atmosphere was very strange indeed. With Bert and May evacuated to Dumfries, and Agnes now living in her own house across the landing, Bill and I often had the house to ourselves. It could be deafeningly quiet at times. I was really beginning to miss the daily hustle and bustle that was the norm. Much as he was older than I was, I did get to know more about Bill around this time. If I were doing nothing of an evening he would take me down the British Public Halls where I would sit and watch him practice billiards. More frequently though he would take me to the Sacred Heart youth club, sometimes with James and Frank, where he would teach me how to play - under the ever watchful eye of Father Butler. This short, but happy, period was brought to an end when Bill, with absolutely no hint or dint, let it be known to mum and dad that he was going to join the Navy. The first reaction of mum was to stop him on the grounds that he was too young - he was not yet eighteen. His argument was that he would be eighteen in two months and that he would then be conscripted into the army. If he volunteered to join the navy now, he would be accepted. After much argy-bargy between him, mum, and dad, it was decided to let him have his way. I felt empty at this decision; it made me feel very lonely. A few weeks later relief was at hand with the receipt of a letter from the evacuee home of May and Bert. May was happy and content there, but Bert disliked the place and wanted to come home. He was back the following week.

It was Sunday morning, 3 September 1939, when war was declared. I was sitting at the table with Bert, having breakfast, when the music from the radio was interrupted by an announcement that the Prime Minister, Mr. Chamberlain, had an important message to make to the nation. With solemn rhetoric, he explained that Germany had invaded Poland in contravention of the agreement he had made and signed with Herr Hitler. As a consequence we were now at war with Germany. After a brief hush to take it in, mum made a contemptuous retort, as if to the radio.
"He goat that bliddy wrang, didn't he? It wus only the ither day that he telt us that he'd made the world safe fur us, and that there widnae be any war".
She sounded very angry, but said no more. Bert and I sat looking at each other as if begging the question: Where do we go from here?

Reality Kicks in - War Declared

A total blackout was immediately declared. Using curtains and sheets, everyone was ordered to completely black out their windows. Not even a chink of light was allowed to leak through.
"Put out that light", was the cry of the wardens, as they patrolled the streets at night. Repeat offenders were fined. Masking tape was also issued to protect windows from being blown inwards causing dangerous shrapnel. Walking the streets after dark, though, was eerie, as the street lamps were no longer lit. Torchlight was now a prerequisite for getting around, but had to be extinguished immediately at the first sound of the siren. By now every single person was in possession of an Identity Card which was required by law.

In the ensuing weeks and months the social and domestic life of Glasgow continued as normal. In the absence of Bill and May, it was now down to me and Bert to go for the messages. Our pet hate was standing in the queue at Gormans, the butcher in Nuneaton Street. It was always a long wait, and very cold in the winter. In the past Bill had made this task unnecessary, as he would purchase our weekend needs from the butcher in Rutherglen, where he worked. Now, with no ifs or buts, Agnes would ensure that we took it in turn as required. As far as the impending air raids were concerned, 1939 passed uneventfully. It was now being referred to as a phony war, and continued to be sneered at well into 1940.

The first air raid on Glasgow happened mid morning, on July 19, 1940. Such was the indifference to war at this time that it took everyone by surprise. Not even the siren sounded out until the solitary plane was spotted over the Clyde Graving docks at Yoker. Four bombs were dropped at the rear of 34 Langholm St., just off the Dumbarton Rd, The gable end of a tenement was completely destroyed. Three people were killed and many injured. A shelter was also destroyed by a direct hit. Fortunately, owing to the lack of an early siren warning, it was empty. So much for the early warning lookouts that were supposed to have been posted.

Reality Kicks in - War Declared

Recrimination followed, but the truth was that the phony war had degenerated into apathy. I was in the shop with mum and dad when the siren did sound out. Our first reaction was that it was a practice run by the wardens. This notion was quickly dismissed when we saw a warden scurrying around screaming at people to get into the shelter. We immediately closed the shop and took ourselves over to Granny and Granda's place. It was a curious situation. They were standing talking to their upstairs neighbours when we arrived. I expected that we would all go straight round the back to the Anderson shelter. Instead, we filed into the living room while Granny said she would put on some tea. It was as if we were waiting for something to happen before we took any decision; we needed some kind of proof that the attack was real. We eventually took ourselves round the back but made no attempt to go into the shelter. In any case, Granny and Granda had by now made it clear that, at their age, there was no way they were climbing into a hole in the ground.

While mum and dad stood there, scouring the sky in search of planes, I stepped down into the shelter to explore. Despite the morning light it was still very dark in there. It was also damp and cold which was enough encouragement for me get out. It felt like the raid was never ending but in truth it lasted for less than an hour. The all-clear sounded and we made ourselves back to the shop. It was later that afternoon that we learned of the single bomb landing just off the Dumbarton Road. The West Side of Glasgow was much too far away for us to have heard it, I thought, but the raid was real and mum and dad took it very seriously. In future, mum said, we were all to head straight for the shelter at the first sound of the siren, and that we were to stay there until the all-clear sounded. There was now a real sense of uneasiness in the city, and a mood of certainty that there would be more raids.

Reality Kicks in - War Declared

Some three months passed before the next attack. It was mid-day when a solitary plane was spotted coming in low from the northeast of the city. The noise of bombs being dropped, without any warning, shocked everyone. It must have been two minutes later that the wailing noise of the siren sounded all over Bridgeton, By this time everyone was either in the shelters, or making their way with great haste. We were no sooner in the shelter, huddled together, when suddenly, through the opening to the shelter we saw the sky turn luminous with an intense flash of light. Seconds later, there was a loud explosion, and the ground trembled. I was absolutely petrified and grabbed hold of dad. A few moments later it happened again, followed by yet another one. I was now shaking with fear, and tensely waited for the next one to be even closer. But that was not to be. A strange quiet ensued, and after a little while I calmed down, but still held on to dad. We stood at the opening to the shelter, looking up at the sky. More huge flashes appeared in the distance, but still no noise. Dad said that the flashes were coming from the direction of Clydebank, and that they must be hitting the shipyards. The flashes continued at intermittent intervals. This went on for over an hour. The all-clear sounded out only for the alert to wail out again. It was 4 o'clock in the afternoon when the high continuous pitch of the all-clear was again heard and we ventured outside the shelter. Gazing around the sky our eyes were quickly drawn to a small nearby area of glowing red.
"There's somethin' burnin' over there", said dad.
"It's got to be close to Dalmarnock station", added mum.

In the course of the day the full extent of the damage was made clear. A landmine and a cluster of incendiary bombs had hit the sidings, south of Dalmarnock Railway Bridge. The nearby gas works also suffered a near miss. The following morning the newspapers reported that Clydebank had taken the brunt of the attack. A gun cruiser, HMS Sussex, had been hit and partially destroyed. Tenements had been hit, some destroyed, but the damage had been minimised by the high number of near misses.

Still, lives were lost and many injured. Like Bridgeton, there was sporadic damage in other parts of the city, without any loss of life. Two months later there was a similar attack. This time Bridgeton was unscathed, but Cambuslang and Burnside were reported to have received a hit. Once more, Clydebank had taken the brunt of the attack with similar losses and damage reported. The myth that the tenements could stand up to these attacks was now well and truly buried in the debris of destruction. With great haste, the council proceeded to reinforce the inner walls and roofs of tenement closes with strong timber, thus providing a degree of shelter from partial hits. The raids continued at intervals through to late December. Going in to 1941, all was quiet for two months. As was later said: 'it was the calm before the storm'.

On Thursday, March 13, the siren wailed out its warning. It was 9.15 in the evening. As we fled to the shelters we could see the eerie greenish glow bathe the sky over Clydebank. This was caused by streams of flares that came to be known as Molotov Chandeliers. It was like a huge dome of light suspended above the west side of the city; but much more extensive than that from previous raids. This light heralded the start of the most devastating and brutal attack, on Glasgow; and in particular, the people of Clydebank. This light, augmented by the devastation of the incendiary fires, would not diminish for many nights.

For our part, we huddled in the shelter with the fearful expectancy that it must be our turn next. We thought it had arrived, when the tenement in Allan St, just off Dalmarnock Rd, was completely destroyed. As we later learned, part of the bomb casing, with its parachute still attached, came to rest in the nearby power station yard.

In the aftermath, it was reported that an estimated 250 bombers took part in multi wave attacks. Clydebank suffered a major disaster with

9,276 houses extensively damage and a further 2,881 destroyed. In Glasgow as a whole 647 people had been killed and a further 1,680 had been injured in two nights of bombs, parachute mines and incendiaries. The job of removing the dead went on for weeks. With short respites, the blitzkrieg went on through to the end of April. Thereafter, daylight attacks by single aircraft continued through 1941, but most of them were aimed at maritime targets. The last raid took place on April 25, 1943.

The one abiding memory I took from this was the sight and smell of Allen Street, two days after the attack. It was no more than a ten minute walk from the shop, and I persuaded dad to take me round to see it. The street was cordoned off, and like us, there were many local people eager to satisfy their curiosity. It was a shocking sight. Most of the four -storey tenements that had lined Allen Street were reduced to a mountain of rubble. Firefighters and wardens were clambering all over this mass of broken stonework. One of the onlookers said that they were searching for bodies. The pungent smell of cordite was still in the dust-laden air. There was also another, quite repulsive, smell that I could not identify. Patiently moving forward as others left, we finally got ourselves close to the cordon where we could clearly see the whole scene. Suddenly, there was a call from one of the wardens who was frantically trying to clear stones in front of him.
"Over here", he called.
He was immediately supported by others who quickly cleared the stone to reveal a body. A stretcher was passed up to them. With masks over their face, and gloves to protect their hands, they lifted the dead body onto the stretcher. They slowly made their way down the rubble to the street. At this point the cordon rope in front of us was dropped and an ambulance backed up over it. The stretchered body was carried towards it. As they came closer, the smell that I had detected earlier was now a revolting stench. Everyone around us was now holding their hands over their nose and mouth. It was the first time I had smelt decaying flesh, and I felt nauseous. I turned

away, followed by dad, and never looked back. My curiosity for the aftermath of air raids had been dispelled forever.

Chapter V

Reality Kicks in

Reality Kicks in - The Black Market

In addition to the blight of the air raids, the introduction of food rationing compounded the malaise felt in the early war years. Everyone had to register with their preferred butcher and grocer in order to obtain their weekly ration of meat and groceries. In return for a weekly meat coupon they could buy up to a value of 1/2d. Similarly, for a weekly grocery coupon, they could obtain 3 pints of milk; 4oz of cheese; 1 egg; 8oz of sugar; 2oz of tea; 4oz of bacon; and, not to forget us weans, there were special coupons that allowed us up to 3oz of sweets a week. To the families in the tenements it was yet another imposition that had to be accepted, and absorbed. Typically, its impact was much alleviated by their "share, and share alike" culture that would see them exchange their coupons with each other in an effort to balance out their needs. It led to an even greater bonding that expressed itself in their outgoing spirit of togetherness, and their readiness to laugh at even the bad jokes.

The shortages added to another growing problem in the city. Breaking into shops and warehouses had always been the domain of the racketeer, and the petty thief, with the latter being mostly responsible for the 'fell-off-a-lorry' syndrome. This had always been an acceptable face of large, industrial cities. But with the impact of rationing, and the increasing shortage of other goods elevating them to luxury status, the demands of deprivation created a Black Market that had to be serviced. As a consequence large-scale burglary was rife, and petty break-ins became rampant. Almost anything could now be had on demand, at the right price.

Bars, which were the social center of every district in Glasgow, were now also the domain of the small business community. In Bridgeton, as in other areas of the city, there was little that happened that was not known, or even preplanned, in the local bars. Ironically, it was the small shops, despite their exposure to break-ins that were the mainstay of this thriving market. Given that nearly every tenement at street level was lined with integrated shops, Glasgow was one huge bazaar of merchandise. It was this volume of shops in the tenement districts that provided the distribution outlets for a market that was at one with the needs of the people, and therefore wholly natural in its exploitation.

Our shop was no exception. Dad would expect at least four attempted break-ins a year of which two would be successful. Even his indulgence of the local beat bobby, Jake, with his evening mug of tea, laced with a wee dram, got him little protection. But from mum's protective standpoint, Jake could rough it with the best, and provided a comforting presence. He was middle-aged and, as dad described him, one of the old school. He was only interested in the real villains and mostly turned a blind eye to anyone trying to earn a living, even if you did sell the odd extra ration.

"If you offered nae hurt", he would say, "then you couldnae be aw' that bad".

He would always wave over to us as we stood at the closehead. Occasionally, he would remind us of his awareness of us flaunting the law.

"Nae fitbaw, the day, lads"? he would jocularly ask. In one instance, James Cheekily answered him back.

"Naw, we only play on Saturdays 'n Sundays".

"That's good tae know, James", he called back. "The next time we raid yae, ah'll tell them to look oot fur the boy wae the rid hair. Ok"? This took the smile off James's face and brought a lot of jibes from the guys down on his head, much to the amusement of Jake.

We were standing around the close one day feeling a bit bored and restless for something to do. The only sign of interest was the sight of auld Mc Fadgen and his horse drawn milk cart coming down the road from the direction of Celtic Park. I could never understand why he never had a first name. It was not as if he was that old. Still, everyone called him auld Mc Fadgen and he had no qualms about it. The top of Sorn Street was always one of his regular stops. He would ring his hand bell to announce his arrival; accompanying this would be a call for everyone to come and get their fresh milk. Soon he had a small crowd of his regular customers around him, each with their milk jug at the ready. He carried three canisters on board from which he would ladle out the milk as required.

Reality Kicks in - The Black Market

One of his specialties was sour milk, which was much loved by many of his customers, especially granny and granda. Even dad was very partial to it. To this day I still cannot understand how people came to like the stuff. To me, sour milk was fresh milk gone bad; and it was absolutely vile. But there you go; I just accepted that there were certain things in this world that would forever remain a mystery.

As I watched granny collecting her milk, there also was granda, bucket in hand, shoveling up the horse droppings, and loading it into his pail. This was fertilizer for his dahlias, which he grew with great pride in his garden. Occasionally, he would offer me a tanner to follow auld Mc Fadgen's horse and collect a bucket of manure to feed his beloved flowers. Mind you, when I did so, I always made sure it was well out of sight of my pals.

Having dispensed his milk, auld Mc Fadgen walked out in front of his horse, and, making clicking sounds with his tongue the horse followed him. He walked towards the shop where he brought the horse to a stop. He climbed into the back of his cart and retrieved a medium sized block of cheese. This was dad's weekly ration, which in addition to his payment, auld Mc Fadgen would receive customer coupons corresponding to the weight that dad had ordered.
As we stood there aimlessly watching the horse and cart, impatience got the better of Frank.
"Anywan fancy a hudgie oan the auld yin's kert?" he asked. "Whit aboot you, James"?
"Naw, yae know am no' intae that".
"Yae cin also count me oot. A'll be waanted indoors, shortly", said Charly Gillan.
"Don't look at me, Frank", I said. "You know I've been well warned against this kind of thing."
"Ah suppose it's doon tae me, then", said Archie. "C'mon, a'm gem fur anything", he added.
They both made their way across the road and waited. Soon, auld Mc Fadgen appeared. With two upward steps he was up on the font seat of the cart, clicking his tongue and shaking the reins. As the cart

slowly moved off Frank and Archie jumped on to the back step. I had seen this situation many times before. Auld Mc Fadgen knew they were there, and in the past they would have received a mouthful of obscenities. In time, he had become so fed up with the hassle that he decided to ignore them, provided they confined themselves to the lower step.

We watched them clippety-clop down towards Baltic Street. We could see Frank leaning over the back door and having a good ol' look around. He then unhooked the door and stretched himself along the floor. We were not in the least surprised when Frank reappeared, still low to the floor level and pulled the door closed. As the cart approached Baltic Street it paused, at which point they both jumped off and ran back towards us. They stopped and looked back only to see auld Mc Fadgen turn into Baltic Street and out of sight, At that point they turned and raided aloft their booty in triumph. "They've nicked a cheese", said James.
He had no sooner said this, than Frank, with an underarm release, rolled the cheese at speed down the middle of the road. They both chased madly after it. When they caught up they took it in turn to flick it with their hand to keep it rolling. Just before they came into the shop's line sight, Frank picked it up and partly hid it in his arms.
"Well done", said Charly. "Whit ur yae gonnae dae with it noo? There must be at least 4 pun o' cheese there. Who the hell is gonnae eat 4 pun o' cheese? Even if yae shared it oot, we'd be eatin' cheese fur the nixt month. On toap o' that, who likes cheese anyway?"
"Fur a start", retorted Frank, "ah'm no' sharin' this wae anywan except Archie."
"That's fine", responded Archie, "but ah don"t like cheese eether. So whit ur wae gonnae dae wae it?"
"We'll sell it tae Barny's dad an' make a few bob."
By now I was getting a wee bit embarrassed especially at the proposal to sell it to dad. Also, as I told them, when auld Mc Fadgen discovers his loss, he's going to be retracing his steps. "And who's to say that he didn't spot the both of you getting a hudgie."

"If he does", said James, "we'll hive tae git rid of it, fur ah don't waant oor mither an' faither involved in this." Frank nodded in agreement with him.

"Ok", said Archie, "supposin' we take it over tae big John, an' ah'll tell 'im that ah found it, an' that it must hiv fell off a lorry."

He had to be joking, I said. How could dad ever believe a story like that, just after he's taken a delivery from auld Mc Fadgen? What I suggested was that we all go over and see dad, and that we stick to the truth as close as possible, without getting anyone into trouble. We would tell him that as auld Mc Fadgen was heading along the road to Baltic Street, that the back door of the cart flew open, and that one of his round cheeses fell off and rolled along the road. We picked it up and brought it in to him for advice on what to with it.

"That sounds good tae me", said Frank. "An' maybae we'll get a reward", added Archie.

We had a final look at each other for comfort, and filed into the shop. Half way through the story, led by Frank and Archie, and glossed up bit by Charly and James, dad called an end to it. "Enough is enough", he said, and went on tell us that he was going to do with the cheese. He was going to get in touch with auld Mc Fadgen and ask him if he was missing a cheese. When he said yes, he would tell him that a cheese had been found lying on the road and that it was badly damaged. When he came round to collect it, dad would offer to buy it from him for half the price. If he accepted this offer then each of us would get a tanner for our honesty in returning it.

The following day dad told me that auld Mc Fadgen had accepted the offer and that I was to go and tell my pals to come and collect their money. I was also to warn them that when they collected their money they were going to have their ears battered to the effect that if they ever pulled a stunt like that again their parents would be the first to know and, including me, it was fairly certain that we would all have a sore arse at the end of it. When I told the lads, it came as no surprise that not one of us claimed the reward.

Reality Kicks in - The Black Market

The word was out, and spreading to all of dad's customers and beyond that an extra cheese ration was available at big John's.

Chapter V

Reality Kicks in

A Taste of the Real World

War Declared

The Black Market

<u>Uncle Harry</u>

My Final Year at School

Reality Kicks in - Uncle Harry

Conscription was now the order of the day. If you were aged eighteen and above then enrollment was compulsory. Exemption was only allowed on the grounds of being a proven conscientious objector, a 'conscie', or engaged in work that was deemed essential to the war effort, or the support of city services. Dad, for example, was exempt, partly on health grounds, and partly his position as a shopkeeper. At the time I had no awareness of him having a health problem, but as later emerged, he had a ruptured groin that he would never admit to, despite the pain and discomfort that it must have caused him.

In keeping with my expanding knowledge of their persona, Uncle Harry and Uncle Geordie used their employment status to avoid the dreaded call-up. The Dalmarnock foundry, where Geordie worked, was being converted to an armaments factory and, as he openly boasted, he was first in line to register for exemption. Harry, on the other hand, had some experience of working in the dockyards in Partick, and chose to go back there. It was also convenient as he lived in Partick with his girl friend, Betty, in a single-end in Castlebank Street. Its location was no more than a mile from the heart of Clydebank, and whilst there had been no direct hits in the street, it was an integral part of the hellish devastation in the area. Until I later came to know better, it was his one saving grace that he and Betty lived there; yet never once did he talk of it in fear, or make any reference to the suffering that he must have witnessed. This I found strange. My curiosity would sometimes make me ask a question of him, but it would be quickly dismissed with impatience. Yet I would sometimes overhear him in conversation with dad, vehemently cursing the bombing. But he made it sound like it was more of a nuisance than a problem.

The truth emerged one day when I overheard him having a heated discussion with dad at the back of the shop. The gist of it was that the merchant ship that he was currently unloading had a cargo of fruit on board. Fruit at this time was very scarce and much in demand. He wanted to move a few crates of bananas, and was demanding that dad take them off his hands at a price. Dad's stance was that he was not averse to selling on some of these bananas to his customers but there was no way he was taking the risk of taking on the volume that Harry was talking about. Harry was far from pleased at this and started to taunt dad with previous deals he had put his way, and the profit he had got from it. Harry was getting angrier and dad was refusing to budge. Having witnessed Harry's temper over the settling of Geordie's debt, I was fearful that he was going to get violent. It did not come to that as dad came up with a compromise. He offered to ring Walter McLaughlen and ask him to take them off his hands. For a start, Walter's shop had a much greater storage area, and he was always open to deals that he could turn around quickly. Also, dad was still happy to take some of them for his customers. Harry being agreeable to this, I was told to run back home and tell mum or Agnes to come and take over for a bit.

I was now going on 13 years of age and was becoming more and more involved with the running of the shop. As a consequence, I was also getting greater exposure to Harry, and his way of life. I soon learnt that his newspaper stands were just a front for his other dubious activities. His work in the docks was a double-edged source of income, as well as giving him exemption. In my naivete, I wondered how he could manage to cope with so many jobs. It was partly clarified by my learning that he worked permanently on the early shift at the docks. The shipyards and the docks, as did all war-related industry, worked on rotational shifts, but somehow he had wangled it to avoid being rotated. This allowed him to have the afternoons free to organise and run his other activities.
But where did all his money go? He clearly had to be earning a lot. Yet, there would be occasions when he would borrow money from dad. With further exposure, it soon became clear that he, like Geordie, had a passion for gambling. As dad used to point out, you could always tell when the main events in the Scottish racing calendar came round. Harry's normally depressed, and angry looking face would have a readiness to smile. The Hamilton, and Ayr, horse tracks were his favourite racing events.

Reality Kicks in - Uncle Harry

At such times he would always try to gather in as much money as he could lay hands on. If he got enough, he and one of his 'hard' friends would set up a book together. This always gave him a buzz. Failing that he would just indulge his in-the-know knowledge. His other great passion was dog racing. The White City, Shawfield, and Carntyne were the three main tracks in the city and were well known to him. But the Carntyne track, just off Duke Street, was his second home. It was not far from Bridgeton, and seldom, it was said, did he miss a meeting.

He was the acknowledged guru on dog racing (among his own kind). His favourite dictum was that, "gambling oan dogs wis a mug's gem". Another piece of advice was that if you want to keep ahead of the bookie, never back a dog to win, always back it to be placed. That way, you have two out five places to get a return.

Because of the simmering friction that was always present in the encounters with Harry, it was always my wish that meetings with my parents would be few and far between. Unfortunately, circumstance contrived to make this impossible. Granda, who had continued to suffer from infections to his abdomen, was eventually committed to hospital for treatment. On closer examination his condition was found to be very serious, and untreatable. He died some weeks later and was buried at Dalbeth cemetery. Granny was grief stricken and thereafter refused to leave her home.

Mum and Agnes attended to her needs every day. Bert and I were told to visit her as often as possible. We were also told to use the spare key held in the shop to let ourselves in. I had a special relationship with Granny and was only too pleased to call in each day after school. It was on one such visit that I called out to her as I entered and got no reply. I was shocked and scared to see her sitting on the living room floor with her back propped against the wall. She smelt strongly of alcohol and my first conclusion was that she was drunk and that she had slid down the wall and fell asleep. To support this I could see her bottle protruding from the cleft of her diddies. I called to her by way of trying to wake her up. Her eyes opened and she looked up at me. This prompted me to slide my arm under hers with the impossible aim of trying to help her rise to her feet. She gestured with a shake of her hand for me to stop.

"Go an' git yer maw, John."

I ran straight to the shop where both mum and dad were in attendance. I shouted out my news and told them to hurry. They told me to stay and mind the shop and hurried out. I stood and watched as they both ran across the road. Granny was found not only to be drunk, but very, very ill. She was taken to hospital and I never saw her again. In the space of three months I lost two very special people in my life.

Granny was buried beside Granda. The following day, Harry and Betty moved in.

Chapter V

Reality Kicks in

A Taste of the Real World

War Declared

The Black Market

Uncle Harry

My Final Year at School

Reality Kicks in - My Final Year at School

I was in my final year at Sacred Heart, and I was very much looking forward to joining James and Frank in Pirn Street Secondary. It would be Frank's final year, and my first and only year. My 4 years at Sacred Heart had not been particularly memorable. Starting as I did in the juniors whilst being 2 years older than my classmates did make me feel a little self-conscious. Helped, though, by the presence of James and Frank in the playground, albeit in classes 3 and 2 years respectively ahead of me, I was determined to try and make up some of the leeway, in line with what I had been allowed to do at Burnside.

In my first year, owing, I thought, to my age difference, I came first in my class with flattering marks. As in the case of Burnside, I had mum make a request to the school, that, on the basis of my age and results, I should be advanced in class by one year. Despite my success mother's request was turned down on the advice of Father Butler, who reportedly said that it was much too early to make a judgement on the basis of first year results. All things considered it was held to be an acceptable judgement.

My second year results were much in line with the first year and showed me to be ahead of my year. Again, mum applied for an upgrade, and again it was turned down. This time the reason given was that the review board, headed by Father Butler, was unsatisfied with certain areas of my work. I asked mum as to which areas of my work they meant, but she did not know. When I asked her to go and see Father Butler, she was very reticent, and seemed almost embarrassed at the thought of her questioning the priest. She asked if I had given any trouble on the playground. Failing that was I keeping up with my catechism. On the latter, at least, I had to admit that I found the unremitting rote boring, and often struggled to keep awake. There was also the odd incident in the club when we would have an argy-bargy over a game of snooker. Of course, there was also the cheeky, (maybe provocative), fun that Frank would poke at the father. But there was never any real harm intended - or, was there? Well, certainly never by me. I was being branded by association, I think.

In my third year I lost some of my drive but still managed to come third. No doubt, I thought, that Father Butler would have felt amply justified in his previous decisions. Especially, as I was manifestly losing interest in his rote, and no longer felt guilty at missing mass, despite having to face another kind of sermon from mum for doing so. My fourth year passed with much impatience to be gone.

My year at Pirn Street was a joy. The teaching levels were of a much higher quality, and geared to a more academic drive for attainments. What religious instruction that took place was distinctly low-key. To me it was like a breath of Burnsidian-fresh air, with a large dollop of reality thrown in. I enjoyed every moment of it. I was also teamed up with Frank again, and that meant some added fun in the playground. James, who was now 14, had left. The year just flew by, but it still left me with a few vivid memories. One of these was from the playground that was manfully ruled by Mr. Connolly, a math's teacher. A fearsome disciplinarian. I am sure that had he also been ordained with the talents of Father Butler, he would have surely gone to some heaven.

My few encroachments on his playground laws were entirely down to me - Frank made no contribution. But one sin in particular stood out. A ball broke loose to me, one day, from a hand ball game, and I had the foolish audacity to kick it back. The consequence was instantly heralded by a roar from across the playground. I had never heard my surname called so loudly. Tall, slim, very dark hair, and ashen faced, he strode towards me, his black tawse dangling from his wrist. If I said I wasn't scared, I would be lying. He stood there like an Adolf image from one of the cinema newsreels.

"You play enough illegal football on the streets, McBarron, without bringing it on to my playground", he bawled. "Hold out your hand". I nervously raised it towards him. "Hold it flat, boy!" he called.

He was lightning fast as he brought the tawse down. I felt my face go scarlet as I struggled to suppress the pain. I looked up at him, and was about to mumble some kind of an apology, when I saw Frank behind him smirking. That was all I needed to regain my composure. It was my first and only strapping and it was infinitely more painful than the 'unprovoked' smacks with the pointer that occasionally came my way from Father Butler.

My other memories of that year were of the challenges that this higher mode of learning presented. In particular, maths provoked and stimulated me. My first acquaintance with the symbolism of algebra was fascinating. Combined with a higher standard of English, History, and Art, it presented a whole New World of stimulus and hope. This is not to say that my previous learning at Sacred Heart had no related basis. The difference was that my time at Sacred Heart had been so prejudiced by other factors that clarity of thought, and ambition, had been replaced with confusion. Pirn Street, on the other hand, showed me a way forward; it gave me direction, and an element of self-control. Unfortunately, I was not to use it wisely.

At end of year my reports were good. Mum and dad were pleased. They were also flattered when they received an invitation from the headmaster to meet with him to discuss my future. The outcome was that I was offered the opportunity to stay on and complete my secondary education.

Reality Kicks in - My Final Year at School

Mum and dad were delighted for me. They knew how much I had enjoyed my year, and here was an opportunity to finally catch up. They strongly urged me to take it, and promised to back me in any way I wished.

Deep down, without any doubt, I knew that I wanted to accept this offer. But at the front of my mind there were other drives at work. The option to walk away and socially grow apace with my age group was enticing. The chance to be free of the strictures, the discipline, and the penalties, was also a very easy option. Sacred Heart had done a good job here. But, there was also the fear that I was still out of sync with my age group in academic terms, and for me to continue at school would set me apart in social terms. The academic difference was not a problem, but the social difference was. At the time, all of these thoughts and drives had no rational clarity. They were emotions with vested interest; each pushing and shoving to get control. In the end I took the easy option and said no. Mum and dad were sadly disappointed. So much so, that guilt made me come very close to changing my mind.

It was the first of two very serious mistakes I was to make.

Chapter VI

The War Years

The War Years - Life in the Shop

The year was 1942; I was now 14 years of age and eligible for work. Dad proposed that, if I wanted, I could work full time with him in the shop. This pleased me no end as I had already considered this possibility. Mum and Agnes were also pleased that it gave them more time for other pursuits. In particular, and to my utter astonishment when they told me, my brother Michael was about to be born. I remember being greatly confused by the news. But such was my excitement at the prospect of working with dad in the shop that I put my confused thoughts to the back of mind

My hours were to be 9, 'till 5, with an hour's break for dinner. My pay was to be in the form of pocket money amounting to 5 shillings a week. When I turned up for work on the Monday following my last day at school I was scrubbed up, and well turned out, in my first tailored pair of long trousers. I was truly proud of myself that day, as was dad.

Looking around the shop that morning it took on a whole new dimension. Everything on these shelves was now under my control. Their replenishment was now down to me. New brands and new ideas; I was now to be involved in these decisions. Such was the energy I felt my every free moment was spent visualizing the moving of display cabinets; maybe reposition the serving counter, and certainly the shelving could be restructured to provide more space. I could not believe that I had the power to do these things. Ok, there would have to be discussions with dad before any of these changes could really take place. But, slowly, slowly, I thought. All was in the future, but they were going to happen. In the meantime I was going to concentrate on getting to know the customers better, and try to improve our service. The customers already knew me, of course, but only as a schoolboy helper. Thoughtfully, dad reintroduced me to most of them in the course of the day. I was his full time assistant, and that they were to trust me to serve them as well as he would.

In the course of the next few months I was to learn much about our customers and their little ways. There were many surprises, especially from people whom I had previously thought I knew. Mrs. Hargreave, for example, James and Frank's mother, and one of our regular customers, suffered from sinus headaches, which she treated with Askit powders, a local product that was very popular in Glasgow. Despite any medical advice that she may, or may not, have taken, she firmly believed that it was the only medication that gave her relief. But, not only that, she required six of them every day and, without exception, she would buy them in twos; morning, noon and early evening.

Then there was Charlie Gillan's mother who, like many other customers, could be seen carrying a load of belongings, wrapped up in a sheet to disguise it as washing, to the pawnshop in Dalmarnock Road. Come Friday, when the weekly wages were handed over by their husbands, or other working members of the family, they could also be seen returning from the pawnshop having redeemed them. When I first came on to this my naive logic believed their actions to be ridiculous. Why redeem them on the Friday with interest, only to pawn them again on the Monday. Why pawn them at all, and save the interest. As dad explained, that to do this would mean them losing control of their spending. It was a common and essential practice with people on low incomes.

The other practice that surprised me was the amounts of tick (credit) that dad allowed his customers. I remembered well my embarrassment on a previous occasion, when I was caught browsing through the shop 'tick book'. In my new situation I was now not only empowered access to the book, it was now my responsibility to keep it up-to-date, and to make judgements on when, and when not, to allow it. In my initial examination of the tick book I counted over 50 people with unpaid amounts against them. I knew nearly every one of them, and many were close friends of mum and dad. It took me a while to grasp the extent of all this credit, and what it meant. In one such browse I estimated that the total outstanding was in the region of 300 pounds.

Getting more and more into my job I eventually got the confidence to ask mum and dad to explain to explain the reason for this massive credit. Their explanation was a very light-hearted one. They even joked that we could all be very rich if everyone paid what they owed. But that was never going to happen, they said. For a start some of them had moved house and would be very difficult to track down. Also, it was highly unlikely that their income had improved. But what about all these other people who live locally, surely they have to pay if they are to continue receiving tick, I asked?

"It disnae work that way, son", said dad. "Debt is a way o' life fur people in this area. Withoot tick they couldnae git through the week. An' withoot tick they widnae buy here either."

"It's a vicious circle", added mum, "but that's life...People pay whit they can oan a Friday... They're no stupid, they know whit they owe, an' we jist try an' keep a check oan it... But if yae think somewan's tryin' it oan, then jist you hiv' a word wae yer da' before sayin' anything... We're always gonnae lose some... but, we make a livin'." That pretty much summed up the heart and mind of my parents and their business acumen.

Then there were the cheats. The most common ploy was to divert your attention from what they wanted to steal by asking to see a product from one of the shelves, thus forcing you to turn your back. The till could be vulnerable to this. As was common in most small shops the till was made from a solid block of wood with carved, polished dimples of varying size and depth to hold coins in disparate groups. This would be located in a drawer under the counter and out of reach of unattended customers. The more determined ones, usually tall, young and agile, would ask you for something, as you were retrieving change from the till. This ruse, timed right, could make you forget to fully close the drawer. They would then lift themselves backwards on to a sitting position on the counter, from where the could lean back, reach over and grab what they could. This happened to me twice when I was on my own. Fortunately, the paper money was always tucked underneath the till.

Cigarettes, which we stored in a free standing display cabinet at the end of the counter directly above the till drawer, were also a target. Owing to the war, they were on restricted supply and hence, very scarce. The most common cigarette at that time was Woodbine which we sold in packs of five, and only to our regulars. Just occasionally though, there would be offers of a few fell-of-a-lorry extras, at which times we would be less discerning in who we sold them to. Again, the same diversionary ploy would be used to have you turn your back and so allow the more dexterous to slide open the cabinet and retrieve a 5 pack with their fingers. The most persistent one of these, despite the many warnings from dad, was Davie Smith. I would catch him regularly trying to exercise his particularly long fingers. There was one occasion when I was on my own, when he was so persistent, and got me so angry and frustrated, that I tried to scare him off. I warned him that if he did not stop I would introduce him to my Uncle Harry. For a while this worked a treat, but it left me annoyed with myself for even considering the thought of Uncle Harry being involved. And, talking about keeping it in the family, not even uncle Geordie was above thieving a few cigarettes when I was on my own.

****

On being released from her commitments in the shop, mum took it upon her self to make, what she called, her contribution to the war effort. She and a close friend of hers from Sorn Street, Nessie Moss, came up with the idea of holding dances in the backcourt shelter at number 40, facing the shop. They would provide sandwiches, and ginger drinks, anything stronger you brought yourself. There would be an entrance charge of sixpence. All proceeds would go into a fund that would be shared out to all local lads and lassies that had been conscripted into the armed forces. The idea was that anyone who came home on leave would be given a donation from the fund. It would be a fixed sum of 10 shillings and was intended to augment their spending money while they were at home.

A committee was formed to share the workload. Leaflets were printed and distributed throughout the area. Mum was elected treasurer, and the main contact to get your donation. The ARP was consulted and gave it their blessing. Their view on it was that in the event of an air raid there could be no safer place to be. It proved to be great fun, and soon the news spread all over Bridgeton. Other areas took up the idea with their own variations. It was a marvelous success, and, as the occasion arose, it extended itself into parties for family events.

Mum was now in her element. Unlike dad, she was a spontaneous extrovert who loved nothing better than to party. Invite her to dance, or singalong, and she was there. More often than not she required no prompting. As each dance night arrived she would be beside herself with pleasure. On the night no one escaped her prompting. She was absolutely brash in her teasing of others but with a charisma that could not offend. Shyness in others was not even a challenge. Invited to sing or dance they would obey her every whim. Dad, with his ever-present grin, would stay in the background and admire - until she spotted him, then dance, or sing, he would. As for me, she often embarrassed me at these events, but my protests were more feigned than real. Part of me always wanted to be dancing with her.

****

Those early years in the shop with dad were a bonding period that was to hold dear to me in later life. To simply admire dad, was not to understand him, but to do as others did. To understand the simple thoughts that underpinned his generous acts was a lesson in humility. To see him provide sustenance (tick) to others without one hesitant thought, and to see him struggle for words when he could not was a lesson in penance that could never be taught. My dad was not a clever man. But he was a man who could watch his son presume to be; as when he restructured the shelves of his shop; when he relocated its counters and displays; and when he renewed its internal ceiling and lighting. This was his other gift - he knew when to trust, and to accept its consequences. It was this spirit of unquestioning trust that allowed me to grow without fear of my mistakes - and there were many.

The other surprises that lay waiting for me as I grew into the shop, was its predictability, its pattern of usage. It would be very busy in the morning between 7, and 9 o'clock. This period would service the needs of workers going to work, and children going to school.

The War Years - Life in the Shop

Between then and 4 o'clock, when the children returned from school, trade would be sporadic with little volume. It was in this period that you would take most of your deliveries from suppliers, which, for a small shop, was not many. It would also be the time when dad would go to the fruit market in Bell Street, and to his other suppliers, to reorder stock and pay his bills. In this period he would occasionally take some time out to visit his business friends Walter McLaughlen, and George Daily. If it were close to dinnertime they would usually meet up in George's bar in Nuneaton Street and have a 'quiet' drink. Consequently, it could be said that there was always time in the course of the day to do other things which, if not fully utilised, could be a problem for a progressive mind.

Most of my free time in that first year was spent planning my grand scheme for the shop. Dad was always a patient audience. He had to be, as my proposals for change were never constant, and changed from week to week and sometimes daily. He did point out one omission in my scheme of things, and that was cost. Where was the money to come from? Ah, yes, but this was not a problem; it could be done in stages. Besides, my first project was to restructure the shelves, and, as I intended to use my woodcraft talent, taught me by Jimmy Miller, I would rebuild the shelves myself, and hence, the only cost would be the wood. Secretly, though, I knew that if I got any technical problems, Jimmy would help me out. On reflection, maybe dad also knew this, as he had no qualms about the possible outcome.

My Grand plan proved to be much slower than my impatient mind would have otherwise. But it progressed, with much wheeling and dealing on its costs, over a period of two years. On reflection it was more a series of highlights than a plan. This, as I wrongly thought at the time, was borne out by Jimmy's response when I asked for his opinion on my efforts. Shaking his head and grinning in amusement he said "after aw 'ave taught yae; yae still know nothing".
I felt badly put down by his response. But this feeling changed to confusion when he ruffled my hair and added, "yaeíre a great kid, John".

The War Years - Life in the Shop

In all it did teach me the first principles of business, ergo "Mr. MiCawber", and led to me setting up more formal accounting controls for the shop.

My other pastime in this period resulted from my daily exposure to the war headlines that jumped up at you from the morning newspapers. There was no escaping their impact. As the morning rush subsided, dad and I would sit down with our mug of tea, and browse through our favourite paper. Mine was the Express, mostly because of its wider, bolder banner line, and its graphic maps of the war zones in Europe. This took on an even greater fascination with the announcement of the D-Day landings in Normandy, in June 1944. As the allied forces fought there way into France and onwards I would track their progress daily by means of the graphic illustrations from the newspapers. Located at the back of the nearside display window, and out of sight of the customers, I set up my own war status board. By selectively cutting out the maps and other illustrations from the Express, and tacking them on to the board, I tracked all the major battles across Europe. What started as a casual pastime, soon grew into an absorption with all data on the war, and later, its motives.

Finally, it was over. On May 8, 1945, VE Day, Victory in Europe was proclaimed. The celebrations in Glasgow were hugely spontaneous in its joyous emotion with its focal point in George Square. But it was all but a prelude to the global end of the war by the surrender of Japan, which was brought about by the awesome aftermath of the Atom Bomb being dropped on Hiroshima.

Young Joe, Mungo, Dad, and Frank

James and Frank trying to make me look tall

Charlie Clark and me at the back, fronted by
Paddy, Frank, Archie, and Charlie Gillan.

Agnes, Charlie, me and Mongo

Chapter VI

The War Years

Life in the Shop

The Winner Loses

Those were the Years

Annie Gillan - The Sad Pleasure

My Teenage Years

The War Years - The Winner Loses

My release from school coincided with that of most of my friends, and brought us back in line with those who had previously left, such as James, and Charlie Gillan. Everyone was now working and enjoying their increased spending power. Our social pastimes and exploits were rapidly changing. We now saw ourselves as adults, and hence, above many of our previous pastimes. With the exception of street football, which became more forceful, most of our other games and pursuits were put away, whilst others evolved into a more adult version. We still met up at the closehead most evenings but in less predictable numbers. As most of us would now have jobs, the talk now centred on these other people with whom you worked. They quickly came to be important images in your life. The daily exchange of stories on their background, and their work status, created a new aggressive way of speaking. Self-importance took on a new meaning. It was no longer a desirable conceit, it was an essential requirement of your identity and standing, in the workplace.

The work available to school leavers at 14 years of age was very mundane. The local butcher, baker, and grocery trades would absorb a small number. But the biggest uptake of young labour was in the shipyards, the docks, and the mass production factories. With application, and good luck, you would be encouraged to take up a trade or other skilled work. Welders and crane drives were much in demand. Locally, small factories were also beginning to appear as spin-offs from the expanding manufacturing base supporting the war. James, for example, who had left school the previous year, had got himself a job in Black and White's whisky bond. A year on he was claiming to have worked himself into a good position in the bottling area.

Frank, on the other hand worked as a storeman for a soft drink (ginger) manufacturing and bottling plant in Shettleston. He enjoyed the more physical work of stacking crates of ginger, and loading the delivery lorries. In the course of a year his strength and stature grew quickly. He was now around 5 foot 8 inches tall and very muscular. As he often made it clear at the closehead, no one messed him about at work. Charlie, Archie, Mungo, his brother Paddy, and the others were all in jobs, but not all of their own choosing. Listening to the guys constantly talking up their jobs, and its increasing importance to them, left me feeling a little bit estranged. It all came over to me, as if the teachers had been replaced by foremen, and that the teacher-bullies had been given new fearsome powers. Then maybe I was just a bit jealous of them. I felt as if their lives were being extended by new friends, while mine was static. My job was great but, compared to theirs, I naively thought it was restrictive. I felt as if I was on the outside looking in on their New-World Life, which was filled with many highlights in this period.

The pecking order in our gang at this time was also changing. The little trials of strength that go on in all groups were becoming more active. They were usually resolved, though, without any serious hurt or loss of pride. Then, quite unexpectedly, it happened. I should have seen it coming, but you seldom do. We had gathered around mid-day on Sunday, and were waiting around for a few more to turn up so that we could have our usual 6-a-side game of football. There was the usual argy-bargy going on, accompanied with a bit of pushing and shoving, but with very little intent. Suddenly, without warning Archie started in on me. "Why dae yae hiv tae wear a straightjacket, Barney?" he asked.
James was the first to spot what he was up to and moved to shut him up. "You know bliddy well why he's wearing it, so shut it, Archie."
"Ah didnae mean any herm", retorted Archie, "Ah jist waanted tae know."
"It's Ok, James", I said, in order to stop him taking it further. "I'll tell him why. "
My thought was, that if I gave him a straight answer, he would drop it, and that would be the end of it. I went on to tell him that as far as I knew, I had fractured my spine when I was four years old, and that the hospital had told my parents that I had to wear a straightjacket well into my teens in order to keep the spine straight while it healed.
"That's a load o' shite." responded Archie. "Anybody knows that if yae break a bone, they pit a splint oan it, an' it heals in nae time. You

must hiv that jaiket oan fur at least seven years noo...Ah still think yer talkin' a load o' shite."

"Look Archie, I've told you, as I understand it. If you don't believe me, then fine; just bugger off."
"Who dae yae think yae ur tellin' me tae bugger aff, ya wee bauchle?" shouted Archie. And with that he gave me a heavy push on the chest.
With all the guys standing around, there was no going back. So I responded by grabbing him high up with both hands and, mustering all the strength I could, I pushed him so hard that he went staggering back, tripped himself up, and rolled over in the dirt. Archie was now, really, really angry. He glared at me with fury as he got to his feet. Without any hesitation he came after me with his right fist sorely clenched. To the encouraging shouts around us I managed to avoid his flailing fist and grabbed him round the body. We wrestled for supremacy before tumbling on to the ground. I then managed to get on top of him, and to my surprise, I found myself to be the stronger, and easily held him down by the shoulders. I called for him to pack it in, to which he responded by grabbing me by the hair and tried to pull my head down onto his chest. I resisted this, with some pain, and managed to get my head back up. But there was no way I could get him to release his hands, without me first releasing my grip on his shoulders. The pain from this position left me with no option. Trying not to hurt him too much, I took aim at his forehead and brought my head down on top of it. Because he was pulling my head down the impact was greater than intended, also, because of the direction of his pull, my head came down on the bridge of his nose. There was a simultaneous screech of pain and a release of his hands, and I rolled over free.

With battered pride Archie was quickly on his feet, blood streaming from his nose. Shouting vengeful threats at me and promising retribution from an older cousin, he ran off home. Everyone was pent-up with the excitement of my victory. They made mock punches at my chest accompanied with shouts of 'well done'. They also shouted to each other, with great surprise in their voice, that

The War Years - The Winner Loses

Barney hid stuck the heed on Archie. It was as if I had performed the renowned act of the 'hard man' , and they were jealous of it. In my mind the opposite was true. My act was never meant to hurt him, but to free me from pain.

Despite my feelings of guilt, I swanned for a few moments in the aftermath of their praise. What it was really telling me, was that I had been seriously elevated in the pecking order. But this elevation was short lived. Sure, it brought me a bit more respect from guys like Archie, but again this was brief. As I looked round the gang I could tell their height and strength were clearly visible. James, Frank, Mungo, and others must have been around 5 foot, 8 inches at this time, whilst I seemed to be stuck at around 5 foot, two.

To be honest, it had never really bothered me before. I had always been smaller than the others without it having any significance for them. The attack by Archie changed this. It prompted many thoughts; not least of them being why he attacked me in the first place. Why had it suddenly become a focal point for him? It posed other more important question. Was the straightjacket really restricting my growth? For how much longer, exactly, was I expected to wear it? As prompted by Archie, was there another reason for me having to wear it so long?

This all spilled out when confronted with mum and dad over the fight with Archie. They had heard of it from the neighbours and wanted to know the causes. They also seemed to be over concerned with any damage I might have received. As a consequence, I bluntly asked them to tell me why I still needed to wear the jacket, if my original injury was only a fractured spine. They were both taken aback by my directness, and went silent. They looked as if they were either unwilling, or unable, to answer. I broke the silence by further insistence on my need for an answer.

It was mum who broke their silence. With much sadness on both of their faces she went on to explain the need for the jacket. It was true, she said, that I had suffered a fractured spine, and that this had been caused by a fall down the tenement stairs. However, on admission to Mearnskirk, their examination discovered that I also had tuberculosis of the spine which, in the form that infected me, was called Potts disease. It attacks the vertebrae and if not cured it can cause extensive spinal collapse. In my case they had successfully operated on me to remove the infected pieces, but to prevent collapse it was deemed essential that I wear the jacket to hold my spine erect. It was believed that if I wore the jacket well into my teens that my natural growth might compensate for the loss of vertebrae bone.

While this explained all, it did beg one more question. How soon would I be able to remove the jacket for good? But they did not have the answer. Only the doctor could answer that, they said. They also insisted, that if I had any such thoughts then I must get clearance from the doctor. I agreed to this and the appointment was made. Two days later we went to see our local doctor. He was very friendly and seemed to be well versed in my condition. He was also very sympathetic towards my wish to dispense with the jacket and even joked that I had every right to be wanting rid of it.

My jacket was removed and he examined my spine and the small boney bump that I knew to be there. It's looking quite good, John, he said. Lets see how strong it his, he added. He made me bend over and touch my toes, which I did with ease. I was then asked to pick up two reasonably heavy pieces of metal from the floor, which, again, gave me no problem. Other tests were carried out that were clearly intended to assess the strength of my spine under load. I felt very strong throughout and had no qualms about the possible outcome.

Throughout the examination my mum and dad sat in the background looking on. Finally he told me to get dressed. Hoping to have him tell me otherwise, I pulled on my jacket with disappointment. When I finished dressing I took a seat beside mum and dad. The news is very good, the doctor said, but maybe not quite as good as you would have liked, John. Your spine, while not fully recovered, shows signs of containing the damage, but it could still do with a bit of help. You still have a few years of growth ahead of you and I think we should harness this over the next few years to give you more stability. Reacting to the disappointment on my face, he added that if I were to dispense with it now, there would be a risk of some collapse. How much he could not say. It would depend on the loading. But this would put it back under my control, I concluded. Instant rationalization took over.

On returning home there was much debate on the pros and cons of the doctors findings. Out of concern for me they wanted me to continue for another year. But they were also full of sympathy for my desire to be rid of it. Pressed heavily on this sympathy, they finally gave in to my persuasions. Overjoyed, I there and then stripped off my shirt, discarded the Jacket, and re-dressed. I stood there in front of them with a joyous smile on my face. I could feel the freedom as I stretched myself erect. I was certain that I was at least an Inch taller. Mum and dad gave me a hug and said that they were so pleased for me. But, as I chose to ignore the doctor's advice, their pleasure was not as certain as mine.

****

Where were you then, my Bonny Jean,
When guidance was not at hand
To steer me from a frailty,
My impatience could not withstand

Chapter VI

The War Years

Life in the Shop

The Winner Loses

Those were the Years

Annie Gillan - The Sad Pleasure

My Teenage Years

The War Years - Those were the Years

It was the classic era of the cinema; the classic era of the dance hall; the era when football became 'more than a game'; the era when Friday evening and Saturday, the 'weekend', was the be all, and end all, to us. We had money in our pocket, freedom of choice to spend it, and friends to share your pleasure with. Wrap all of these up in the drives they now call hormones, and your memory makes an indisputable statement that 'those were the years'.

Everyone remembers their first cigarette as the beginning of a life-long habit, or the most easily rejected pleasure they ever tried. I remember mine well, not so much for the taste, but the fact that I nicked it from the shop - it was curious how the loss went undetected by the clever stock control that I had set up. Not only that, it was a five pack of woodbine I had removed. Smoking in our gang had begun early with a few of them. Paddy Cloherty, Mungo's brother, always seemed to have smoked even at school. The other older ones, such as Frank McQuillan, and Davie Smith, were regular smokers. It was only when I joined them, that I came to wonder how they could afford it, as a five pack of Woodbine cost a tanner at that time. As for my first cigarette, I didn't like it at all. But, of course, I went through the motions. You had to, as everyone else was into it.

Mum and dad were totally against it so I tried to confine my newly formed habit to the weekends where it could be kept out of sight. Davie, Frank McQuillan, and the Cloherty brothers smoked five a day and were regarded as heavy smokers. It was not unusual to borrow a fag from each other and, with the exception of Paddy, there was always a willing response to the request: "Hiv yae goat a fag oan yae? Ah'll see yae right the morra."
In the case of Paddy, and obviously for ease of access, he always appeared to keep his fags in his top breast pocket. But when asked for one, he would always retrieve a woodbine packet from this pocket with the response that it was his last one. With few exceptions, it was always his last one. As no one had ever seen him smoke this last fag, he came to be known as the guy who always smoked his second-last fag first.

The War Years - Those were the Years

The cinema to us was always an essential source of pleasure. It fed us with dreams, hopes, and ambition; it gave us an insight into another world that we aspired to. We would extract wonderfully visual images that we would use to enrich and supplement our own world. Who can forget the madcap input from 'A Night at the Opera', in the company of the Marx brothers. In a variety of ways it would feed back into our mischievous teens.

And what about the unbelievable input to our senses from the dream-like values portrayed in 'Snow White and the Seven Dwarfs'. Who can forget the joyous fun in accompanying Judy Garland along the 'Yellow Brick Road'; how she enlightened us with music and prose. And the pain and pleasure of first love, in 'Meet me in St Louis'. Then there was the other genre of 'Cowboys and Indians', which was taken to new heights of excitement with 'Stage Coach'. Its vivid portrayal of human frailties gave me my first exposure to the stress of birth. That great scene when they all sit down to eat at 'Apache Wells'. And, of course, the climax of the chase by the Apache Indians followed by their rescue, by none other than the cavalry. This was followed by other great films in this genre, such as Jessie James, Destry rides again, and many more. Great action movies set in the most magical location of the time, the 'American West'.

If romance on a grand scale was your favourite movie then consider the impact that Clark Gable and Vivien Leigh had in their portrayal of Rhett Butler and Scarlett O' Hara in 'Gone with the Wind'. The scale of its background, awash in gloriously vivid colours, stamped images of immense proportions. And if this was not enough it, was followed by the most moving film that I had ever seen, 'Wuthering Heights'. A few years later in 1942, we had another romantic masterpiece, 'Casablanca'. Bogey, and Ingrid Bergman, in that foggy, black and white atmosphere, created haunting images, not least of them, being the fragile beauty of Ingrid Bergman herself. To this day, she never knew that she had a distant admirer in the back streets of Bridgeton, whose torch burnt brightly for her.
It was also the era of Betty Grable, the girl with the million dollar (insured) legs; and the musicals, whose tunes continued to be sung in

your head long after the film. Among them at the time was Yankee Doodle Dandy, which stunned everyone with the images of James Gagney, singing and dancing. After all, you don't expect your favourite gangster to be a song and dance man - that's not on. But he was, and we loved it. These were indeed, the epic days of the Cinema, and I have only mentioned but a few. In those years, those blitzkrieg years, we feasted on some of the greatest creations of our time. They were pleasures that knew no barrier in their dispersal. If you had a tanner to spend you were rich indeed. You had access to dreams and pleasures; flights of fantasy that took you all over the world.

They would change the main film twice a week, Monday and Thursday, and move them around the districts to ensure that no one missed out. The more popular films would always be released first in the town centre. Sauchiehall Street, Renfield Street, and Argyle Street were the weekend Mecca for new films and would attract huge queues. Entertaining the queues was a profitable pursuit of the street singers, and speciality acts, which Glasgow was famous for. Allied to this were the up-market bars with their plush lounges for the wenches, who would drop in for a drink prior to taking up a place in one of the queues. With your pocket money still intact, Friday night up town was where you wanted to start the weekend.

****

Another source of great pleasure, were the dance halls. Up town, the primary ones were the Locarno, the Berkley, the Playhouse, and the most famous one of all in the war years, the Barrowland. Each had their own special attraction. The Barrowland, though, could rightly be said to be the social heart of Glasgow's East End. It was built by the Mc Iver family as an integral part of Glasgowís famous market place, from which it took its name, 'The Barras'. It was also a tribute to their mother who, by her energy and hard work, created the market. She was a well-known street trader in the east end of Glasgow who, like most other street traders at that time, sold her wares from a hand cart (a 'barra'). Despite her subsequent success, she could still be seen plying her wares in the market.

The Barrowland also faced on to another famous social landmark - the Saracen's Head ('The Sarry Heid'), the oldest pub in Glasgow. Built in the 17th century it grew to fame in the early 18th century as an Inn when it was regularly frequented by literary figures of the day. Sir Walter Scott, Thomas Gray, William Wordsmith, and Rabbie Burns (as a tax collector) were known to have indulged its food and ale. Still standing today, in isolation from its history, it is sad looking relic of its former glory. But it was still a well loved pub in and a favourite meeting place for the Barrowland dancers.

The Playhouse was the biggest of the uptown halls. With its vast dance floor it attracted the 'big' bands of the day, and would always pull the largest crowds. On the other hand the Berkley would attract the 'true' ballroom dancer, where the quality of the dance, and partner, was perceived to be more important. The Locarno in Sauchiehall Street, was said by brother Bert to draw the most attractive girls in Glasgow, and on the basis of this, was a Mecca for American service men during the war years. It also had a certain notoriety for the occasional fight between the them and the locals.

They said that the girls were so pretty, and the competition so severe, that the locals were forced to defend their pride. To control this, the management loudly proclaimed in notices around the hall, that any one causing, or involved, in a fracas, would be thrown out and barred for life. A story circulating Glasgow at that time told of a fracas in the Locarno, upstairs in the balcony area, where an American service man was pushed over the balcony, and by good fortune broke his fall on the protruding chandelier and landed on a sofa from which he bounced back on to his feet to much applause. He was immediately accosted by the bouncers and escorted into the manager's office where he was warned that if he ever performed that fuckin' trick again he would be barred for life.

In addition to the city dance halls, most districts in Glasgow could boast of a primary dance hall, with probably the Dennistoun Palais in Duke Street, and the Plaza at Eglinton Toll being the most prominent. In addition to this most districts had a community hall that were used for diverse social functions, but would often be used as dance halls at the weekend.

It was in these halls that we pubescent teenagers were expected to practice the graces that would forever confirm that girls were girls, and boys were boys, and to dance was a way to meet. Unlike the modern dance halls, the protocol adopted in the community halls was of another era. There was an implicit rule that the sexes be kept apart when not dancing. Hence, on entry, the girls would spread themselves along one wall, while the boys would take up a position on the facing wall.

At first sight it was all very strange. But, for the shy and the demure, it had its advantages. It protected you from the need to mingle and talk until you were ready which, for many of us, was very difficult. You would stand there with your mates and feed off the stronger ones in an effort to put a face on your nervous confusion. The more macho would stare across at the girls trying to search for one pretty enough to match his self-esteem. It was all posturing and strutting as they looked intently across the floor at their intended partner, hoping for a hint of a smile, or any gesture that would confirm they had clicked. Regardless of whether they had, or not, the unabashed ones were in their starting blocks, waiting for the band to start up. On the first note being hit, they were off. If she was pretty you knew that you had to be quick. If you were beaten to it, you were expected to graciously stand off and accept it, whilst inwardly wishing that he had tripped and fallen in the rush.

"Are yae dancin?"

"Are yae askin'?".

A smile, and a minimalist nod of the head, would complete the proceedings and you were on the floor. Mind you, the question was always tinged with that little bit of fear that she would turn you down.

"Are yae dancin'?"

"Naw, ah'm waitin' fur ma friend...but thanks anyway."

The dreaded turn-down did not end there, as you now had to make your way back across the floor, looking very noticeable as you picked your way through the dancers. The more sheepish of your mates who never tried, would feel justified, but their turn would come.

****

Football had become our passion in those early years. A memorable occasion was when was when Celtic won the Scottish Cup in 1937. But this was surpassed the following year when they won they won the Empire Exhibition Cup playing against oposition that included a few of the best teams in England. It was therefore a great loss to us when it was announced that all league football was to be suspended for the duration of the war.

Football continued to be played at Celtic Park during this period but, owing to the team being stripped of its better players by the armed services, the quality of the play was so poor that it lost its support. No more Saturday afternoon excitement at Celtic Park; no more heroes, such as Jimmy McGrory, Jimmy Delaney, Bobby Hogg, and Malky MacDonald, to feed our dreams. On top of that, in what was to be the last pre-war season to be completed, we lost 3-2 to Rangers at home in front of a record crowd of 92,000. To compensate for this deprivation our street football took on a new dimension and was played at every opportunity subject to the indulgence of our local bobby, Jake. Also, to the delight of dad, the shop sales of tanner balls soared. But fired by our distorted memories of the great players and teams from the past we knew that those times would return when the war ended. And so they did.

The war years and its many its many ups and downs, were now in the past. 1946 saw the resumption of league football and the start of a new season. It was now obligatory that six of us, and often more, would be at Celtic Park each week. We also took up the same position on the terracing to the right of the main stand. None of us knew why this choice of location became our favourite position, despite the fact that this end of the ground was known to be the 'Rangers' end' when they clashed at home. At these games, those of us who were 'Tims', would move to a corresponding position at the Celtic end while the others, such as Charlie Gillan, Charlie Clark, Archie Gemmel, and Jimmy McQuillen, who were 'Gers' fans would stay put.

The home game against Rangers would always be the highlight of the season. The whole East-end of Glasgow would be buzzing from early morning. To this day nothing has changed. The first of the Rangers' supporters' buses would arrive around 11 o'clock. They would always park as close to the ground as the police would allow. By 12 o'clock they would start to park at the top of Kinnear Road, and Springfield Road, and thereafter they would progressively park all the way down to Sorn Street. Around 2 o'clock dad would close the shop, and shutter the windows to protect them. It would remain closed until after the game, and all the buses had left the area.

In the pre-war years I was not allowed to go to the 'big' game. Instead I would sit at Grannies window and watch the masses of people flaunting their scarves and twirling their ricketies as they progressed up Kinnear Road. Among the elderly locals, such as Granda and Grannie, there was always an air of gloomy expectancy of what was to come. Towards 3 o'clock kick off time, Kinnear Road would become quiet, with not a person in sight. If you were not at the match you were aware of the hushed silence just before kick off. Suddenly, the silence would be broken by the piercing sound of the referee's whistle, which could be clearly heard at the bottom of the road. The joyous roar of the crowd would immediately follow it as the game got underway. Thereafter, the roars, and groans, of the crowd would punctuate their pain and joy as it matched the ebb and flow of play.

This being the first Celtic and Rangers game that I was allowed to attend we had been warned by our parents to leave the ground 10 minutes before the end of the game to avoid any trouble. But such was the tension of the match, that we got carried away with our own excitement to the final whistle - we were beaten 3-2. Leaving the ground we hurried across the London Road to Kinnear Road with the intention of keeping ahead of the crowd. But it was not to be. The taunts and insults being thrown at the Rangers' supporters as they returned to their buses were too much for some of them. Bottles started to fly through the air. Some smashed against the parked buses, and some caught the railway sleepers behind. James, Frank and the others immediately took off down Kinnear Road to safety. I went to follow but hesitated as another bottle struck a nearby supporter and pulled back behind the bus for protection.

For some perverse reason, that I have never understood, I was not afraid, but excited, and wanted to see the outcome. I felt immune (the arrogance of youth) to the obvious dangers as I skirted in and out behind the buses. Some of the supporters were screaming at the drivers to get the bus started and get the hell out of it. But, parked closely as they were, this was not all that easy. Besides, some of them were also under attack. It now got a bit heavy as supporters with blood running from head and face wounds were dragged on to the bus. At this point the shock and danger did come home to me and I took off. Staying low and close to the inside of the parked buses. I ran down Kinnear Road. The noise of the police siren was now everywhere. Now clear of the danger I got across the road and ran down towards the corner of Sorn Street. I was met on the way by dad who was frantic with worry as he came searching for me.

The War Years - Those were the Years

It was all over as quickly as it started. Inside an hour all the buses had departed and all was quiet again on Kinnear Road. The only remaining signs of the melee were the remains of broken bottles and a few smashed windows on ground floor houses. The street cleaners would soon clear the debris on Monday morning, and the factor would replace the windows. By Monday, all would be well again in this normally quiet area of Bridgeton.

****

Our Sunday 12 o'clock meet up at the closehead had now become a bit of a ritual. Originally, its main purpose was to bring together as many as possible for a game of street football and, if needed, to sort out the whip-round to buy a new ball. It had now evolved into a forum for carrying out a post-mortem on the previous day's game, and to generally gab about work, which was now such an important factor in most of our lives.

There would be quite an extensive analysis of the game that was usually good for a few opposing opinions on the merits of Celts, and the Gers. It was good for a laugh, with much taunting and baiting. Strangely enough, there was very little aggro between us, despite there being a fairly even split on who supported whom. Only Archie, true to his gutsy attitude, would attempt to pose a more powerful distinction between us by insisting that he was a Prodie, and that he had no time for Papes, when it came to playing Rangers. Curiously, it was nearly always James who responded to Archie's attempts at manliness.
"Shurrup, yae ignorant little shite. yae know as much aboot religion, as yer own arse hole."
Typically, this response was more than enough to deter Archie from any further bravados. In any case, come work on Monday,
where you would always expect a bit of stick depending on who won, it would all be forgotten till their next meeting. To us it was not a problem. Looking back at this period I am still amazed at how little we were impacted by the the deep rooted sectarian hatred that was

the norm at these 'old firm' meetings. Given that we were all born on the doorstep of Celtic Park, why were we not caught up in this odium? Why did we not hate our 'Proddy' friends, and they, their 'Pape' friends? I still ponder.

After the game had been put to rest, the gab would always return to the happenings at your place of work, with the usual litany of moans and groans that were mostly directed at those, whose opinions and self importance you were opposed to. The black and white views expressed on these matters ensured that the waters could not be muddied by varying shades of grey, and that the answers to the questions raised would be clear-cut. Besides, the subjects and their associated problems were too important for us to allow any smart mouth comments from anyone thinking that they knew better.

Dominating most of these discussions would be Frank, who was now beginning to hold sway over most of us. For some time now, he had been sounding out about one of his work-mates, who was trying to lord it over the rest of them, and that one of these days he was going to get his comeuppance. There was no doubt among us, that if Frank chose to have a go at this guy, whose name, we were now told, was the Sheriff, there could only be one winner.

Having now got everyone's attention, Frank went on to flesh out the character of the Sheriff. Based on what he told us, we now had some reservations on the outcome of his intended rammy. That Frank, owing to his work as a storeman, was very muscular, and very quick on his feet, as he regularly demonstrated at football, was not in doubt. But the Sheriff, he told us, was a razor guy, and that he always carried his weapon with him, even at work. He sniggered at our suggestion that this put him at a fearsome disadvantage. It was his belief, he said, that he could take the Sheriff out anytime by pushing a stack of boxes over on him. The Sheriff had been warned that this would be his fate, if he ever pulled a razor on him. By now, we were all entranced at Frank's elevated position at work, and his lack of fear at facing up to the threat of a razor. As if to dispel any lingering doubts on the truth of his story, he suggested that he take us to meet up with the Sheriff, next Saturday at the Shettleston Welfare dance hall. This was the Sheriff's local haunt, he said, and that he always went there on a Saturday, with his girl friend and some of his gang.

"Who's up fur it?" he challenged..." What about you, James?"

"Ok, I'm with yae", said James.

The confident response of James proved to be the catalyst. Without any further hesitation, a minimum of six of us opted to go. None of us had been as far as Shettleston before and we looked on it as another adventure.

The excitement of our impending Saturday night out had us meeting up at the closehead, each evening. We talked of little else other than our planned night out. Being the centre of attention, Frank was in his element. Under his persuasion it was decided that we would set off around 6.30, and that we would walk there, and get the tram back. According to Frank, who made this trip daily, Monday to Friday, it would take us just under an hour to walk the distance. Consequently, as the dancing did not start until 8 o'clock, it meant that we had an hour to spare. Mungo and Paddy thought that this was perfect as it would allow us time to do other things. With further questioning, Mungo said that he and Paddy knew of a good snooker hall in the Shettleston Road, not far from Parkhead Cross, where we could stop in and have a game. This idea went down well when Frank added that we could also have a drink there. Saturday could not come soon enough.

We were well decked out when we met up around 6.15. Charlie Gillan had agreed to join us, which made our number up to seven. We set off up Sorn Street and on to the Springfield road. Each of us had at least five shillings in our pocket, which gave us a feeling of affluence and self-assurance. In the case of Archie, it was not enough to feel good, he had to be seen to feel good by rattling his shillings around in his pocket. A lot of banter was directed at him by way of getting him to stop; but he just rattled all the more to taunt us. Caught up in this and our chuntering about who was playing who

at snooker it seemed like no time had passed when we passed
through Parkhead Cross and on to the Shettleston Road.

We entered the snooker hall, which, at this early time, was fairly
quiet. I went to sort out a couple of snooker tables, while the others
got the drinks in. I was just about to book when I got the call to hold
on. Looking back, I was given the nod by Charlie to follow him and
Archie over to a table in the corner. As we sat down Charlie told me
that Paddy and the others were getting in some beer.

"Whit if the Polis come in?" Asked Archie.

"That's no' likely, this early", retorted Charlie. "Besides, the barman
knows we're under age, an' he widnae take a chance if he wisnae
sure."

"Ah goat yae a Mackeson sweet stout, Barney", said James as he
approached with a tray of drinks. "The rest of us are hiv'n a pint".

"If he's ok aboot it, we'll hiv another yin before we go tae the
dancin", added Paddy as he sat down.

I had no relish for beer at that time. Its bitterness was a taste I could
not bring myself to acquire, despite the many urges by the others to
do so. It had an aversion for me that went beyond its taste, and which
I chose not to analyze. James knew this well, hence his offer of a
sweet stout. Mackeson's was a very popular drink, hence, I could sip
away at it and still give a passing resemblance of being able to take
my share with the others.

What about the snooker? I asked them. Are we going to have a
game? With the exception of Paddy, who was keen to sit there with
his drink, they all stood up in response. We also agreed to leave our
drinks on the table in case the barman pulled us up; we could always
trek back and forward while we played. Archie, as usual, was up to
his tricks and challenged me to play him for a tanner. With all the
coaching I had received from Bill, allied to the fairly regular games I
had with Bert down the Hampden hall, I felt I would be taking
advantage of him. The guys knew this too and made him back down.
In the end I played Charlie Gillan, and the others played a foursome.
Charlie was a fair player and we pushed in two games easily. The
others were half way through their second game when it was decided
that, as it was now 8 o'clock, they would break off and make their
way to the dance hall.

The War Years - Those were the Years

We got to the dance hall just after 8.30, by Mungo's watch. We stood in line in a small queue to pay our entrance fee of sixpence. Owing to it being a warm summer evening, none of us had coats to check in at the cloakroom. We therefore filed straight in the hall. According to Mungo, a lot of the girls had arrived early to take up their favourite spot on the right hand side as you entered. Having never been here before, we paused just inside the entrance to take things in, and eyed up the left side for anyone who resembled our preconceived image of the Sheriff. Despite him being known only to Frank, we confidently assumed that he had not arrived. We therefore made our way partly down the left side of the hall, still close to the entrance, where we could see everyone coming in.

The band started up and, there still being too few guys around, many of the girls came on and danced with each other. As they danced past the guys gave them the glad eye. In particular there was one girl whose movement around the floor caught everyone's eye. I must admit that I was not as skilful as the others in assessing the attractions of girls. To me her dance movements made her look quite elegant. She had a slim waist and a very ample chest, and when she smiled in response to Frank's teasing as she danced past, she looked strikingly pretty.

When the dance ended, James, Frank, and Mungo unanimously decided, that they were each going to be the next one to dance with her. As the band struck up they each made a beeline across the floor towards her. As a bit of fun they stood shoulder to shoulder in front of her and dared her to choose. Given the manner in which she had previously responded to Frank's teasing it was no contest. She ignored James and Mungo, and followed Frank on to the floor. Mind you, they were not to be wholly outdone as they got the nod from her two friends. I was so engrossed by their antics that I never noticed that Charlie, Paddy, and Archie, had wasted no time themselves and were now up dancing. Much as I would have loved to have been up there myself, I just did not have the courage to make that first hurried move across the floor, A bit of this had to be the fear of the dreaded turn-down. But I rationalised it to the back of my mind. After all this was my first real dance hall. Time was on my side. I would sort it.

Left to my own thoughts, I lit a cigarette; listened to the music, and watched the movement and steps of the dancers. My eyes also tracked to the entrance in the expectation of seeing the Sheriff enter. Considering that I had never seen him before, it had to be daft to think that I would recognise him. But I was wrong. The guys were into their second dance when a group of fellows entered and positioned themselves in front of the doors. They were well dressed and clearly looking for attention. I had seen this kind of posturing before by would-be hardmen and was about ignore it when suddenly he appeared from the centre of the group.

There was absolutely no doubt in my mind that this was the Sheriff. He had no hat on his head, nor did he have a guitar slung over his shoulder, but in every other aspect, he was straight out of a Gene Autrey film. His dark suit was something else. He was every inch an up-front western dude who demanded to be seen. His short leather boots and pointed toes, overlaid the bottom of his close fitting trousers. But, it was the jacket that really set him apart. Truly made to measure, it sported two lower and two upper pockets. The lower ones had straight flaps that were trimmed with yellow piping. The upper pockets had no flaps; instead they had curved slits that were also trimmed with yellow piping.

As I stood watching him closely, his eyes wandered all over the hall as if looking for something or someone. The friendly smile that he wore on entry was now beginning to wane, and his eyes were now focused, as if he had located what he had been looking for. I followed his line of sight and drew the obvious conclusion that Frank was dancing with his girl friend. He waited till the dance finished and the floor had cleared before walking straight over to her. At the same time Frank and the others left the floor and rejoined me. I gave Frank a nudge and nodded over to where they were now standing. He was giving her a dressing-down, and she looked close to tears.

"So, he's arrived", said Frank, turning to face us. "What dae yae think of 'im, then?".

"A bit flash", said Paddy, to which everyone nodded in agreement..."He's goet quite a few fellas wae 'im", noted James.

"That's his so called gang", sneered Frank...

"Well, whit ur yae gonnae dae noo?...Yae're surely no gonnae ask her to dance again, ur yae?", asked Archie..

"Why not. She's a nice bit o' stuff, isn't she?" retorted Frank...

"Aye, there's nae doubtin' that, but dae yae think he'll take that lyin' doon?", asked Archie.

"Ah don't give a fuck!" said Frank with a contemptuous sneer...

"He's cum'n over here", said James with a nod.

As he approached I noticed two thin pieces of mother of pearl curving outside the lower point of his slit pockets. Shit, I thought, these must be his weapons, and what I was really seeing were the curved handles of two razors. To say I was a little fearful would not be true; I was shit scared. Catching Charlie and Archie's eyes gave me no comfort either.

With a raised finger pointing at Frank, his angry voice began preaching a sermon on his rights; and that he was prepared to defend them against anyone.

"Ok, Frank, I'll accept that yae didnae know it then, but yae sure as hell ur gonnae know it now. Her name is Fanny -.she's my girl, an' she's always his bin my girl. She knows it; an' everywan in this hall, except you it seems, knows it...But now you do know it. Hiv yae goat that clear noo? Fur ah don't waant any misunderstandin' between us."

"Ah've always understood yae, Sheriff, An" now that ah know yur girl, an' that her name is Fanny, ah now know an' understan' yae even better", replied Frank.

"Ur you try'n tae be fuckin' sarcastic?"

"No' me, Sheriff, no' me", answered Frank, whilst holding his hands up in mock alarm.

Still pointing his finger, he came back at Frank. "Wan final fuckin' word tae you. Ma name is Sid, as well yae fuckin' know. So bi warned. If ah ever hear yae call me Sheriff, again, yer gonnae answer fur it. Ok?"

"Ok, by me" replied Frank, studiously omitting his name.

Silence descended on us as the Sheriff left to rejoin his crowd. James eventually broke it.

"What's it to be, Frank...Ur we gonnae call it a night and go doon the road? Or, ur we gonnae cerry oan an' hiv a few more dances? "

"I'm fur definitely cerry'n oan." answered Frank. "Ah'm gonnae sort that cunt oot wance an' fur all."

"Yur surely no gonnae ask Fanny fur a dance?" asked James, while trying hard not to burst out laughing. "He would cut yur ears oaf before you goat a word oot."

"Naw, ah widnae ask her tae dance. Ah couldnae dae that after givin' him ma word...But he didnae tell me that ah couldnae cut in when he wis dancin' wae hur."

James, Paddy, and Mungo, doubled up with laughter at the sheer cheek of what Frank was suggesting. You are mad they said. But Frank, with a grin on his face, was not agreeing with them.

"Yae widnae, wid yae?" asked James, while the rest of us stood gawping in disbelief.

"Will yae back me, brother?" asked Frank...They looked long at each other for a short while; then James started slowly nodding his head.

"Yer oan. Ah don't like 'm eether"

"Count us in." said Paddy and Mungo.

And what about us three, I asked? With our height and build, there was no way Charlie, Archie, and myself could play any part in this. It would be fearsome enough just to stand and watch it.

"Naw, you three hiv nothin' tae dae wae this.", said James. Jist slowly move yerselves up to the door, an' at the furst sign of trouble, yae get the hell oot o' here as fast as yae can. Ok?"

We nodded, and slowly made our way to the exit door and positioned ourselves so that we could have a clear view of the dance floor, whilst ensuring that our exit would not be obstructed.

The band struck up and Fanny and her girl friend took the floor. The Sheriff, meanwhile, was having a heated discussion with his pals. He would occasionally break off and stare over to where Frank and the guys were standing. Finally, without any warning, he turned away from his audience, and stood facing the dancers as they swirled past.

Fanny and her friend soon appeared. They also looked like dancing past him when he stepped forward and tapped her friend on the shoulder and appeared to excuse himself, which was the usual courtesy when cutting in. Taking Fanny by the waist he rejoined the dancers. Our eye immediately looked for some kind of reaction from Frank. But he just stood motionless and ignored them as they danced past. But not for a second time, as was made clear by Frank walking on to the edge of the floor causing some dancers to skirt round him. The tension rose as the Sheriff and Fanny danced past us and on to where Frank was waiting. As the dancers in front, who screened Frank from the Sheriff's sight, moved to bypass Frank, the confrontation was inevitable, as it was surprising.

With shock and anger, the Sheriff came to a halt as Frank came in to view. A fearful blush came over Fanny's face and she tried to beak away, but was prevented by the Sheriff's hold on her waist. He stood and stared at Frank; then lifted his left hand and pointed at him.

"Ah did warn you, Frank." he said.

"Haud oan a minute, Sid. Yae warned me not ask yer girl fur a dance, an' that's ok by me. Bit yae never said a couldnae cut in. C'mon, that's the custom, an' am only payin' yer girl a compliment."

The Sheriff released his hold on Fanny, who instantly fled off in fear, and close to tears. This fear spread to the other dancers who had stopped dancing and were slowly retreating from the floor. Even the doormen were none too keen to respond. Maybe they also were fearful of the Sheriff's reputation, I thought.

"Ok, smart arse...yae asked for it...An now yer gonnae get it."

His face took on a ghoulish look. With that he spread his legs slightly apart, and in the same movement, both hands reached for the mother of pearl handles looping from his slit pockets. With a practiced flick of his fingers the handles slung back to expose the blades. There was an almighty scream from the girls. Most of them headed for the exit while others cowered together in fearful curiosity.

"Ok.. Yae bastard...have these." Both blades, aimed straight at Frank's face, had barely moved , when an even louder scream of pain filled the hall. One of Frank's heavy brogue shoes, truly aimed, had been delivered in an upward movement, at incredible speed, and had buried itself in to the Sheriff's groin. Groaning in terrible pain he dropped to his knees still grasping his razors and, as if to ease the agony, he bent forward slowly till his forehead was resting on the floor.

My final images, before I took off with Charlie, and Archie, was of the Sheriff's gang running over to help him; and of James, Paddy, and Mungo, tripping them up on to the floor; and of Frank standing on one of the Sheriff's wrists, and shouting abuse at him.

We took off as fast as we could, and headed for Parkhead Cross. We had not gone far when we heard the noise of people running behind us. This made us run even harder in fear that we were being caught up. It was Archie who risked a pause and looked back.

"We're ok", he shouted, "it's only Frank and the lads behind us; but keep running, they've got fellas still chasing them".

We ran like hell, I tell you, 'with lungs fit to bust'. We were still a bit short of Parkhead Cross, when we met with a sight that was an indescribable pleasure to us. Two policemen stood in our path with outstretched arms ready to pull us in.

We happily gave ourselves up then, gasping for breath, we struggled to answer their questions. By now we were joined by the others, and looking back we could see the chasing gang coming to a halt. The unwelcome sight of the police was enough for them to take off. In reply to their questions, we told the police that there had been a gang fight at the Shettleston Welfare, and that we had been chased by some of the gang. With some serious doubt in their voice, they took our names and addresses and let us go.

Having regained our breath, we jokingly conducted a post-mortem on the evening, while walking home. There was much laughter as we wisecracked and colourfully enlarged on certain moments, such as Franks cheeky 'cut-in'. On this point I asked Frank what he had said to the Sheriff on the floor.

"Ah jist told him, that if he waanted to be a Sheriff, he wid hive tae be a loat quicker oan the draw. Ah also told him, that if yer gonnae face up tae somewan, then don't threaten 'im; jist dae it. It's the furst blow that always counts."

Frank was now in his element. That evening, he moved on to another plane.

You pull that stunt again an' yaer barred fur life!!

Too slow on th' draw, the Sherrif gets his come-uppance

Chapter VI

The War Years

Life in the Shop

The Winner Loses

Those were the Years

Annie Gillan - The Sad Pleasure

My Teenage Years

The War Years - Annie Gillan - The Sad Pleasure

My attraction to Annie Gillan, Charlie's sister, was not a
spontaneous one. Initially contrived, to counter, and defend, against
the growing expectations of my peers, our relationship was no more
than a convenience to both of us. It could not even be said of her that
she was pretty. Her whole appearance was one of straight lines.
Erect and slim with but the merest sign of latent curves on her chest.
Her face was long and pallid, topped with a lavish growth of brown
hair which, again was straight with every indication that this was its
preferred state; no wave, nor curl, would be welcome there. When
not unsure of herself, her attractive eyes would be fully open, and
visibly tinged with blue. Her nose was not unduly long and straight;
her lips, when not at rest, were less than fulsome.

My mother first introduced us to each other at one of the Backcourt
shelter dances. I was only there because she insisted that I was of an
age when I should be 'enjoying' myself. Mum always had a way with
words that, though clear and well intended in her own mind, could
be very confusing to others. When she caught you grinning at her
odd use of words, she would humorously dismiss it with the retort,
"Whit're yae laughin' at? Yae know whit ah mean." In this case, her
meaning was very clear; in collusion with Annie's mother, it was
boy-meets-girl time. We were nudged, and cajoled, in many ways
but without success.

Finally, they ran out of patience and with as much delicacy as
'leading a horse to water', we were taken onto the floor by our
respective parents and bluntly told to get on with it. At the end of the
dance they again descended on us and, with gleeful intent, they
ordered us to stay there till the next dance started. In the course of
the evening we managed to subdue our shyness to the extent that we
promised to meet up again on what, we timidly agreed, would be our
first date. There was no real excitement in this arrangement. It
simply fell out that we found it easy to talk to each other and were
happy to meet up again as friends. She even sensitively joked that as
I maybe need a girl friend to keep face with the others, so likewise
she could do with a fella; and that maybe it could help us to be more
confident.

The War Years - Annie Gillan - The Sad Pleasure

Our first date went pretty much as expected. We went to the pictures, supported by a bag of boiled sweets and had a good giggle at the Marx Brothers' 'Day at the Races'. I walked her back home; had a short chat at the closehead in which we agreed to another outing; waved her goodbye and walked home. It was all pleasantly uncomplicated, and in no time, it seemed, our meetings became a regular Wednesday affair. If the films being shown at the Strathies (Strathclyde Cinema) or the Plaza were not to our liking then, it being summer, and weather permitting, we would just go for a walk.

On such occasions we usually ended up in one of the small park areas that flanked the bowling greens halfway up Kinnear Road. Although they were part of the Bowling Green complex, both of the parks were surrounded by iron railings and blinded by tall hedging, which gave them an element of privacy. Annie would always prefer to sit, or lie, on the grass as the mood took her. On one occasion we were lying chatting away aimlessly browsing the sky when I started to feel restless. The sun had hardened the ground and I could not get comfortable. With an insight that I had come to know and respect, she did not inquire of my discomfort but told me, by way of common sense, that my back could never be at ease on hard ground and that I should be lying on my side. As she spoke, she also adjusted her posture in line with mine. I looked at her with a certain fondness, and smiled. "Do you mind if I kiss you?" I asked. She returned my smile and shook her head. I leaned over and did so with a pouting peck on her lower lip. To my surprise, it was soft and warm, and pleasant.
"What brought that on", she asked, with her usual honesty.
"I just wanted to say thanks", I replied.
Our innocent pleasure at that moment was only made possible by our blissful ignorance. Annie was now more than my friend, she was my soulmate. In the course of the year our relationship became more openly confident. We were now recognised as being a match, and to a few, we were even envied - much to the delight of our parents.
As I became more aware of Annie's maturing figure - the emergence of curves where formerly there were lines - her latent breasts now

more pronounced - the thought did cross my mind that the hopes and wishes of our parents, could be self-fulfilling. But there was the emerging problem of my sexual ignorance. It felt like, as in many other areas of growth, I was trailing behind. As usual, any enlightenment after your school years came primarily from the experience and anecdotes of your peers. And as most of this was coloured by the need for self-embellishment, it was as much use to you as the exploits of "Oor Wullie" in the Beano.

My greatest fear at this time was that the slowly maturing Annie would move on to a knowledge plane that would marginalise our friendship. Such unkind thoughts that she would do so only made me feel guilty and confused. But a little help was to come from an unlikely source. Archie, who had formerly partnered me in my Wednesday pictures slot, was a little bit put out at being replaced by Annie. I even suspected that he was jealous of what he considered to be our closeness. He claimed to be very knowledgeable in this area, and often boasted of his success with girls at his place of work. In agreement with the other guys, I believed that there was as much substance to this, as there was to his many other claims that were shown to be bravado. Irrespective of this there was an occasion when, owing to Annie not being available, I agreed to go to the pictures with him and that we were to meet up at his house at 7 o'clock.

Come Wednesday and on time, I knocked on his door and got no response. I knocked again, and after a short wait, he opened the door to me whilst holding up his trousers with his other hand. "Did I catch you on the pan", I asked, thinking that he had come from the lavatory.
"Naw, ah'm havin' a wank", he replied and darted up the hall into the living room.
There was clearly no one else at home for him to be acting like he was. My first thought was that he was playing the fool again, just looking for attention. Surely, he would never have opened the door unless he knew who it was. This was fully borne out when I entered the living room. He was sitting by the fireplace with his trousers at

his feet. His penis was firmly gripped in his fist, which he was stroking rapidly up and down. As my knowledge of wanking was entirely hearsay, the reality shocked me. My first reaction was that this must be painful. But I had no sooner thought it, when he started to get a bit excited.

"Ah'm cum'n, ah cum'n, Barney," he whooped. And with that he ejaculated with rapid squirts of semen falling back to rest as droplets of emulsified liquid that saturated his still-active fist and penis. Too late for its purpose, he hurriedly grabbed a dish cloth that was lying beside him and plunked it over the embers of his wank. As he did so he let out a sigh, and looked up at me with unabashed pleasure.

"Oh, that wis great, Barney, that wis a good yin", he said as he proceeded to mop up his hands and other parts.

Thoroughly shocked and confused by what was my first introduction to masturbation I struggled to respond

"Surely, that must be sore on your wullie?", I asked.

"Don't bi daft" he retorted...If yer haun's a bit rough, yae cin always rub a wee bit o' butter, or olive oil, on it before yae start. But c'mon, don't tell mi yae don't dae it yersel"...Or maybi yae don't need tae because yae've goat Annie. Eh, eh?"

I felt myself getting angry with his ugly comment. He was so ignorant, I told myself. But, if I were to keep face with the other guys, then I could not be seen to disagree with Archie on this subject. As a diversion I asked him what he was going to do with dish cloth.

"Ah'll jist throw it in with the waashin".

"What if your maw finds it?"

"She'll waash it wi' the other claes. Whit else dae yae expect her tae dae wi' it?"

All the way through the picture, I could not my get mind off Archie's wank. I was still reacting to the shock and trying to understand its consequence for me, if any. It preyed on my mind over the next few weeks, but a greater problem was soon to replace it.

In the course of hanging out at the closehead I would frequently meet Annie to-ing and fro-ing from the house for whatever reason.

Likewise, I would frequently see her from across the road in the shop. I was therefore surprised that following the episode with Archie, I failed to see her over the next few days. I casually mentioned this to Charlie, who explained that she had not been keeping too well of late and that their mum was confining her to the house for a while. He added that I should not worry about it. There was no further news over the next few days and I therefore decided that I would ask Mrs. Gillan, herself when she next came into the shop for her bits and pieces. Sure enough she did turn up, but without her usual cheery greeting. She was also very subdued. "How is Annie?" I asked. "Charlie told me that she was not keeping too well."

"Naw, she's no' keepin' too well at aw", John. We dont know whit it is. If there's no improvement by the 'morra, we're gonnae call the doact'r in. But don't yae worry, John, ah'm sure its jist some bug she's caught."

The following day I was serving a customer when dad called out to me, that an ambulance had just pulled up across the road. I instantly knew that it had to be for Annie, and without hesitation I dropped what I was doing and ran across the road and up the close where I was met at the door by Mrs. Gillan.

"Is it Annie?" I asked. To which she sadly nodded her head.

"The doact'r disnae know whit the problem is; so he's have'n her taken in tae hospital for a check up. Ah'll let yae know how she git's oan, John."

They carried her out on a stretcher. She looked very pale, and appeared to be sleeping. Mrs. Gillan accompanied her on to the ambulance and, as they closed the doors behind her, I had an incredible feeling of loss.

Despite my frequent requests to visit her in hospital, I was refused. I was given many reasons for this, but they always sounded more evasive than explanatory. It was mum who finally deigned to tell me that the reason for my exclusion was that Annie was suffering from tuberculosis. Pressing her further, she told me with great honesty, that her condition was deteriorating. Some three months later, Annie died. The Bane of the tenements had struck again.

The War Years - Annie Gillan - The Sad Pleasure

Much as I felt it to be expected of me; much as I wanted to; I could not bring myself to visit to express my condolences to Mrs. Gillan. It was she who came to me. She dismissed my misgiving about not coming to visit her as being a natural feeling. But she did have something to ask of me.

"I know yae wur very close to Annie, John. She of'en talked tae me, aboot it. An' ah waant yae tae dae me a favour. Ah'm no a religious person. None o' ma family ur'. But, ah jist feel that ah cannae let'r go withoot somewan blessin' her wi' a prayer. Ah know yur a catholic, John. An' ah know that yae're religious, as yae go tae the chapel every Sunday wi' yer maw... So, ah wis wunderin' if yae wid dae mi a big favour, an' say a prayer fur her at the funeral before she goes to be buried."

I was absolutely shocked by what she was asking me to do. For a start, I knew nothing about funeral ceremonies; I had never even attended a funeral. But such was the pain on her face as she asked that, stunned and confused as I was, I did not hesitate in saying yes. To see the joy on her face, at my response, made me feel honoured. It crystalised my thoughts, and in that moment, I believed in what I had just agreed. She thanked me, and kissed my cheek.
"Yur a good boy, John. If only it had bin different."
It was not much later that reality kicked in. The ramifications of what I had just agreed to do left me stunned, and overwhelmed by the consequences. What did I know about burial prayers or ceremonies? Nothing, was the quick answer to that. As for being a religious person, in the context of what Mrs. Gillan believed, it inferred that by right of me being a catholic, and going to chapel on a Sunday with my mother, that I had insight into the mysteries of God and his blessings.

The truth was that any thoughts of me being a religious person in the real sense had been seriously dented in my later years at school. I just felt that I was in over my head. But, the very real loss I felt for Annie, was stimulus enough for me to try and do something to ease the sadness and pain felt by her mother,

The first reaction of mum, when I tried to discuss it with her was very much akin to my own. We're listeners, John, not preachers, she said. Nevertheless she was sympathetic towards my predicament and suggested that I go and get some advice from Father Butler. But, given my dislike for him, this was not a consideration. Not best pleased at my dismissal of her advice she reacted as normal with her own dismissive comment.
"Ok, if you won't do it, I'll do it myself", she retorted.
I felt a little guilty at having provoked her, but true to her word she pulled on her coat, and set off to see Father Butler.

She was hardly gone an hour, when she was back. With fury in her voice, she said that she had been treated badly by Father Butler. She had been severely chastised for not knowing better, she said. He considered it blasphemous that she, or any of her family, should preside over a catholic ceremony, or prayers, for some one from another faith. He ordered me out of the vestry. He also told me to attend confession as soon as possible. Who is he to talk to me like that? She went on all evening about it. Even dad, who was coming home for his supper after a long day in the shop, was in danger, I thought, of having to cook his own meal.

She eventually calmed down, but not before making it clear that if I chose to say a prayer at Annie Gillan's funeral; then I was going to say a prayer; and that she would provide it for me, chapter and verse. She then announced that she was going upstairs to see Moira McAlister, and with that she stormed out. It was generally known that Mo' was a devout catholic, and a very compassionate one at that. The neighbours held her in high esteem. In their opinion what she did not know about the catholic religion, and its protocol, was not worth learning.

On returning from her chat with Mo', she had noticeably calmed down and was more like herself. She had obviously got what she wanted, as she praised Moira as being such a lovely woman with a heart of gold. She went on to explain that Moira had made light of the problem. There were many prayers, she had said, that could be offered up, that would not offend your own faith. Given the circumstances, she recommended one that could be appropriate. Mum handed me a prayer book, on loan from Moira, which she said, was bookmarked with a piece of card, and asked me to read it. As I read the verse to myself its poetic depth moved me.

Do not stand by my grave and weep
I am not there, I do not sleep.

I am a thousands winds that blow.
I am the diamond glints of snow.

I am the sun on ripened grain,
I am the gentle autumn rain.

When you awake in the morning's hush,
I am the swift uplifting rush,

Or quiet birds in circled flight.
I am the stars that shine at night.

Do not stand by my grave and cry,
I am not there, I did not die. "

****

With prayer book in hand, Mrs. Gillan led me into the front room whose only light was from the candles that stood on a shelf at the rear. Their yellow light festooned the head of the coffin and cast flickering shadows on the walls. I positioned myself at the foot of the coffin, with Mrs. Gillan beside me. Annie lay there in her white funereal gown, her pallid cheeks in conflict with the flickering light. The family filed in to the room and took their place around her. Throughout these preparations I stood there with my head bowed trying to concentrate on my prayer. As silence again filled the room I lifted my head to see, only for it to fill with bizarre images. There was I, barely sixteen years of age, standing at the foot of a coffin, surrounded by mostly strangers, all staring at me with amazement and expectation in their eyes.

I could feel a tear flow down my cheek as I lifted my prayer book. I looked at the first line of verse and the single tear was joined by others. This was unreal. I could not do this. I'm sorry, I said, and walked out of the room and out the front door.

I am sure that I would have run had it not been for the inchoate howl that preceded my uncontrollable crying. I sat on the closehead stairs and was joined by Mrs. Gillan. She was also in tears as she wrapped her arms round me.

"Ahm so sorry", she cried. "Ah should never hiv put yae through this. Yae're still a baby. All I waanted wis to share ma grief."

Wish you were here to ease my mind
And to explain this mysterious lore
That seems to have no compassion
For verities that are evermore.

That distinguishes from others of different creed
When painfully laid to rest
In the earth from where we all were sprung
As was Annie's only bequest

She was neither lover, nor sinner, before she died
Too early in her innocent teens
I am told that she is now in heaven
And to believe in what that means

Chapter VI

The War Years

Life in the Shop

The Winner Loses

Those were the Years

Annie Gillan - The Sad Pleasure

<u>My Teenage Years</u>

The War Years - My Teenage Years

The loss of Annie left a void in my life. Though very much doubted by others, our relationship was never sexual in nature. We did become very close but always platonically so. The prescient sexuality displayed by others was well outwith our experience, The shyness that had dominated our lives, was only held at bay by our honesty with each other. It is true that we used our friendship as a protection against the flaunting confidence of others. But it was only intended to buy us time to patiently find our own way though the hormonal jungle without the painful taunts and well meaning ignorance of others. I missed her sorely. She was the reality-surrogate for Jean, the soulmate I parted with in Mearnskirk.

Initially, there had been much sympathy from the guys when meeting up at the closehead. For a while there was also the danger of my closer affinity with Charlie displacing that with James and Frank. This was brought to an end, though, by Charlie clicking with a girl at the dancing. Soon, it seemed that everyone had a girl friend, and that we were no longer meeting up as often as we had in the past. In this period other differences began to surface. With their increasing affluence from working, many of the guys were now meeting up in the pub for a couple of pints, or going down the snooker hall. I would always join them at the weekends where it was still the drill for us to go out as a group. But as my taste for drinking had never got beyond a couple of bottles of sweet stout, I was never going to be a drinker. In addition to this there was still a few of us who were legally under age - but for them it only added to the buzz.

This apart, I would still occasionally join them for a game of snooker. As it turned out, though, meeting up with the guys midweek was now a matter of chance, with the pictures still the most popular outlet. In truth, the only pursuit that was still passionately shared by us all, was football; Celtic on Saturday, and our own game on Sunday.

The War Years - My Teenage Years

These changing social habits were slow to impact on me. It must have been a year later (I was 17) when it finally dawned on me that I was in a Monday-to-Friday rut. It was not just the social changes; it was the whole damned daily routine. And at the heart of it was the shop. Yes, I was working there from choice; but that choice was now three years old. In my emerging teenage grasp of the world you not only had the right of choice, but also the right to change. Slowly and painfully I rationalised that if I gave up my job in the shop and took another one, I would be free of the over-familiar daily restraints and therefore have more independence. Taking this train of thought further I also concluded that I would be able to meet more people and, depending on the job, I could be more affluent. Rounding it all off with a few more self-satisfying thoughts I decided to put my conclusions to mum and dad.

The following day, in the mid morning quiet of the shop, I was presented with the opportunity to do so.
With much guilt and a severe leak in my confidence, I took it. They listened to me attentively; and with a little smugness, I thought.
"What do you think?" I asked.
"Go for it", they replied without any hesitation.
The promptness and manner of their response surprised me. I was, of course delighted that freedom was at hand, but the ease with which they conceded pricked my vanity.
"Are you sure you can manage without me?" I asked.
"Of course we can. If we are stuck, we can always call on Agnes to help out. Besides, we only want what is best for you. So take yourself off and do your own thing."

****

The War Years - My Teenage Years

As luck and circumstance would have it, my first job was in Kinnear Road. Located halfway between the shop and Baltic Street, a small factory had just been set up to manufacture 'firelighters'. They were popularised as a quicker method of kindling your fire in the cold winter mornings. If you could afford the extra penny, they were a welcome alternative to the bound bunch of sticks (chopped wood) that were sold in most shops.

Being a new startup company looking for workers, I was readily offered a job as a packer at 10 shillings a week - the same as I was paid in the shop. This in itself was hardly a reason for taking the job, but it was a start; and given that I was now mixing with some 10 new faces, it was stimulating. The factory itself was small and consisted of a yard flanked by two brick built sheds with sliding doors. One was home to the packaging and consisted of a long bench surrounded by stools for perching on. The other shed contained the manufacturing plant which, on first whiff, bordered on the obnoxious.

On my first day at work I was shown round the factory and its workings by a very tall, muscular man who introduced himself as the owner and manager. He gave me a very brief overview of how the firelighter was made which, as he put it, was nothing more than a piece of bog peat dipped in a diluted form of naphthalene. In the ensuing days I expanded on this to mean something more complex and more dangerous.

The process was divided into two operations. The peat block as received, was dry and trimmed to a regular shape. Each block would be passed through a saw table of seven blades to produce eight slices of peat 1-1/2 inch thick. These slices were then passed through another table of seven blades that made 1 inch deep incisions. The resulting slices then looked like a tablet of eight pieces that, held together at the base, could be easily snapped off as a single unit - a firelighter.

The War Years - My Teenage Years

They were then carefully stacked in large wire baskets and passed on to the next operation at the other end of the shed.

Here they would be lowered into a foul smelling tar-like substance until the basket was fully immersed. The basket, while still immersed, would then be given a vigorous shake. The shaking continued as it was withdrawn. It would then be placed on a line of metal rollers where it would roll down to join the others and left to dry. Surprisingly, they dried and cooled very quickly. You could also tell when they were dry as they sparkled brightly under the light.

Much as my parents were happy at my striking out for independence, they were not best pleased when they discovered my choice of work. They made it clear that they had higher hopes for me; that I could certainly do a lot better than work in a filthy sweat-shop. They asked me to leave and find something else. Their pride was hurt, yet still they acknowledged that is was my choice and that they would not press me.

When next I met up with the guys they were even more annoyed at me than my parents.

Your a fool, John, said James. How can you give up the comfort of the shop to work in a place like that.

"Your mer than a fool, added Frank, your a fuckin' eejit. Whit dis yer maw and da' say to it? Don't tell me they're behind yae, fur ah don't believe yae"

Archie also added few choice words, all in the same vein. Likewise did Charlie, whom I respected. The fierceness of their abuse absolutely stunned me. They all of them thought I was just plain daft and voiced their willingness to change places with me any day. Try as I may, I could not rebut them. But angry pride would not have me back down. They all chose what they wanted to do; so they were no better than me. They would not be convinced. In the end there was a muted acceptance of both positions and we agreed to differ.

The War Years - My Teenage Years

Looking back on this episode I still clearly remember the anger and arrogance of my teenage pride and know it to be wholly natural. As Jimmy Miller would have said, "if yae don't' make mistakes, yae cannae learn". Mind you, there was more to follow and not all of them worthy of Jimmy's philosophy.

Regardless of the well meaning advice, I continued in the manufacturing of firelighters and so impressed the manager that after only two weeks on the packing he trained me to run one of the saw tables. Mind you the training could not be said to be difficult as it was primarily aimed at the art of protecting your fingers from the whirling blades. In the course of a further two weeks I not only mastered both saws but also got an opportunity to try the dipping. Now this really was a memorable experience.

As I withdrew my first basket from the hot naphthalene the ever-present smell intensified. Its gushing fumes filled my nostrils and almost overpowered me. As my youthful energy made light of the task of lifting and dropping it on to the rollers I was greeted by words of praise from the manager. "Well done', he said. "You were a bit unsure with that first basket but you'll master it in no time", he added.
Be that as it may, it wholly convinced me that it was not a task that I intended to master. Indeed, it was the defining moment when my stubborn pride acknowledged reality. My final decisive thought in this reappraisal of my future with the company was when I walked out from the gloom of the shed into the light and looked at my overalls. From the chest down they were covered with a damp film of naphthalene. Also, as they quickly dried in the cool air, they started to sparkle. Much as this was the accepted face of the dipper it never occurred that this was other than normal. As I stood there sparkling with the success of my labours the truth dawned. I

was nothing short of a human firelighter. One match, (and I did smoke), was all that was needed.

Did I exaggerate? I never returned to find out. My second job in life was at an end. Apologies all round to my parents and friends thankfully accepted; they were right and I was wrong. As a denouement to this episode, a small fire did occur in the firelighter factory (no one hurt) that required the attention of the Fire Brigade. Following their inspection the factory was declared a fire hazard and was closed down.

To this day I can still recall the faces of those women perched around the packing table. All their worries and hopes would spill out in their daily banter. And I being the only male member of their group, the banter could be merciless in its treatment of me and always with a sexual slant at my ignorance. I will never forget bringing them down in hysterics when I innocently referred to our manager as being right horny - I was referring to his 'corny' jokes.
A few other jobs followed. Each brought their own experience to bear on my teens. From them all I learned much, and yet so little. They certainly expanded my knowledge of working life in Glasgow. More importantly, though, it taught me that my emotional confusion, far from being unique, was a common experience in the work place.

****

In this period two other people contributed to my learning curve. My uncles, Harry and Geordie, could hardly be said to be a source of wisdom; nor could they be said to be kindred spirits. In truth my growing dislike for both of them since Granny died was never far from expression. None the less, they were an obligatory part of family life. Curiously though, in an odd little way, Harry would insinuate a fondness for me. On one such occasion in the shop he was talking to dad about his favorite pastime, dog racing. Dad was also fond of a bet on the dogs and , for a change, they were on common ground. He let it be known that he was going to Carntyne that evening and was trying to persuade dad to join him. However, as dad's social affinity with Harry was barely above tolerance, it was never going to happen. Turning his attention to me, he asked if I would like to join him. Before I could rebut his invitation dad expressed the thought that I might find it interesting. Persuasively, he talked up the fun of it being a new experience for me and that I might even get lucky. If you have nothing on this evening why don't you give it try, he added. With dad so keen there was to be no refusal. This seemed to please Harry no end and we agreed to meet at 7 o'clock.

Glasgow sported three very popular tracks at that time: Carntyne, close to Parkhead Cross; Shawfield, just down from Bridgeton Cross; and White City, close to Ibrox. Carntyne was only a 10 minute ride in the tram from Springfield Road at the end of Sorn Street. My first impression as we entered the racetrack was that of a football ground surrounded by an oval shaped track brightly lit by lampposts set at fixed intervals round its inner length. Also like a football ground, the track was surrounded by terraced steps with a medium sized grandstand fronting on to its centre. The other factor that quickly became apparent was that only the grandstand, its fronting terracing (the silver ring), and one end of the terracing (the regular ring) was used by the racegoers. The regular ring, which we had entered, was by far the busiest of the two. Harry gave me a overview of how it all worked. All the bookmakers, he said, were located in a line round the top of the terracing. He took me up the terraced steps to get a closer look. Each bookie stood on his stool with his raceboard perched on its stand at eye level. Beneath the board, at waist level, hung a large leather bag with most of them having the bookies name imprinted in bold letters.

The War Years - My Teenage Years

I was a bit awestruck by it all. With loud garrulous calls they competed with each other to get the punter's attention. Owing to the close presence of our own Backcourt-bookie I was long since familiar with the bookies betting strategy when pricing his odds - or so I thought. This was all so different. To me this was betting on a grand scale. There was a buzz of excitement everywhere. Turning our attention to the track we walked down the terracing and took up a good position where we could watch the dogs being paraded. We scanned through the programs that Harry had bought for us on entry. I opened it at the first race and read the blurb describing each dog's background and past performance. But, with the exception of confirming that there were five dogs in the race, it had little meaning for me.

Harry, for his part, was now nodding his head knowingly whilst tapping his finger on the name of a dog in the race list. This is what I want you to do, John. I've got a tip that Black Jim is going to be a trier tonight and I want you to bet a shilling 'place' on it. Now the bookies don't take place bets on the course so you will have to go to the Tote, he said, pointing to a row of windows positioned close to the stand. I'll meet you back here before the race starts. I got up to the Tote and joined the smallest of the five queues. It cleared quickly. I passed my shilling through the window and called out my bet. With a muted response the clerk slid a race ticket back to me. Was this to be the first step on the road to a new career in gambling? Surely not. Clutching my ticket I made my way back to our chosen position on the rail. True to his word I had no sooner got there than Harry arrived.

The dogs paraded past us for the last time prior them being put in the traps. Black Jim is number 4 and it's got an inside draw on the rail, said Harry. The dogs were quickly loaded into their box. From half way round the bend behind the traps the hare spurted forward on the rail. It picked up speed at an incredible rate and flew past the traps; they were off!! Black Jim got a flyer out of the box and was up on the first bend well in the lead. I found myself screaming at him to stay there all the way round. The screaming became a roar as he sped over the line; he was never caught. Harry and I were grinning all over ourselves. "How much did I win?" I asked him. "You'll hiv tae wait till it's displayed on the Tote", he said, pointing to a huge display board at the other end of the ground. "There it goes now. It's showing 4 -1 for a win and even money for a place. You've won a shillin'."

"I could have won 4 shillings had I backed it to win", I instinctively responded.

"True", said Harry, "but you wid have lost a shilling had it come in second. Instead, yae hid two chances to win a shillin'."

His logic of having two finishing places out of five to win was sound but, as I discovered in the course of the evening, it was a bit boring. As I went off to collect my winnings it struck me that Harry made no effort to do likewise. Instead, he seemed intent on studying the next race in his program. On my return I was astonished to find that Geordie had joined us and was in deep conversation with Harry. My arrival went unnoticed and, not wanting to intrude, I stood there looking on. Geordie pulled a wad of notes from his pocket and handed them to Harry.

"Is it all there?" Asked Harry.

Geordie assured him that it was and offered to count it for him.

"Naw, ah trust yi", replied Harry with his lopsided grin that so easily could be mistaken for a sneer. He drew a couple of the notes from the wad and handed it to Geordie, who eagerly accepted it with a tinge of grovel. They looked like a couple of crooks with a well-defined pecking order. A tarty looking woman now appeared and with much familiarity took hold of Geordie's arm. At this point Geordie became aware of my presence and with evident guilt hastily withdrew his arm and stepped aside. He greeted me with an apology for not seeing me and, for an awful moment, I thought he was going to introduce me to his friend.

The next race came and went without any tip from Harry. I lost my previous winnings on a dog that looked very lively in the parade. Harry and Geordie also lost but, from their lack of concern, it could not have been much. They immediately turned their attention to the next race and conversed in undertones.

"Ok Geordie", this is the big yin. Yae know whit to dae, don't yae?"

"Sure", responded Geordie, "ah'm ready when you ur".

In the course of this exchange, Harry pulled out his wad of notes and peeled of what appeared to be half and handed them to Geordie.

"Ok, ah'll see yae back here after the race."

"Sure thing", replied Geordie and hurried off with his friend in attendance.

He then turned to me with a smirk on his face.

"Now, Johny boy, ah've got anither tip for you. Number 2, Monsoon. The one in the blue hap", he added as he pointed to the dogs assembling for their parade.

"And remember; the same rule; a 1 shilling place bet. Ah'll see yae back here fur the start of the race." With that he headed off in the direction of the bookies.

On the way to the Tote I considered the risk of making it a 1 shilling each way bet. Persuasively, I convinced myself that that even if Monsoon failed to win it need only come second for me to get most of my 2 shillings back. It was done and, naturally with increased expectation and excitement, I returned to our vantage point to watch the dogs being paraded. Soon after, Harry, Geordie and his woman friend returned looking very pleased with themselves - especially Harry.

The dogs were now loaded in to their boxes and all eyes were focused on the hare as it started up. Like a slingshot it whipped off the bend and sped past the traps - they were off. Monsoon in trap four got off to a good start and headed the other dogs into the first bend but was still running wide. Going into the second bend it tried to come inside and took a hit from the closing inside runners. Down the back straight it recovered to take the lead going into the third. It maintained its lead going into the last bend but again ran wide allowing two of the inside runners to come upside with it. They ran abreast towards the finishing with Monsoon appearing to draw away. Then, without warning, the inside dog veered to its right causing the outside two to clash badly. Monsoon, who was leading by half a length , took a whack on its rear and finished third.

One moment I was beside myself with excitement; the next, I had a hollow feeling of disappointment. When all the jumping and cheering abated I was confronted by an ugly sight of Harry and Geordie 'effing an' blinding' about their bad luck. "Wid yae Fuckin' believe it?" Harry screamed. "We wur beaten' by a fuckin' snapper. Cin yae credit that fur fuckin' luck."

As for Geordie, he was also cursing their luck but in a manner that was aimed at placating Harry. As for the snapper this, as I was to learn, was a term for dogs that were prone to fighting and were known to snap at other dogs in the race to protect their advantage in the chase.

Having calmed down a bit, Geordie ventured to ask Harry how much money he had left. Glaring back at him, as if the question was an unwanted reminder, he pulled a few notes from his pocket - his wad was gone.

"Ah'm also skint", said Geordie with a tinge of self-pity.

"Ah've got a couple of pounds left", said his woman friend.
"Let's go and drown our sorrows wae a couple of drinks", she added.
"We might as well", he responded, whilst looking at Harry for assurance. "Are you staying on, Harry", he asked.
"Ah'll see yae later in the Springfield", replied Harry, and with an impatient gesture of his hand, he turned his back on them.
"Well that's been a blidy bad night for me", Johny boy.
"Ah've barely enough left to piy ma papers in the mornin'. Mind yae, ah can always fob them off to the afternoon", he added, more to himself than to me.
He was still simmering with anger but was clearly trying to hide it from me.
"Now, whit about you? Yae must be down a 1/- shillin' noo."
Not to have him know that I ignored his advice, I casually agreed with him.
"Well let's see if we cin get your shillin' back. Ah don't hiv any mer tips, but ah still know a thing or two aboot dogs he boasted. There's one in this race that's not won fur a while and for me he's always bin a trier. He's good fur a place bet; and yae should get better than even money fur it. So have a go at it. Or do yae waant to call it a night?"
There was now a distinct impatience in his voice. It was as if he was eager to leave. Not wanting to disappoint him, and equally not wanting to accompany him back home in his current mood, I told him that I was going to stay on for a couple of races.
"Ok", he responded. "Ah've had enough. I'll get masel' back doon the road." With that he abruptly turned and headed for the exit.

He had obviously lost a great deal of money on that one race and I was eager to know why. It had to be some kind of scam if it required the help of Geordie. Why else would he involve him? The following day dad confirmed this in response to my query. No doubt Betty would have taken the brunt of it when he got home, he added. As to the scam, dad thought that if Geordie was involved then it had to be a layoff bet. It was commonly used by bookmakers to protect themselves against heavy losses when they have taken more money than they can risk on any one dog. When that happens they sell part of their risk off to other bookies. It was dad's thought that Harry must have had a good tip for a dog that he knew would open at high price with the bookies. He would get Geordie to bet (say fifty pounds) on the highest opening bet he could find, say 5/1. With such a high opening bet the odds would be immediately slashed to 3/1. As the other bookies reacted so the price would stabilise at these odds. Harry would then get a friendly bookie to lay off his bet at 3/1. Thus, in theory, Harry couldn't lose. But if he failed to get the lay off and the dog lost then the scam was a bogey.

****

In my later teens brother Bert was never too far from my thoughts. He was the loveable rogue of the family. Without the nastier side of Harry, he was not above some of his dubious wiles and fondness for alcohol. At that time he worked as a delivery van driver for Connell's 'ginger' factory in Mordaunt Street. Never one for talking too much about the perks of the job, he clearly possessed an insight into the working practises of the successful working man. Socially, he was a typically gallus Glaswegian; full of cheeky confidence and a ready smile, he could trade the local humour with the best. Connell's ginger works provided him with an affluence that sat well on him. It funded his generous lifestyle and gave him an aura of worldliness that would ebb and flow with the times. This period was to hallmark his persona for life.

Our elder brother Bill was an entirely different character. His life in the navy during the war had left him with a love for travel and an unremitting urge to revisit those exciting ports of call. To Bill, the war was no more than a backdrop for new experiences of an order he could only have dreamt of. They were the fount of many stories that he would embellish over the years. The implicit structure and ranking of the navy also impacted him. It gave order and confidence in his pursuits. This was exemplified in the ease at which he would take up sports and other activities that he put his mind to. In most of these pursuits he would achieve a high level of competence. One in particular, Billiards, he excelled at. So good did he become that for a couple of years he was ranked in Scotland's top ten.

Golf was another sport that he pursued.. He took it up in his early twenties and encouraged by the prompting of his girl friend's father, allied to lots of practise on the 9 hole on Alley Palley (Alexandra Parade), he reached a single figure handicap in the course of two years.

He was also very fond of ballroom dancing. Not for him, the Barrowland. It had to be the Palais or the Berkley, which were mostly frequented by 'proper dancers'. Again he took his competence to another level when he won a bronze medal for the foxtrot and a silver for the waltz. It was a pursuit that Bert also excelled at. But, in keeping with his gallus personality, he preferred the Barrowland, or the Locarno. As needs must they also had a common addiction for fashionable clothes but could differ in their tastes. With his greater affluence, Bert would constantly indulge himself and, against the fashion trend at that time, he was never above buying the occasional piece off the peg. Bill on the other hand, whilst more thrifty in his spending, would always have his suits made to measure and also the odd shirt. Competition between them could be quite rough at times with more serious problems being averted by the intervention of mum or dad.

The War Years - My Teenage Years

There was one incident that Bert always laughed off. Bill had just bought himself a new suit for a forthcoming social event (he was big on status events). He certainly looked a picture when he tried it on in front of mum and dad, who were generous in their praise. When Bert set eyes on it he was more than a little envious of it and asked Bill to let him try it on. In response, he got a scathing look from Bill, and was bluntly told that the suit would remain in the wardrobe under lock and key until the event. But this only made Bert all the more determined to try it on. He tried to persuade mum to get a loan of the key but she would have none of it. By sheer chance I came home one day and caught him in the act of prizing off the rear panel of the wardrobe. He was not put off by my presence except to ask me with a mischievous smile on his face not to shop him. I wanted no part of it, I told him. This was down to him and Bill. But I had to admire his cheek when he put the suit on. Posing in front of the mirror he liked what he saw. I could only laugh when he turned to me and said that he was off to the dancing. When mum, dad and Bill learnt of Bert's doing, all hell let loose. Many a week was to pass before Bill and Bert could sit at the same table let alone talk to each other. But, despite their many fracas and fiercely competitive nature, there was still a bond between them that showed in a their passion for activities that all three of us shared.

In this period the one social activity that was second only to football was the dancing. While Bert did his own thing at the Barrowland and the Locarno, it was Bill who first introduced me to the allure and mysteries of ballroom dancing at the Palais. It was a wondrous experience that gave me much joy and not a little pain. For many months I would accompany him on a Wednesday to learn the basic steps, as he put it. He would always meet up with the same group of guys and girls who were somewhat older than me and very definitely more experienced. As a consequence, and despite their encouragement, I was very much on the fringe of it all. By way of trying to give me more presence, Bill suggested that I buy myself a made-to-measure suit. He also tactfully advised that I should have the jacket bloused at the back, which was quite fashionable at that time. Whilst I was not particularly conscious of the growing curvature of my spine when among friends, the impact of Bill's words struck home. I was about to pay the penalty for the hasty disposal of my straightjacket.

When I saw Bill dancing for the first time I was overawed by the unexpected grace of his movement as he glided round the floor with his partner. And they were so close to each other, I thought. It made me feel clumsy and self-conscious yet I was still being driven to try. But after many weeks of viewing and practising in my minds eye I eventually succumbed to the invitation of one of Bill's partners. My confidence was not helped by Bill's mischievous call for her to be kind to me. As we stood waiting for the band to start up she explained the basic steps of the foxtrot - slow, slow, quick, quick, slow. She held me at arms length as she guided me round the floor. When I clumsily got out of step she would patiently stop; recap on the steps and movement and resume dancing. Although I was awkward and self-conscious it was my first dance and I enjoyed it. Before the evening ended, and no doubt prompted by Bill, I was again invited by one of the group to dance the foxtrot with her. I went home that evening feeling pretty good about myself and with every intention of making the Palais a frequent rendezvous.

After a few months I reached a reasonable level of confidence and was able to get round the floor with not too many mistakes. Bill's friends were now beginning to leave me to my own devices. As a consequence I was now exposed to self-doubts. Could I really ask a girl to dance without the security of knowing her? Shyness, the bane of my life, returned; it was never too faraway. I rationalised it every which way I could.

The War Years - My Teenage Years

If I was to make any progress at dancing then I had to overcome it. Eventually my pride took over and I partially suppressed it to the extent that I was able to ask with overt politeness for a dance. On the basis that I got fewer rejections I also found an area in the hall were I could be at ease. This was helped, I think, by the same groups of girls always positioning themselves in the same space each week. They soon picked up on my shyness and, providing I waited until the early rush of dance requests subsided, they were quite content to dance with me. Needless to say they were seldom my first choice; then again I was was quite certain that I would not be their first choice either.

With every little success my vanity grew a little stronger. Soon my eyes were becoming more selective. One girl in particular stood out from the group. She had stunning red hair with straggling curls that were softly bound at the back by a band whose colour would vary each week. Her freckled face seemed always to be primed with a latent smile that readily effused on eye contact. She was no taller than me and was a delight to dance with. This pleasure was seldom available owing to her popularity. But there was the odd opportunity as when she would return late from a visit to the cloakroom or other diversions and find her friends already dancing. On such occasions I would present myself and was seldom refused. Like the other girls in that area she was aware of my shyness but her confident self-assurance would always put me at ease. She even corrected my self-conscious dancing posture that prevented me from getting too close.
"Try to relax, John", she prompted. "And you must get closer to your partner", she added with a playful pull of her arm. Her name was Kate, and over a period we developed a familiarity with each other. I even gathered sufficient courage to ask her for a date; but this was not to be.

The War Years - My Teenage Years

In the two years that followed I continued my Wednesday visits to the Palais. Sadly, the visits of Kate became less and less frequent until finally they stopped. From one of her friends I learned that she had married. Still, there were many other pretty girls frequenting the Palais. So much so that every week I would fall in love with one of them; and every week I hoped that I would succeed. Whilst I look back with fondness at this period it did expose a frailty that was to be the bane of my life.

Chapter VII

A New Beginning

A New Beginning - In search of Something

The confusion of my teenage years led me to taking up many activities only for them to be exhausted and dropped. In my early twenties now, only one of them, the dancing, truly captured me with its tantalising prospects of filling my void. But it was not to be. Its painful exposure of my frailty impelled me to seek other means.

As an alternative pursuit I took up weekly lessons on playing the accordion. This had come about more by chance than intent. It was the outcome of me tinkering with the accordion keyboard at one of mum's Backcourt dances. These dances continued for some time after the war, much to the delight of mum. Jimmy Miller, who was untrained, but quite competent, was one of her stalwarts on these occasions - was there no end to this man's talents? In the interval between dances he would allow me to try my hand on the keyboard. Eventually, I became passably good at playing one or two popular tunes of the day, such as: "aul' scotch mother mine", which was always good for a sing-along waltz. It was he, who suggested to mum, that she send me for lessons. Not only did she do so, at 2/6d a lesson, she also got Jimmy to get hold of a good second-hand accordion for me, which must have cost her a few pounds. I could see what was in her mind, but I was happy to go along with it on the basis that it was only once a week. Inside no time I had extended my repertoire, but I was still "playing by ear". Reading music would come later, I thought, but with little conviction.

I was flattered one evening at being given the honour of a one-time-only-never-to-to-be-repeated chance to stand in for Jimmy when he took a break and received a smattering of applause for my effort. Little did I know at the time that my musical career was about to come to an abrupt end. It happened on my lesson night. I picked up my encased accordion, and opened the door to leave, when I was confronted by Frank and Archie. Forget the accordion, you're coming with us, they said. A smart-arse mug down the Hampden hall has challenged us. He's challenged James, Mungo, and Paddy, to play him for five bob a head. They've told him that they would each bet him five bob on one game only, providing we can choose anyone of our guys to play. He thinks that all of our guys are in the hall and he's dead sure that he can beat anyone of us. So we're going to pull a flanker on him by slipping you in the back door. There's a half-hour wait for a table so we have to hurry back. The guys had pulled this stunt before and they would never have lived it down if I reneged on them now.

Before I got back that evening mum had returned and found my accordion in the back room. Not only that but she found our kid brother, Michael, who was now eight years old, banging noisily on the keyboard. May, who was supposed to have been looking after him, saw no fault in this. When angrily questioned by mum she unwittingly let it be known that I had gone down the snooker hall. On my return that evening I was told to hand back my 2/6d lesson fee and, on doing so, got a severe dressing down. It was not that I had missed a lesson that angered her; nor do I think it was the money, which was reason enough. I think that she felt cheated out of her hopes for my musical talent. Two days later my accordion had gone; not another word was said about it. As for the outcome of the challenge; yes, I won. Not only that, but the guys had put an extra five bob on it for me. Still, I would have preferred to keep my accordion.

****

I was now in my twenties and yet I still had this feeling that I was younger than my years. James, Frank, and the others seemed to be more self-assured, and more single-minded in what they wanted for themselves. It was as if they were privy to experiences that were passing me by. Try as I may to keep up with them, they were slowly creeping ahead. This was borne out by their mid week pursuits, which were mostly associated with meet ups in the many bars strewn all over Bridgeton. This did not come natural to me, and therefore I could not compete. Consequently, I found myself with time on my hands, looking for an outlet.

A New Beginning - In search of Something

It was dad who picked up on my boredom, and suggested that I go to the library and find myself a book to read. I had never been inside a library before, and it stirred my curiosity. In the absence of anything better to do I decided to explore, and being a nice evening, I walked down to the public library at Bridgeton Cross. It was a huge red sandstone building whose colour and ornate frontage made it stand proud of the tenements that flanked it. It would often catch my eye when I passed it on the tram. As I walked through its doors the first thing that struck me was its size. Every inch of its walls were shelved and filled with books. In addition to this there were freestanding bookcases positioned in orderly lines along its floor. The sheer scale of presentation was awesome. I spent the rest of the evening trying to fathom out how it all worked. By the time the library was closing I had only scraped the surface of its complexity. As a first cut I worked out that the books were organised into subjects, most of which I had not even heard of. To take it further than this was going to be difficult; it was a challenge. But as I left, I thought, this will do for the moment. There was enough here to bring me back.

Over the following weeks, and with the help of the librarians, I not only got to know its organisation, and how to locate books, on any subject, I now had my own membership card, and was free to borrow any book of my choice. This led on to the discovery that the library held a complete range of lesson books on primary and secondary school education. I got quite excited at this find. It meant that I had access to my missing two years of secondary education. At my own pace and in my own time, I could try and catch up, I thought. It would not be structured as in school, nor would any examinations be taken. But it would greatly improve my confidence to know that I was at one with those missing years, and that the void had been filled. Unknown to me another contribution to my confidence-building was close at hand.

****

A New Beginning - In search of Something

Holidays had always featured highly in our family. As kids, mum and dad regarded it as essential that we got a holiday break away from the tenements during the Glasgow 'Fair', the last two weeks in July. This tradition stretched all the way back to Victorian times when the original fair was first held in the Saltmarket. Since then, it had evolved into a major annual summer event for Glaswegians, and the traditional period when the majority of them took their holidays. There was always a major exodus from the city at this time, mostly to the Scottish resorts located in the estuary of the Clyde, and usually referred to as: "Gon' doon the waater". You boarded one of the many paddle steamers available at that time, and in the space of an hour, you could be at Rothesay, or Dunoon. Going a bit further, and for a bit longer, you could visit many towns on the Argyle shoreline; or on to Broddick in Arran or, creme de la creme, overnight to Ireland.

Broomielaw, Glasgow (Off Down the Water)

In the case of large families, such as ours, the preferred accommodation was a large bell tent. Or, if you could afford it, the luxury of a chalet - a wooden hut with bunk beds. Cooking on an open fire was the order of the day. It produced burnt sausages and chops of a flavour nowhere to be found in the city.

With vistas over the estuary, comparable to none, and a setting sun over the Irish Sea, all for free, this was an idyllic luxury for a tenement dweller. I grew to know every inch of the Clyde absorbed from many trips, and a few of the pleasures of Ireland provided by ancestral family. Looking even further back, one of my favourite memories was when, in the company of dad and George Daily, I witnessed the launch of the Queen Elizabeth in 1938. I was ten years old and the impact was massive.

Now 24 years old, family holidays were no longer mandatory. We now had the choice of doing our own thing. Mum and dad, and anyone else who wanted to join them, continued to have their break. At such times, control of the shop would be handed over to whoever dad and mum considered trustworthy. Mostly it would be Agnes, or, by default, Geordie. In the event of it being Geordie, dad always took the view that if he broke even, he was happy.

Around this time one of their holiday trips took them to Tynemouth, where they met up with Jenny and Polly, and their respective husbands, Jack and Billy, who were on holiday from Newcastle. Such was their pleasure from this holiday thereafter they continued to meet up with them at regular intervals. They went on to form a very close friendship that was to bring much pleasure to both families. Accommodating their visits would have been difficult for mum, but for the offer of Betty, begrudgingly agreed to by Harry, to share their house in Sorn Street.

On one such visit, Jenny brought her daughter, Edna. It was all a great surprise to me, as I knew nothing of Jenny's family at this point. She was a slim, attractive girl, around the same height as myself. She smiled easily, and was even more attractive when she did. We took to each other immediately, no doubt aided by behind-the-scenes prompting by our parents. They were there for the week and in the course of this I took her up town to the pictures. On another occasion I showed her around Sauchiehall Street, Buchanan Street, and a few other areas of Glasgow which I thought would interest her. In no time at all, it seemed, the week had gone and I was shaking hands as they prepared to leave. Why don't you come to Newcastle and visit us said Jenny. Your mum's coming down in a couple of months. I'm sure Edna would like to see you again. Is that not so, Edna, she prompted. Yes, I would like that, she said with a smile. I diffidently agreed to try. She left me feeling that she meant it, which was quite pleasing . The end of the year was now encroaching. A year that had started on a deep low was now, thanks to Edna, looking to end on a high.

****

We were now in November, and heading fast towards the end of the year and the 'Old Firm' match on New Year's day which, with Celtic playing at home, was going to be huge. Our anticipation of the match was heightened by a preceding event that was even more important to us and due to happen on the last Saturday in November - the Celtic and Rangers reserve game. It was an event that could crown our own footballing exploits. Our street team, called the Kinnear boys, had replaced the street football of previous years and was very successful around Bridgeton.

Street teams were common in Glasgow, with most games being played on a Sunday. It was well supported by the council who provided some 50 pitches on Glasgow Green. At the height of the summer these pitches would average 4 games apiece on a Sunday, and would also be heavily used midweek in the evenings. At that time the quality of our team had been expanded with the inclusion of guys from other streets. So much so, that I was lucky to get a game on the right wing. The core of the team was still our own guys with James, Frank, Archie, Davie, and the Cloherty brothers, much to the fore. But our undisputed star was Mungo Cloherty, who played right half. He had been approached a few times by scouts patrolling the Glasgow green, and had been offered the chance to join one of the leading 'junior' teams. On instructions from his father these offers were always rejected. His father, who had contacts in the ground staff at Celtic Park, was intent on getting him an interview with the reserve team trainer. He eventually succeeded with the outcome that he was offered a trial in the reserve team.

In those days, even a reserve match would draw a good crowd at Celtic Park. For this reason we got ourselves up there early in order to secure a good viewing spot. At reserve games we always stood in the main enclosure instead of our usual position on the terrace. It got us closer to the players and besides that, there was only one price at reserve games. As kick off approached we eagerly listened for the team announcements. First surprise was that Mungo was playing right back instead of his usual position at wing half. The other one was, that against him was Torry Gillick on the left wing. Torry was one of the all time Rangers greats. But, he was coming to the end of his career, and the last time we had seen him play he had lost most of his pace.

The game started well with one or two good tackles by Mungo, on Torry. Thereafter, though, things started to go seriously wrong for him. Although Torry hadn't the speed any more, he had not lost any of his old skills. He started to play little one twos with the inside left, that would leave Mungo stranded. As the game went on his lack of experience at this level began to show up badly, and Torry was now going past him with hardly a tackle. Frustration finally got the better of Mungo, and his tackling became a bit wild. His confidence had now gone, and I am sure he was glad when the half time whistle went. Torry ran over to him as they left the field, and shook his hand. Mungo did not reappear when they ran out for the second half.

The great era of Bobby Evans, John McPhail, Bobby Collins, Bertie Peacock, Charly Tully, Neil Mochan and others, was now replacing that of the dire post war 40s. Ah! If only Mungo could have joined them: another hope, another dream, was gone. We all of us felt it.

Celtic's line-up against Falkirk in a League Cup tie won by 5-1 at Celtic Park in August 1955. Back row, from left to right: Haughney, Fallon, Bonnar, Evans, Stein, Peacock. Front row: Collins, Fernie, Walsh, Tully, Mochan.

My Favourite Team

Chapter VII

A New Beginning

In Search Of Something

<u>Happy New Year</u>

The Move to Possil'

Earning a Living

The Newcastle Years

A New Beginning - Happy New Year

Hogmanay was close at hand, and for some reason, best known to mum and dad, plans were well laid to make this one a beezer. As part of this plan, it was also decided that tradition would be resumed, and that despite the absence of Granny and Granda , our "First foot" would be at their house in Sorn Street, regardless of its new ownership. Music, song, and dance were to be present in abundance. Jimmy Miller was to head up the music with his accordion and Thistle, our cousin, whom mum regarded as a daughter since her mother died, was to be the sing-along songstress, at which she excelled. Needless to say, mum would be the Master of Ceremonies and take care of the dancing. As for dad, his expectation would be to knowingly grin with content at the proceedings and, if questioned on the depth of his enjoyment, to reassure with the utmost sincerity: 'If she's happy, then am happy'.

The booze, provided at reduced cost by George Daily, our friendly publican, was already being stored in advance of need; an action that was not pleasing to Agnes, who was asked to keep it in a 'safe place' in her house across the landing. With her well-known, deep-rooted aversion to all things alcoholic, this did not go down well. Such was this aversion, that it was not unknown for her, in the morning following a party, to empty all bottles containing alcohol down the sink and, thereafter, to 'swear blind' that every last drop had been drunk. Come Hogmanay, however, such attitudes would be swept aside by the fervour generated by the memory of pleasures past, so infectious to the uninitiated, and the catalyst for what was to follow.

Such was the build up that year that my curiosity was stirred to ask how Hogmanay started. It was many years later, though, that a bit of idle research in the library revealed that its origins went back to pagan times, when sun and fire worship was practiced in mid-winter. This is said to have evolved into the Saturnalia, an ancient Roman winter festival of Saturn, which was held in the month of December - a period when people indulged in unrestrained merrymaking. It is also held to be the predecessor of Christmas. The Vikings celebrated Yule, which became the twelve days of Christmas, or the "Daft Days" as they came to be known in Scotland. It went underground during the reformation, but re-emerged at the beginning of the 18th Century and has continued to evolve to the present day.

While Hogmanay, the last day of the year, is said to begin the celebrations, "First Footing", the first person to enter your house after the stroke of midnight, is the act of ensuring that you are first in line for a party, failing that, the second - who cares?. Traditionally, though, it has been held that your new year will be a prosperous one if a "tall, dark stranger" appears at your door with a lump of coal for the fire, or a cake or coin. In exchange, you offered him food, wine, or a wee dram of whisky. The tradition that he should be dark is from the ancient fear of the blond Viking stranger knocking on your door. What was more likely to happen these days is that groups of friends or family would get together and do a tour of each other's houses. Each year, a household would take it in turn to provide a meal for the group. It was along these lines that our dinner table was laid in waiting.

With Bill now 'demobbed', Bert home on leave, and the presence of Thistle, our 'new sister', it was the first time in many years, that the whole family would sit down to supper. The table was set out with traditional Hogmanay fare. The meal would begin with soup, usually Scotch Broth. This would be followed by an option of sliced boiled ham, or the more traditional, and more popular, Steak Pie, cooked and served from an 'enameled ashet'. To round it off, there was a biggish clootie dumpling with its lustrous outer coating showing it to be well fired. For the more picky, there would be fruit bun stuffed with currants, raisins, and glazed cherries. Beside each place setting would be your dram glass. All was now ready, and the expectation was that everyone would sit down around 9 o'clock and woe betide anyone who was late without good reason. Around this time a knock on the door announced the arrival of Uncle Geordie and Auntie Rachael. With all of us now being present dad took his seat at the head of table with mum to his right, the rest of us took our place at random.

As the meal progressed there were the usual compliments for the food, especially for the steak pie, which was deemed to be excellent by everyone. This would lead to a drawn out discussion between mum, Rachael, and Agnes, on the merits of Gormans, the butcher who supplied it. In the course of this, dad served up a glass of whisky to mum, Mick, Geordie, and Rachael, and bade them good health. Bill and Bert poured themselves a beer, and offered me a Mackesons' stout. Agnes, May, Michael, and Thistle, set about the dumpling supported by glasses of iron brew. Things moved along quite chattily with Bill and Bert letting it be known that they were going to do their own 'First Footing', and would join us later round at Harry and Betty's. We knew Bill to be going out with a girl and no doubt had to see her first, whilst Bert was going to drop in on a mate.

Around 11 o'clock Jimmy Miller arrived carrying his accordion, but looking a bit doleful. He explained that his wife was not keeping well and while it was nothing serious he was not going to leave her by herself at the 'Bells'. Whilst showing concern for Jimmy's wife, mum was clearly disappointed at losing her musician. As ever sensitive, Jimmy went to great length to reassure her that this would not be a problem. He pointed out that one or two of the people expected at the party were just as good as he was on the accordion, and that was why he had brought it with him.
"You take it with yae, Aggie, he said, "there'll be people there who will be only too pleased to play it."
That's true, agreed mum, but ah wis so looking forward to you leading us roon to Sorn Street with a bit of auld-lang-syne music.
"That's no' a problem", he said, raising his finger and pointing at me. "John is mer than capable of playing you roon to Sorn Street."
I responded with shocked disbelief at what he was saying. To which he addressed me with a raised finger.
"Yae know yae cin dae it. Now yaer no gonnae let yer mammie and me doon. Ur' yae?" He asked with a grin on his face.
I grinned back and nodded. Ok, I'll do it.
He then shook hands with dad, gave mum a hug, and wished us all a Happy New Year, and left.

The Bells were now imminent, and with the exception of Agnes, May, and Thistle, dad poured us all a wee dram of whisky in preparation for the toast. The radio was switched on to have Big

A New Beginning - Happy New Year

Ben's confirmation. Conversations started to peter out and silence ensued. We all of us stood there, fully attentive and glasses raised, as the first peals of the New Year rang out. "Happy New Year" we all cried in unison, and drunk from our glass. As the remaining strikes peeled out their notes we moved among each other and embraced. An odd tear was shed here and there but not without an accompanying smile. Following on from this a curious restraint enveloped us. It was as if we were asking the question: "where do we go from here?" The question was soon answered by a loud knock on the door. Our 'First Foot' had arrived, and it was Sconey and Peggy from the close. With gleeful hugs; the presenting of gifts; and the offer of drams from respective bottles, our neighbours descended on us. New Year's day had arrived, and the party was underway. What no one knew nor cared, was when it would end.

It was going on 1 o'clock before we all assembled at the closehead. Every tenement window, it seemed, was ablaze with light and boisterous neighbours. When I appeared with the accordion strapped on there were further boisterous calls for me to play their favourite song. The embarrassment that I felt as I walked down the stairs was now replaced by outright fear that I would freeze. After all, I could only play "by ear"; and the songs that I had learned were very few and far between. But the one most appropriate to the moment was one that I did know: "Auld Lang Syne". My hope, at that moment, was that if I got started then people would join in, and my limitations would go unnoticed. And so it proved, for I had barely got started when people picked up on me and, led by mum and Thistle, launched into song. My confidence grew in response, especially as Thistle, who was familiar with my limited repertoire, would prompt me for the next song.

We made our way along Baltic Street and in to Kinnear Road, where not so many windows were raised, nor hands waved. Harry and Betty greeted us as we approached. Harry was gushing with pride, and expressed surprise and flattery at my playing . We entered to find that a few of the neighbours were present. Not only that, one of them was quick to let it be known that he also played the accordion and that he would be more than happy to relieve me if I wanted a break. Without pausing to exchange comments on our relative skills, I handed it over to him, much to his surprise and delight, and his assurance that he would look after it.

Much as I had got a buzz out of playing the pied piper, I was glad to be shot of it. Had I continued, it would only have been a matter of time before I embarrassed myself. It was with much relief, that I made my way outside for a break and lit a cigarette. It was a clear night and not so cold for that time of year. There was still the odd group of people, bag in hand, heading for a party.

There was one old fella coming down Kinnear Road, from the direction of Baltic Street on the shop side. He crossed over towards Sorn Street and was approaching our corner when he seemed to trip on the pavement and fell. As he did so there was a dull thud as if he had hit something. I hurried down the path towards him, to see if he was injured. As I did so I could see Bert crossing the road towards us. He was carrying the same paper bag as when he left the house to go First Footing.
The old fella was sobbing when we got to him.
"Whit's the matter ol' son? Hiv' yae injured yursel'?" asked Bert.
"Naw, ah hiv'nae injured masel' ", the old fella replied.
"C'mon then, whit ur' yae cryin' fur, then?", Bert asked.
"Ah wis gonnae furst fit ma son an' 'is wife", he replied.
"Where dae they live? Jist tell us, an' we'll get yae there?'
"Yae don't un'erstaun'", he replied with a sob. "Ah cannae go there noo...Ah've broken ma furst foot boattle."
"C'mon, aul' son... Don't be daft...Let's get yae on yer feet", said Bert.
With both our help the old fella got to his feet.
"Now, where dae yae live?"
"Jist up the road, there, in Patna Street"
"Are yae sure yur able to walk, noo?"
"Yeh, sure. Ah'm jist a daft aul' fool.. Ah'm ok, noo."
"Gee's yer arm", said Bert, and before the old fella could protest, he slipped the handle of his own bag over it.

A New Beginning - Happy New Year

"Now look...Yae never broke yur boattle... Yae only thought yae did...Now, off yae get an' furst foot that son o' yours... An' a Happy New Year tae yae."

The old fella stood there for a moment as if unable to understand what was happening to him.

"Whit's yer name?" he asked.

"Ma name's Bert."

"God bless yae, Bert... An' a Happy New Year tae yae."

Our eyes followed him for a while to ensure that he was steady on his feet. He turned and looked back at us.

We waved to him.

He waved back and went on his way happily singing to himself.

Ah b'lang tae Glasgow,
Dear ol' Glasgow toon.

There's sumthin' the matter wae Glasgow,
Fur it's goin' roon an' roon.

Ah'm only a common ol' workin' chap,
As any wan here can see.

But when ah get a couple o' drinks on a Saturday.
Glasgow b'langs tae me.

Chapter VII

A New Beginning

In Search Of Something

Happy New Year

<u>The Move to Possil'</u>

Earning a Living

The Newcastle Years

A New Beginning - The Move to Possil'

My visits to the library were stimulating and provided some welcome pleasure in the winter-laden months. With less and less midweek socialising being readily available, boredom was being barely kept at bay by my reading. My general knowledge was noticeably expanding, but to no purpose. Throughout the winter months I became preoccupied with the thought that I had to change my lifestyle. My social past was now greatly diluted and had to be replaced. This was no reflection on my friends who were much better adapted to the Bridgeton lifestyle than I could ever be and hence it was accepted that I could not compete. No one could be faulted for this; and certainly not my parents who could not do enough for me.

Under the stimulus of my winter reading I had further insight on my problem. It later led me to the conclusion that it was simply the fault of circumstance; a circumstance that had seen me damaged and nurtured, when young, by two opposing cultures. The clinical culture and values of Mearnskirk were still the cornerstone of my being, and were at variance with the Bridgeton values that nurtured me. It had to be at the root of my confusion and self-doubt. Along with this thought came a certain clarity, and the possibility of a way forward. Yes, I needed a new lifestyle, but it could never be based on one aspect to the exclusion of the other. It had to include both, as they were inseparable parts of the same problem. Once this was recognised my confusion started to dissipate. I could now clearly see a way forward, But I was no closer to the means of making it happen.

A solution was presented to me on one of my visits to the library. Prompted by habit, I was browsing through the notice board when I spotted a leaflet on winter courses on offer from Skerry's College. What caught my attention was its layout, which categorised its courses under the title of academic, commercial, and craft. I got a copy from the librarian and read it through in more detail. It was the academic items that posed the thought. Primarily, they were inviting school leavers to continue their studies with a view to taking the university entrance examination. But, more importantly for me, they were also inviting enquiries from people with aspirations to enter university, whose schooling had lapsed since leaving school at fourteen. After a brief flush of excitement my old self-doubt reappeared. Did I have the talent, or was it simply wishful thinking?

That evening I discussed the matter with mum and dad; including my self-doubt. They dismissed the latter without hesitation. There was no way their son lacked ability. Despite the predictability of both the question and answer I needed the meagre reassurance it gave. They also dismissed any discussion on the cost. Their only stipulation was that I must continue to support dad in the shop, as there was news afoot that Agnes would be moving to a new house in Castlemilk.

The following day, in the company of mum, I walked through the ornate sandstone entrance to Skerry's college for the first time. We were directed to an office that was said to handle all enquiries and enrollments, and were dealt with immediately by a very friendly woman. Mum explained my commitments to the shop and the need for the classes to be in the afternoon or evenings. This was not a problem she was told as classes were scheduled from early morning to evening. An assessment would be made of my current academic status and that a curriculum would then be prepared on the basis of what I intended to study. It was all very friendly. Fees were discussed and concluded with mum agreeing to the sum which she promised would be paid by me the following day. So began my attempt to reach the level that would allow me to take the university preliminary examination.

****

In the early 50's the word going round the tenements was that Glasgow was in for a big shake-up. Rumours abounded that Bridgeton was going to be demolished and replaced with new housing. Closer to the truth was that new housing was indeed being built but in the green belt surrounding the city. These were the forerunners of the 'housing schemes', the generic name used by the councils to describe these new housing projects. Elegantly touted as the council's answer to the squalour of the tenements, they had an in-house lavatory and bathing facilities allied to greatly improved kitchen equipment. They were built en masse around the city and grew to be just as big a blight as the tenements they replaced.

In their haste to be seen as worthy city fathers, determined to rid the city of its worst tenements, they deemed it essential that every inch of the green belt, that had been prized from its former control, was to be used for housing and nothing else. And this they achieved. Such was their foresight and economy in these 'schemes', that not one inch of space was originally provided for shops and social amenities. These were forcibly added later, well after the social deprivation they caused was well established. The wide streets that were at the heart the tenement social amenities were gone. In their place were narrow streets that were barely wide enough, in some instances, to park an ice cream van. There were streets that became inaccessible whenever a shopping van parked and opened for business. In this planning there also had to be an assumption that people who lived in these pretty new houses could not afford to buy a car. As of this assumption, parking on pavements became a necessity, with petty vandalism a consequential protest.

It was the exciting offer of one of these houses in Castkemilk that made Agnes and her first child leave the family comfort zone of Baltic Street. For Agnes, like others, it was not even a choice. The prospects of having your own indoor toilet and bathing facilities was irresistible and could not be refused. Besides, it was no longer a rumour that the older tenements in Baltic street, Nuneaton street, and Mordaunt street, were scheduled for future demolition. Slowly but surely, the depletion of this area of Glasgow became noticeable. It was now only a matter of time before we were made an offer to vacate. Sure enough it eventually arrived. With respect to the corporation housing department we were given a multiple choice. We could either move to one of the new housing 'schemes', or we could move to one of the older type houses, such as the grey stone buildings that dominated Kinnear Road, but in another area to the

A New Beginning - The Move to Possil'

north of the city called Possilpark. For whatever reasons, that I was not privy to, it was decided that we would move to Possilpark. It did surprise me as it was quite a distance from the shop and would entail a long tram ride with a change at the corner of Hope Street and the Central Station. For my part, it was much closer to Skerry's College. We moved to Allander Street, Possilpark in 1953. Our house was identical in every respect to that of James and Frank's in Kinnear Road. Also like them we were located on the second floor; but very much unlike them we had a wonderful view of the Campsie Hills. On its other side was Loch Lomond; a scene of beauty and a source of future pleasures. Another personal advantage to me was that Possil' had its own library and was located at the bottom of our street. The following two years were very pleasant, which was mostly down to how well every one had settled in to their new environment. We now had three bedrooms, a living room, kitchen, and bathroom, yet it could still feel a bit crushed at times. Nevertheless, a vast improvement on our Baltic Street tenement. Further ease was also on the horizon, as Bill was now engaged to Nancy, and Bert was going steady with 'big' Agnes from nearby Bardowie Street.

In this period the shop continued as normal. Naturally, dad had to leave that bit earlier in the morning, but, as he said himself, he was an early riser and it did not trouble him too much. There was the odd occasion when he felt under the weather and did not feel up to it, in which case I would have to be unhurriedly up at dawn to do the needful. Socially, I still met up with the guys, but mostly it would be on a Saturday, when Celtic was playing at home. James, and the Cloherty brothers were now married. Frank, was engaged, and Charlie was going steady. Archie was now in cahoots with Davie Smith for reasons that no one seemed to be interested in. Our former closeness was now slipping away. Much as we would always remember our youthful years, our youthful dependency on each other was gone. Our future friendship would now depend on how often our chosen paths would cross.

A New Beginning - The Move to Possil'

As for dad, he still depended on his closeness with the people from Kinnear Road, who were his friends. It was their custom, he always said, that had launched and maintained his presence in Kinnear Road for all these years. It was this presence, his shop, that he had raised his family on, and he was proud of it. However, there were now early signs of his failing health. He was now finding it difficult to recover from ailments that formerly he would have quickly shaken off. He had always been plagued by sinus headaches like Mrs. Hargeave. Unlike her, however, the one Askit powder would usually suffice to deal with it. This was no longer the case. He was also becoming more prone to attacks of bronchitis due to his past smoking habit. And there were other troublesome ailments that he would not discuss. As a consequence, I would frequently find it necessary to miss classes in order to man the shop. This was not a problem, though, as I was now sufficiently confident that I had the leeway to catch up.

My presence in the shop, whilst fairly flexible, was usually from early morning to early afternoon. This would allow dad the freedom, as he choose, to visit the wholesalers, such as the fruit and vegetable market, or drop in for a chat with his friends, George and Walter. This would leave me in charge for most of the morning. Uncle Harry's partner, Betty was now a regular customer and would often brighten the morning tedium. I liked her a lot. She was a big bouncy woman who reminded me of granny, and like all big women it seemed, she always had a ready smile on her face. Given the sourness and simmering cauldron that was Harry, it was a strange match. And from the undercurrents of conversation picked up from mum and dad, and supported by the occasional marks on her face and arms, it was not a happy one. She could also be a blatant tease and would often ask me how my friendship with Edna was getting on. Secretly flattered by this, I would always tell her that it was none of her business, at the same time wishing it was true. Another gratifying outcome of Betty's relationship was that mum was no longer at the beck and call of Harry's housework needs.

A New Beginning - The Move to Possil'

Back home in Possil' there was a great easing of the accommodation problem by the announcement that Bill and Nancy were to get married and that they had been offered accommodation in the new town of East Kilbride. Not long after this, as if not to be outdone, Bert also announced his intention to marry 'big' Agnes, as she was affectionately known. Also, for reasons I could not understand, they opted to live in a tenement ground floor, 'room and kitchen', in Walkinshaw Street, back in Bridgeton. It was not far from the shop, which meant that, working out of the shop as I did, I got to see them even more often than I did in Possil'. This also included the football on Saturday, as Agnes, no doubt with some persuasion from Bert, had become a Celtic supporter.

The greatest pleasure from all of this was that our living requirements had been decimated. Michael, who was now 12 years old and in his penultimate year at school, had taken to Possil' as if he had always lived there. He had made many new friends at school and had aquired a reputation for his cheeky personality. Always up to some mischief yet always readily forgiven.

We now shared the big bedroom, while May, for the first time, had the luxury of her own, which she occasionally shared with Thistle. And there was even more space on the horizon, as May, who had 'clicked' at the dancing, was now going very steady indeed with a guy called John Bryce. What all of this really meant was that mum and dad could freely invite their friends from Newcastle to visit. Thus began a period of immense pleasure for mum and dad, which was to fill their later years.

****

Dad's health was now the cause for much concern. His sinus headaches were now more frequent, as was his proneness to bronchial infections. The diagnosis of the doctor was that his long hours of work over the years were catching up with him and that he had to slow up. He was also a worrier; which did not help. His advice was that he and mum should go off on a long holiday and forget about the damned shop. After the doctor left it was decided there and then, with out any further discussion, that they would both go on an extended holiday with their friends, Jenny and Polly, in Newcastle. As for the shop, I would deal with it. If I became stretched I would call in Agnes from Castlemilk to help. And so it was agreed. They left that weekend, and were not to return for some four weeks. While they were away I became preoccupied with the need to find a solution to the problem of dad's failing health. My first inclination was to have them sell the shop, as it no longer had any place in my future intentions. But this would, I thought, be a painful break for them after all those years of total immersion in the problems and culture of the tenements. They had settled in so well in Possil', it was also possible that I was overestimating the pain they would undoubted feel over the loss. I later discussed the matter with Bill, Bert, and Agnes; especially Agnes, who had invested herself so much in the early success of the shop. Without any hesitation they agreed that it was the only solution.

Mum and dad returned in high spirits and looking as brown as berries. The weather had been good to them, and they had thoroughly enjoyed the company of Jenny and Polly. They were especially enthralled by Joe, Jenny's son, and Phaimie, his wife, who had put them up in their 'Prefab House'. These were prefabricated, standalone houses that had been built as temporary accommodation for people waiting to be re-housed. But in Newcastle they had become so much loved by their tenants that they refused to move. They had clearly expanded their circle of friends and at every opportunity, would talk of nothing else. Bill, Bert, and Agnes, dropped in on the Sunday by way of welcoming them home.

After dinner, with everyone still at the table, I nodded to Agnes, who had agreed to take the lead on what we had agreed. She started by telling them how concerned we all were for dad's health and that maybe it was time for dad to give up working in the shop. But she got herself a bit lost for words at this point and looked to Bill and Bert for support. This immediately told mum that whatever was about to be said, we were all in on it. She now knew that we had something important on our minds and impatiently told us to get on with it. With Agnes now looking a bit selfconscious, Bill and Bert took over and with hurried words they made it clear that we all wanted dad to quit the shop.

"Whit aboot you, John, ah don't hear you saying anything?", asked mum. "Ah wid hiv thought that you wid waant tae keep the shop. It's goat many memories for yae an' wid give yae a good livin'." In years past I would have readily agreed with you mum. But not now. I want to do other things.

"Ok, then", said mum, "ah wull tell yae whit we think. We've thought long and hard aboot this while we wur away and we hiv come to the same conclusion as yursel's. There is no way that am gonnae stand by an' let that shop kill yur dad. He's hid mer than his fair share of its problems over the years. And it was our decision that if John didnae waant to cerry it oan as his aen business, then we wur gonnae sell it. So yur dad and I ur gonnae ask yae John fur the last time - dae yae waant to cerry oan running the shop as a business?"

I felt guilty that they had harboured these expectations of me and struggled for words that would ease my answer. I need not have worried though as they were delighted at my choice. It took some three months before the shop was sold and in that period I ran it by myself with only the minimum of helpful intrusion from dad.

Much as he was adjusting well to the loss of the shop, he had one final task to carry out and that was going to be painfully embarrassing. Heavily prompted by mum as a right, the 'tick book' had to be collected. Deep down they both knew that, as tick was a way of life in the tenements, there was little hope that his customers would have the means to clear their debt and still find the money to see them through the week. The system only worked on the basis that credit was only given on the back of current debt being paid. So to pay off the tick owed to dad they would first have to find a new source of credit which, to say the least, was very unlikely. Dad's only hope of recovering the debt would be to collect it in small installments; the method strongly advocated by mum. But the stress and embarrassment of doing this would have been very painful.

In the end it was decided that they would bite the bullet, and that as and when the shop was sold, so the debts, with a few exceptions, would be written off and the tick book would be burnt. Mum was none too pleased with this; but, by the same token, she would not have dad suffer the indignity of having to collect a pittance each week from his former customers, some of whom had been close friends. It was the end of an era.

****

Meeting up with Frank, and some of the others at home games would still continue for a while, but more by accident than intent this also would lapse. We were now fully ensconced in Possil'; and all day to day ties with Bridgeton had now been cut. Or, so we thought. It was not long after we sold the shop that we heard that Betty had split up with Harry, and that he was not best pleased at having to look after himself - after all, 'housework does not get done by itself'. It was not long before he put in an appearance. With a small gift for mum, he was kindness personified. Betty had left him in the lurch. He declaimed her as a lazy bitch, and he could not figure out why he had tolerated her for so long. She would never cross his doorstep again. Please... could mum find some time to call down and help get his house back in order.

Dad was quietly furious and I was not far behind him. He knew that she was going to get drawn into his clutches. It was clearly his scheming intent to not simply have her do him a favour, but to have her do it on a regular basis. If conceded it would soon be asserted as a brotherly right. And so it proved to be, with mum making a weekly trip to Sorn Street to do his housework.

I came home one day to find May on her own in the kitchen making tea. She said she was making it for mum and dad and readily offered me one. Never one to refuse a cup of tea I gratefully accepted. As

mum and dad were nowhere to be seen I was about to inquire of
their absence when they both appeared from the bedroom with mum
poking a piece of cotton wool in her ear.

What's the matter? I asked with reference to her ear.

Nothing for you to worry about; just a wee accident; it will heal in a
couple of days.

When I tried pressing it further dad told me to forget it; that she had
accidentally knocked it against one of the kitchen cabinets. It was
the manner of the answer, I think; but I just got the feeling there was
more to it. Biding my time I again caught May on her own in the
kitchen and asked her how mum came to injure her ear. May could
never lie; and after one attempt at doing so she told me the truth.
Harry had called round while dad and I were out and wanted mum
down that day to help clear up some mess he had in the house. Mum
said that she would do it tomorrow as she was tied up that day. May
said that he started swearing at her and called her a lazy selfish.
Bitch.....I screamed at him to stop shouting and to leave her alone.
Unable to have his will, Harry had given her a violent push. She
staggered backwards against the wall close to the doorway and
banged her ear on the protruding light switch. The switch toggle
gouged and cut the inside of her ear and when he saw the blood, he
said it was her own bloody fault, and beat it out the door.

Dad and I were so angry at this incident that I vowed there and then
that this frightening dominance by Harry over my parents had to
end. The following day I took time out and went down to Gledhills
in Mordaunt Street, where Bert worked. As luck would have it I
caught him on the verge of leaving on a delivery run. I filled him in
on Harry's assault, which riled him up. He agreed with me that he
had to be stopped once and for all. He proposed that he would get in
touch with Bill, and that the three of us meet up and go and confront
Harry. I was disappointed with this as it meant dragging it out with
the risk of it, yet again, being passed over. My hope was that Bert
and I would go and confront him that day, and tell him straight out
where he stood with us. But Bert insisted that the three of us must
confront him. Predictably our heated intentions petered out. Bill was
busy at work and could not see us until Saturday, when we met up

for the football. Come Saturday, as expected, the heat had gone out of it and all we did was make empty threats for the future.

Still angry and frustrated I had to bide my time. The opportunity arose soon after, on the back of a visit from Geordie. He had been asked by Harry to call on mum and let her know that he was down with the flu. Could she come down and do a bit of housework for him. He also needed some shopping to be done. Without any hesitation, and strongly backed by myself, dad told Geordie there was no way mum was going anywhere near the man. In any case, he added, why can't your wife Rachael help him out...

She was working all day, replied Geordie, and was not up to it when she gets home. Besides she is no good around sick people...

And does that apply to you when you get sick, retorted dad. It strikes me that you both want your pound of flesh...

Geordie's reaction to this was that he was only delivering the message, and that he was not asking mum to do anything. That it was down to her, what she wanted to do, or not do....

"That's kind of yae, Geordie", retorted dad sarcastically.

At this point mum intervened by way of calming dad down.

"Look, leave it wi' me, Geordie, an' ah'll give it some thought."

"An' whit do ah tell Harry?"

"Ah've already told yae whit tae tell him", shouted dad...

At this point I intervened and told Geordie that enough was enough, and that there was not going to be any further discussion on it.

"You tell him what you like; and we'll do what we like. Is that clear enough for you?"

Geordie, who had intended staying on for his tea, decided that it would be better for him to leave. There ensued some concerned bickering between the three of us by which time mum and dad knew that I was fully aware of the cause of mum's injury to her ear. In the end dad gave in to mum's plea that she could not turn her back on her brother if he was genuinely ill. My rider to this was that if she did go down, then I was going with her. This was only agreed to by dad when I insisted that he was not fit enough to be exposed to someone with the flu.

A New Beginning - The Move to Possil'

As mum opened the door Harry could be heard calling from the living room - "Is that you, Aggie?".

Mum confirmed our presence as we entered. He was sitting up in bed which, to our surprise, had been moved into the living room. On reflection, he was obviously living out of one room to minimise his cleaning chores. Mum exuded her usual concern as she quizzed him on his health...How long had he been down?...Three bloody days...Was he sure that it was the flu?...Of course he was bloody sure...Had he called in the doctor?...He had no bloody time for doctors...What was he taking for it...Askit powders; what else could he bloody take for it?...Have you been eating enough food?...How can I be eating enough food, when I can't even get out of my bloody bed. Besides, with nobody to go for the messages, there's little bloody food in the house...Well look, I'll try and rustle up some kind of food in the kitchen, and while your eating it I'll get on with tidying the place up. Ok.. Whatever you say, Aggie...

I was beside myself with anger as mum left the room. Ever ready to pick up on threats, even when none was intended, he became aware of my simmering anger and turned his attention to me.

"So whit brings yae doon here? Lookin' after yur mammy, ur yae?"
"Something like that, I curtly replied..."
"Nae doubt, that yae think that she should nae be here...."
"I do as it happens..."
"Ah'm ill, fur Christ's sake! Whit else wid yae expect mi tae dae?"
He was now talking down to me in a sneering tone that really got to me. I was now emotionally riled, and not in control of my feelings when I blurted back at him. "You could start by not feeling sorry for yourself. And if you are ill call the doctor in." I was now trembling and could not say another word.

He was absolutely shocked by my affront...His eyes grew in size as fury enveloped him....
"Ya' cheeky little bastard...Ahm gonnae teach yae a lesson yae'll never forget..."
He ripped back the bed clothes and swung his legs out of bed......I stood there shaking waiting for the onslaught....His anger stalled as

his flu symptoms came over him. He just sat there trembling and breathing heavily....My own anger subsided as I stood there staring at him. Suddenly I was hit by a waft of insight...His anger was no longer aimed at me.... He was frustrated by his own helplessness...I was still in fear of him, but I was no longer prepared to react to it. I knew that, another day, another time, and he would have thrashed me into a state of pain and tears.... But the man who sat there was himself afraid.... It was as if his future stood there before him...

"Get back into bed, Uncle Harry!," I asked him with compassion. He lifted his legs back on to the bed and was in the course of restoring the bedclothes when, without warning, he again ripped the clothes back with renewed anger, swung his legs out and faced me.

"Yae've not heard the last of this...Yae hid nae right tae talk to me that way."

His tone was now more conciliatory...His anger was clearly drained...The frailty that can beset us all was plain to see...He looked afraid; but not of me...

It was as if he had been to the edge and lost the will to fight. I felt guilty, and fearful, that he might lose his dignity, and break down. Much of this, of course, was down to his medical condition, and I knew that he could well come looking for me after he recovered his strength. But I thought not. The sadness in his eyes spoke of something else; and I could identify with it. He was now becalmed, and there was the sound of a recovering dignity when next he spoke.

"Don't tell yur maw..."

"I promise.... Now get yourself back into bed."

Mum, who had been busy in the kitchen, behind a closed door, had not heard a thing. She now reappeared with a plate of scrambled eggs and toast in one hand, and a mug of tea in the other.

"Sit up an' get that doon yae", she said cheerfully. She then turned to me...

"Ah've made oot a wee list of messages, John. Nip over tae the shop an' get them."

Harry told her to take some money from his trouser pocket, which she dismissed with the cheery retort, that he could square her up later. That he did. For the remainder of his life he was more respectful to mum, and in doing so he reaped the benefits of her ever-willing nature..

****

The year ended with Bill emigrating to New Zealand, and May marrying John Bryce. The house was now spacious and more accommodating for the visits of Jenny and Polly. The stairs, though was becoming a bit of burden for dad's chest. This also applied to Jenny, and Polly, who were fairly substantial in size. On medical grounds, an application was made to the council housing department for a move to a ground floor house. This was granted and we moved to a similar house a few streets away on the corner of Hobart Street. Fortunately the bedroom window still retained a view over the Campsies, which I had grown very fond of.

-

Chapter VII

A New Beginning

A New Beginning - Earning a Living

The hopes and dreams that had been based on the outcome of my efforts at Skerry's College had now been set aside. The preliminary examination that would have determined my preparedness to go on and take the university entrance examination was no longer possible. In the course of running the shop in the months prior to its sale, I had fallen seriously behind in my class work. This in itself was not the be all and end all, as I could have had the examination rescheduled and then continued where I left off. The real problem was the fees which, without the income from the shop, could no longer be supported. The money my parents got from the sale of the shop was far from being a self-supporting income. In truth there was barely enough to secure them against a rainy day. True to their nature they even tried to share it with me.

Employment was the only way forward; I had to find a job. As a necessary step on this path I had to register myself as unemployed by signing on at the 'broo' (the Employment Bureau). This was a weekly requirement and also a prerequisite to obtaining unemployment benefit (dole money). Regarded as your minimal income it was based on your past employment and the benefit stamps that accrued. In my case it was minimal owing to my having worked in the shop, which was deemed to be self-employed and hence wholly dependent on the stamps that dad may or may not have accrued on my behalf. The other requirement of you retaining your benefit was that you had to present yourself to the employment clerk at least once a week.

As luck would have it, on my second weekly visit to the 'Broo' to 'sign on', the employment clerk claimed that he had the right job for me. They sent me for an interview at the Singer Sewing Machine factory in Clydebank for the post of progress chaser. The Singer factory, I was told, was a vast size. In its prime it was said to be the largest factory in the world. It had been seriously damaged in the Blitz, but was now long since back to full production status; so I was advised of by the employment clerk who briefed me for the interview. In response to my protest, that I knew nothing about progress chasing, he frankly admitted that neither did he. But I must have impressed him in some unknown way as he convinced me that I need only turn up to get the job. Sure enough he was right, and I was told to start Monday morning. I was given a card with the names of the department and the manager whom I was to report to, and that all would be revealed to me at that time.

While I waited for Monday to come around I was constantly pestered with unwanted advice, from people 'in the know', on the much-repeated size of the place. Come Monday, I have to say their advice had been seriously taken on board. But first, I had to get there. It would start with a ten-minute walk to Ashfield station where I would take a train to Queen Street. Hopefully, I would then make a quick change on to a very crowded train that was destined to stop at Singer's own station in Kilbowie. When we arrived at the station everyone stood up en masse and pressed towards the exit doors as if desperate not to be the last one off the train.

Caught up in the exodus I found myself outside the station, where everyone rushed away and left me standing with a purposeful question looking for an answer. My gaze immediately fell on a huge black five-storey building with a clock tower adorning its roof. Five storeys high, its size was awesome, and fully justified all that I had been told to expect. This had to be Singers. As I walked towards the building people were to-ing and fro-ing everywhere. I stopped one and asked for confirmation that this indeed was Singers. He grinned as if he was very familiar with the question. Look around you, he said. Every one of these buildings is part of Singers... Where do you want to go? I handed him my card. Ok...This is the central building where the final machines are produced. All these other buildings around us are component assembly plants. Now the plant you are looking for is right at the end of this street. Just ask anyone when you get down there. Show them your card and they will tell you which building it is, and where to find Jimmy Frazer, the manager. He wished me good luck on my first day and went off.

A New Beginning - Earning a Living

When I finally met up with Jimmy Frazer, the manager, I was a bit later than the expected starting time of 8 o'clock. He was a cheerful man and understood my lateness. Don't worry lad, he said, everyone is late on their first day. It will take you a good couple of weeks before you know your way around the plant, especially with the job that you have. He then took me for a brief tour round the ground floor level of the plant. We have four floors in this building, he said, and each one manufactures its own range of components. On our walk round we were joined by another man, who was introduced as my foreman, and that his name was Sammy. He was going to show me the ropes, as he put it, and that I would be reporting directly to him. As he explained, I would be one of a group of six progress chasers whose job was to coordinate the progress of components from one production area to the next one in the chain. Each of us would have our own component lists with completion dates and times. Sammy stressed that it was essential that each manufactured or assembled component quantity must be completed and made available to the next operation on time. I was to tolerate no excuses for any hold-ups. If for any reason I sensed that a component was not going to meet its target then he, Sammy, had to be notified immediately. Complete with clipboard and lists, Sammy then took me round each of the machine minders who were on my list and introduced me. With reference to the minder we were talking to, he would grin and tell me to show him who was boss. I looked at the minder when he said this. His expression was distinctly sour; he was unamused.

It all sounded so easy, and sure enough, by the end of the week I was reasonably well acquainted with each minder on my list. But therein lay the problem. You might well be acquainted with the minders but, with the odd exception, they were not going to be big on friendship. The reality was that there was a them-and-us psychology at work that could make things a little bit difficult. Regardless of how much I would try to be otherwise, they believed that my job premised one thing and that was completion dates and times. Also, to protect my job, it was assumed that I would report them for any sign of a shortfall. But much higher in their scale of ingrained aversion was their hate for someone like me continually checking up on their performance. Despite this, I got along with most of them; but there were a few who bordered on the militant. Truth be told, I could see their point, and very much sympathised with it. It struck me that it was a grossly inefficient way of collecting and circulating production figures. Three weeks into the job I mentioned my thoughts in conversation to Sammy. He dismissed them as utter nonsense, and lectured me on the size of the company, and of it being the ultimate in mass production techniques. That was me well and truly told off, and a reminder, in case I had forgotten or never learned, that my job was but a cog in a mighty big machine. Charlie Chaplin's Modern Times had echoed this sentiment long before, but with infinitely more humour. I quit the following week.

****

The Buroo was not overly impressed by my length of stay at Singers, and I think, by way of punishing me, they were none too particular in their choice of employment that they next lined up for me. The Fibreglass Company was one of the biggest employers in the Possilpark area. It also, from plentiful evidence, had the highest turnover. This was borne out by the alacrity and duration of the interview. They asked for my name and address and then, having written it down on a form, they asked me when I would like to start. Not to disappoint them I said I would start the following Monday.

Despite its notorious working conditions, the Fibreglass was a high tech manufacturing company in its time. From extruded glass they produced a fibre, whose properties had many advanced product applications. It could be extruded to a very fine tolerance, coated with an emulsion, and wound on to bobbins. It could then be woven into fashionable and heat resistant textiles. Its primary output, though was in the form of fibre matting that could be moulded into a variety of commercial shapes, including car bodies, or laminated on to other materials to reinforce its strength, or increase its resistance to many other agents.

On reporting for work on the Monday, I just followed in the path of other workers who were heading for what looked like the entrance to the main factory. As we entered I recognised a similar layout and procedure to Singers. They filed past a wall rack of time cards from which they retrieved their own from its fixed location and clocked in. They would then restore the card and make their way through two overlapping rubber doors, which had plastic see-through windows in their upper half. I stood back from this activity and tried to make myself conspicuous in the hope that some official would arrive to reassure me that I was expected. I began to feel a bit self-conscious as fewer and fewer people arrived to clock in. Maybe I had come to the wrong entrance, I thought.

In the midst of this self doubt the rubber doors opened towards me and hurrying through was a busy looking man with a clutch of cards in his hands. Are you John McBarron? he asked. Quickly reassuring him, he responded by telling me that my works number was 1532, and handed me a time card. He then asked me to clock in which I did with a copycat confidence. He pointed out my card location and, waiting until I had restored it, he then gave me a brief lecture on the necessity of clocking in and out for all periods of work. Failure to do so could result in me being short in my wages. Pointing to the rubber doors he told me to go through and ask for the foreman. Just tell him you are a new start, he added.

On walking through the doors the sight that met me was awesome. Everywhere I looked there were lines of spinning cylinders protruding horizontally from metal cabinets. They were spinning at a ferocious speed and what looked like gleaming white thread, was being wound on to them under the guidance of another small spinning spindle that I later came to know as the butterfly. As I took all of this in I began to see other features of the operation. Each cylinder and its cabinet was shielded from its inline neighbours by three metal panels that stretched from the floor all the way up through the upper floor from where the thread was being led. It was like an elongated box stood on its end to isolate the winding machine on three sides. I could now also see that the colour of the thread being produced was from an emulsion that was being applied at source somewhere above on the next floor. As a consequence of the very wet condition of the thread, moisture was being sprayed every where by the moving butterfly, as it spooled the thread back and forward on a predetermined build pattern on the winder. As an offshoot of this the floor of the factory was constantly wet.

At this point a big burly looking man appeared and introduced himself as the foreman, whose name was Jake. You must be the new start, he said. Right, what I want you to do for starters, is to help the machine minders by keeping their feet clear of all this shit. Pointing to a nearby wall, he said, see that brush over there, well get a hold of it and get stuck in. Without any further need of me, not even my name, he strode off in the direction of someone whose name he was shouting at the top of his voice. Mind you, the machinery did have its own ambient noise. As for the shit he left me to clear, this was unused glass fibre. It was the unavoidable waste that spewed down from above on to the floor when the machine minder, or the winder as he was called, stopped a machine to remove the sleeve containing a fully wound spool of thread.

In my early ignorance of the terminology, what I referred to as being thread was the combined strands of finely extruded glass fibre. When not being pulled and stretched to its optimum gauge by the winder, its individual strands quickly thickened as it fell slowly under its own gravitational weight. If left unattended for a few moments it quickly gathered, as Jake would say, into a huge pile of shit. Another cause, which I witnessed on my first day, and fortunately from a safe distance, was when the fibre being wound was accidentally broken in its passage from source to the winding machine and went unnoticed by the minder. Very quickly the glass would thicken and bulk up to the point where it spilled on to the spinning winder and its butterfly. There would be a soft bang as the spool of fibre exploded into a puff of white powdered glass that backed its way up the sides of its metal box like a huge wad of cotton wool. This could also happen when the spool was not changed in time by the minder. It would continue to build until it made contact with the butterfly. From either cause the result was disastrous, as its associated line of machines would require to be taken out of production until such time as the mess was cleared.

Whilst the conditions could be horrendous at times, I would still say that its human culture was much friendlier than that of a progress chaser at Singers. There was lots off good-natured banter among the guys that would while away the day, and give you a resistance to unwanted realities. In this vein, a couple of weeks came and went and I was still brushing up the shit. It was not that I looked down on the job; that I deemed myself above it; it was simply that I was beginning to pick up too many glass splinters in my fingers and my feet, and it was beginning to annoy the hell out of me. A pair of industrial gloves, compliments of the company, did help a little. As for the feet, a pair of wooden clogs was looming high on my list of needful improvements to my quality of life. My main problem, as at Singers, was my curiosity that was always asking questions at the wrong time. My questions at that time were aimed at finding out more about the mysteries of making the fibre which fed each winding machine. The machine minders of course would answer my questions, but this was not the same as seeing the real thing upstairs. I did ask Jake's permission to do so, but, being only two weeks into the job, I was just a shit sweeper trying to get above my station - and he was right.

To get round it I took a devious approach. I hit the sweeping one morning at such a rate that in no time the minders in my area were in full control. I then persuaded one of them to let me have a go at changing a spool. He agreed and positioned me at the next one off. He broke the feed himself, withdrew the spool, and reloaded a fresh sleeve. Go to it he said. I took hold of the falling strings of glass in my fingers, It had thickened and got hot in the interval and hence you had to pull on it quickly to thin it down and so dissipate its heat. After a couple of aborted tries I got it moving. It soon became thin and very malleable. I kicked the brake off with my foot to start the winder and, just I had seen the minders do it, I lassoed it on to the front rim of the winder. I felt it grip and speed up and, with a little bit of smugness, I gently led it on to the butterfly. "Well done, John...Up and running at the first attempt...That can't be bad, eh!" said the minder.

Over the next few days, with the help the minders, I put in a bit of practice. Soon, I felt as competent as anyone and, surprise, surprise, Jake caught me one day. "I'm impressed", he said... "How would you like to manage a couple of machines part time?... We need some extra production"...Pointing to a nearby line of six machines which were standing idle, he said that he would have two of the machines serviced and made ready for me in the morning. I was well pleased with myself. Against the heavy burden of Jake's opinion of me, I was about to take a giant step. More importantly, as I well knew, that as a fully-fledged winder, I had every right to walk upstairs for discussions with my furnace man.

The following morning I got myself in early so that I could witness the preparations for startup. The place was quiet when I clocked in and, my curiosity being on a high, I clunked my way up the iron stairs and stepped on to the steel plated floor. The first thing that hit me was the ambient heat and humidity. Compared to the cool dampness of downstairs this was hot. It was a fascinating sight, though. Everywhere you looked, there were banks of small, gleaming, red-hot metal boxes; all of them extruding fibre through a myriad of nozzles on their underside. I was standing there, absolutely entranced by it all when I was tapped on the shoulder from behind.

Quickly turning in response I was greeted with a welcoming smile from a guy whom I knew to be a furnace man, or a feeder, as they were referred to by the winders. He looked like he was in his early thirties, slim, and slightly balding. "You must be the new winder", he said, offering me his hand. I grinned in response, and, as we shook hands, I introduced myself. In the course of our chat he told me that his name was Janick, but, for reasons he never explained, everyone called him Stoory. He was from Poland, and had served in the free polish army during the war. Following his 'demob' he had applied for, and was granted, British citizenship. He was now married to a Glasgow girl, lucky him, and lived in nearby Balmore Road. His polish-glaswegian accent was amusing, but sat nicely on him. A fascinating character whom I took to immediately.

Going on from there, and in response to my questions, Janick talked me through the process of producing glass fibre. Without trivializing the true complexity that lay behind it, he had a talent for making it all sound simple. He was in charge of a bank of six furnaces that fed corresponding winding machines down below. The next bank to his left had only two furnaces operating, These were the two that would feed my machines, Having got his own bank running, he beckoned me to follow and watch him as he readied the two that would feed me. As he did so he explained that the furnaces were made from platinum which, being a rare metal, was very expensive. But it was the only metal, he explained, that could sustain the high temperature (1800c) needed, without distortion. The glass supply to the furnaces came from a central hopper in the form of glass bools - the very same bools, or jawries, that provided so much fun as kids. The hopper fed its bools into six tracks that were aligned to feed a corresponding furnace in the bank. There was another small device close to the track that released the bools at intervals. This always had to be checked to ensure that the bools did not foul up on the track. He illustrated this by sticking his picker, a stiff piece of coiled wire, between them to check their movement. It was now time for me to get down stairs and get started before Jake did his round.

But there was one last important lesson and that was to show me how the fibre would be fed down to me. With that he pointed to the

winders down below, which, because of the steady stream of falling glass, were now almost hidden under the debris - sorry, shit. I needed to get down there fast, he said, before Jake turned up. After all, this was my first day as a winder, and I wanted to impress.
The week went very well. Running two machines had been a doddle; so much so that that it did not give me an excuse to avoid the shit brush. But, my reward was at hand.

Owing to increased demand, Jake announced that the production had to be increased significantly; and how would I like to run a full bank of six winders. Also, in view of how well I got on with Stoory, he was going to make him my feeder; he was to look after me. It was tough going the first week, but with the help and patience of Stoory, I was soon up to speed; I was now a full time winder, the shit brush was no more. Not only that; by the end of the month I had nearly doubled my earnings. And it did not stop there.

By a variety of devices I eventually persuaded Jake to give me a trial upstairs as a feeder. In no time at all it seemed, I was working in the upper reaches of a very warm heaven, looking down at my winders working in a very damp hell. I had made it. Success, indeed!

Chapter VII

A New Beginning

In Search Of Something

Happy New Year

The Move to Possil'

Earning a Living

The Newcastle Years

A New Beginning - The Newcastle Years

I now embraced my hellish promotion in the Fibreglass, and its three rotating shift-work cycles. It was not a pleasant experience. But, for the moment, the wider benefits that my earnings brought to our living standards made it tolerable. In addition to this, the stability of income meant that I could free myself to concentrate on the wider reading that I was now becoming more immersed in. For the first time in my life I was totally self-sufficient. I had the luxury of earning more money than I needed to spend. One third would go to mum for housekeeping; one third was more than adequate for my weekly needs; the rest I saved in the local bank. In other words, as Mr. Micawber might have said, my budget was surplus to requirements, hence, all was well in the world. My feelings were that it could be put to a better use, which begot the thought that I should do something about it.

Looking out of the window one day, I gazed at the green hills of the Campsies. I often found the view restful, especially when taking a break from reading. As I pondered, the thought occurred to me that, despite our closeness to the Campsies, only Bert and Agnes, who had their own small car, had viewed them first hand. They confirmed what I could only visualise, that the views were magnificent, and that the hills were very popular with picnickers. As I continued to ponder, the thought came to me that this could be the answer to my unused cash flow. It was so self evident that it almost warranted a 'Eureka'. Instead, I was content in the knowledge that I was going to buy a car, and take mum and dad on many better-late-than-never picnics to the Campsies.

There was one small problem with my grand plan...I could not drive, nor, in the short term, did I have any intentions of doing so. Then plan B kicked in, with Bert in the equation. Buy a bigger car and have Bert drive it. He and Agnes loved their weekend trips up into the highlands, and I was certain that, if asked, they would be more than happy to drive the bigger car and take mum, dad, and myself on the occasional Sunday trip. Bert and Agnes, when asked, were more than keen to do so. They even helped me to choose the car, which was a Ford Consul. The choice was unanimous. We liked its spaciousness with a bench seat up front, and the gear stick on the steering wheel. My particular attraction to it was its simple lines, and minimalist fascia.

Our first trip was a joy. We found a quiet glade with a view over the city, and had our first picnic - sandwiches and a large flask of tea. This was to be the first of many trips that went on to explore Loch Lomond, and the Trossachs between Loch Achray and Loch Katrine. Each trip was a new discovery. In the ensuing six months Bert and Agnes took us on tours of Argyle, and it's glorious lochs.

Our picnics grew in stature. It was now fried sausages cooked on an open fire at the edge of the loch - providing we could collect enough dry wood, or, failing that, our faithful Primus stove would suffice. These were special days with special memories. To think that all this beauty was on the doorstep of Glasgow, a city blighted by the industrial age, with icons of its recent past still standing. To discover that this was my heritage gave a new meaning to the word blessed; and to have known and shared this experience with others close to me was blessed indeed.

The other great pleasure that ensued from our tours, was that mum and dad, with much enthusiasm, wanted to share their newfound joy with their friends from Newcastle. It was of the utmost importance that they be taken for a tour every time they visited us. This, of course, meant that it would often require two cars. But this was not a problem, as by then, with persistent and persuasive pressure from Bert, I now had a driver's license. Whilst often going over the same route, I would never tire of these trips. In addition to the glorious scenery, the picnics were great fun, and always eventful. The jolly nature of Jenny and Polly, especially Polly, was infectious, with never a dull moment. An added pleasure for me was that, more often than not, Edna would accompany them on these visits.

There was always a feeling of inner excitement, and expectation, when it was confirmed that she would be with them. The trips with our families would have another dimension when she was there. Without question, a bond was beginning to form between us, and I would convince myself that new meaning was added with each visit. I would tell myself that it would help to widen our interests, and bring us closer together. Conversation was always easy, almost compulsive. There were many areas of common interest that we shared, such as the theatre, and the cinema, and others that we explored.

In truth, it was a charade, a self-deception that kept at bay our emotions. A walk in the sun; where the background pleasures were the visual stepping stones that plotted our footsteps, and coloured our words and thoughts. We both knew that we were heading down a path of fulfillment, whose end was not yet in view. Pleasure and confusion were at one with each other. Each step taken, would be the one that would reveal all. Just out of reach was that insightful word; that presumptive touch; that look. We both knew it was there, but who would be the first to reveal it. Each parting meant another lost opportunity. Eagerly awaited letters that would attempt to bridge the intervals, but brought a meagre sustenance. If we were to flourish then the space and time gap had to be overcome.

A New Beginning - The Newcastle Years

As I drove down through the long thoroughfare of Gateshead towards the Tyne my thoughts were in turmoil. I had agreed with Edna that the only way to bring us closer together was if I came to live in Newcastle. Many discussions had preceded this decision. Accommodation was to be provided by Joe, and Phamie, who offered me their spare room in the 'Prefab'. Ostensibly, I was on holiday and would stay for two weeks. But my real agenda was to find a job, and take it from there.

As I drove on to the Tyne Bridge, my repetitive thoughts took second place to my admiration of this massive steel structure. This was the iconic entry to Newcastle from the north. At the end of the bridge I took a right on to the City Road, which led me onto the start of the Walker Road. A ten minute drive along the Walker Road and I arrived at the front door of the Prefab. I was warmly greeted by Joe, Phamie, and Edna. It was Saturday; I was expected; and Edna had spotted me parking the car. They gave me a great reception, and assailed me with questions on the welfare of mum and dad and the rest of the family. The conversation flowed through an ample dinner that took us into early evening.

The evening was not to end there, as Joe let it be known that he had promised to meet up with his dad at the Jubilee Club, and that it would be a good idea if we all went and had a drink with him. As I had never met Edna's dad, and was eager to do so, I offered to drive us there. It was no more than a five-minute trip. The Jubilee was a working man's club and, as I came to know, was typical of the social culture that flourished in Newcastle. There was not an area in the city that did not boast of at least one club. As a consequence, there seemed to be fewer corner bars, and certainly much fewer than in Glasgow. Being member based, they also had a greater social atmosphere with everyone having a knowledge of each other. Unlike the impersonal pub, they were also friendlier towards visitors and made you feel welcome. Joe found us a table and sat us down. He spotted his dad at the bar and beckoned him over. He was a tallish, well built man and, like Joe and Edna, quietly spoken. I was introduced to him as Edna's 'beau' and felt flattered by this, and his cheery acceptance. Such was the atmosphere that I seemed to be continually shaking hands with friends of the Alcock family. I even met up with Joe and Edna's other brother, Charlie, whose likeness and family traits almost removed the need for an introduction. It was a fun evening that made me feel very much at home with the Alcock family.

Most of the succeeding evenings went with the same spirit. Not that we visited that many clubs; for it quickly became known that my taste and capacity for alcohol was, by their social standards, very limited. But this was readily accepted by everyone and proved beneficial when we visited Polly and Billy. We were invited round for dinner, and to meet the family. Polly's daughter, Lilly, was surprisingly slim compared to her mother's fulsome size, but just as jolly in nature. I was introduced to Jackie, her husband, and their two daughters who made up the Craigie family. Both Billy and Jackie worked on the railway. Billy was a ticket inspector, while Jackie was a train driver. They both had stories to tell. But it was Jackie, who was a bit gallus, who seemed the more keen to enlighten me on the inner workings of the railway. In the course of this, I was to often refuse his eagerly proffered bottles of Newcastle Ale, or other assorted drinks. Being in the market for a job, I was hoping to sound out my prospects; but the opportunity did not present itself.

After dinner, Jennie, Charlie and his wife, Irene joined us. There was quite a sing-along party going when Joe and Phaimie arrived. Jackie and Lilly repeatedly asked after Thistle.. Her sing-along personality was what was needed at this particular time, as was my mother, he said. By way of expanding on their affection for Thistle I let it be known that she was going out with a new lad called Gordon and that it was all looking very serious. This pleased them no end. It was also put to me at this point by Charlie, that I had to visit my mum and dad's favourite pub, the Crown and Anchor, before I went back home. This was where 'oor Jackie, hung oot' - Jackie Millburn, Newcastle Football Club's favourite son. Mum and dad had met him on one of their visits, and were even allowed to wear the 'International Cap' that he had donated to the pub. Being an ardent football supporter I was more than aware of "oor Jackie's", scoring feats, and assured him that this was a must. The party ended with the usual call for a last song. With Joe and Phaimie in the back, and Edna and Jenny up front, I drove us first to Welbeck Road, where I dropped Edna and her mother off, and then on to the Prefab, in Walker.

In the course of the week, which Edna had taken off work in lieu of holiday, we must have walked every inch of the city centre. We would start the morning by buying a newspaper, highly recommended by Joe for its employment ads. We would then walk in to town and find a coffee shop where we could lay the paper out and scour down its employment columns. If nothing was on offer we would walk from there to Jesmond Dene, a beautiful parkland area rightly famed as one of the city's beauty spots. Sunshine permitting (and it did) we would spend an hour or so just walking and talking while still skirting around our emotions. But, progress indeed, we were now walking hand in hand. The Dene was also home to a famous theatre, called the Playhouse. We browsed its billboard which showed it to be currently doing Bernard Shaw's Pygmalion. We had a brief chat and quickly decided that Friday evening was theatre night. I walked in there and then, and booked two tickets for the stalls. From Jesmond, we would always walk back into the city and make our way to the University Campus at the top of the Haymarket, where we would have lunch. Again, I would buy the afternoon issue of the recommended paper, and again I would browse it with hope.

As we moved through the week my prospect of finding work became distinctly low. I even had talks with Jackie Craigie, and Joe's brother Charly, each of them giving me little hope. Friday came and my plans were now unallied and forlorn. We walked, and talked, and agreed. There was no way forward at this time. Edna had to return to work on Monday. With no further employment potentialities to explore my prospects of financial independence would soon be gone. I could stay on for another week, which I had allowed for in lieu of holiday, but thereafter my job back in Glasgow was in danger of being lost. We were very disappointed, but not down, as I drove to the theatre on Friday. We were going to enjoy a special night out. I parked the car and walked the short distance to the theatre. As we approached, we thought that its stone architecture, bathed by the theatre lights against the evening sky, looked beautiful. Then it would do; it was a special night; and the play was wonderful.

The following morning we met up at the Prefab and went for, what proved to be a short walk. We both knew I had to go and, for whatever reason, I decided to leave that morning. Joe and Phaimie had been told, and my case was in the car. By way of reassuring her, I briefly confirmed, what I had previously explained at length the previous day; that I was going to save like fury when I got back to make myself financially self sufficient. But at every opportunity I would drive down and spend the weekend with her. I gently took her by the waist and with a forced determination I kissed her on the lips for the first time. To my ecstatic delight she responded warmly. I wish you could stay, she said. In response I kissed her again. We stood there, very close, for some time. We had made the break through, and my impulse was to stay on and forget the consequences. Instead, I told her with great certainty that I would be back soon, very soon. As I pulled away I could see the tears welling in her eyes. I kissed her for the last time and got into the car. I knew I had to leave then, or not at all. I gestured a last kiss with my fingers, and drove off.

In the weeks following my return there was a frequent exchange of letters. There was then a period when her replies, though still warm, were not as urgent in their response. My concern at this soon waned when I heard that Jenny and Polly were about to visit. With suppressed excitement, I knew that Edna would be coming with them. She had done this before to surprise me. Come Saturday, I went with mum to the station to pick them up. We were on the platform as the train pulled in. I quickly spotted Jenny and Polly as they stepped down on to the platform. Coming up to them, I eagerly scanned the carriage, which they had alighted from. It was empty. I greeted them both with an affectionate kiss on the cheek.
I was hoping that Edna would be with you, I said light-heartedly to Jenny.
Has she not written to you, she asked with surprise.
Not for a few weeks now, I answered.
That makes me very angry, John, because she should have. She took me by the hand and gently squeezed it. I am afraid she has left it down to me to tell you John. Two weeks ago Edna announced that she was going to get married. My excitement caused me to blush with expectation. This seemed to impact Jenny, who was now staring at me in a meaningful way. Her words came very quickly, and with much sadness. She is not marrying you, John, if I read you rightly. I am sorry

but she has chosen to marry a lad called Ronny. I have seen them together a few times but I never thought anything of it.

Struggling to suppress my shock on the way home in the car, I listened patiently to her as she explained, more to mum, than to me, how everyone had expected her to marry me. They were all as shocked, as John must be now at the news... But he's a canny lad... A commercial artist", Edna said.

****

I cried a tear that was never seen
And slept with no repose

As I dreamt of ways to turn back time
To a love that was so, so close

I embraced that it was not to be
And wished her auld lang syne

And consoled myself with an only thought
That her need was greater than mine

Chapter VIII

The Future

Exorcising the Past

A Loss too far

Leave of Absence

The Future - Exorcising the Past

Impatience, frustration, isolation, anxiety; words failed me when I tried to analyse and explain my feelings in this period. My reading had made me intellectually at one with my surroundings; but did little to explain my inner world. For my years, I believed myself to be ridiculously naive and ignorant of all things emotional. My bookish knowledge only compounded the problem by instilling in the minds of my family and friends an exaggerated respect for my veneer of learning.

It seemed to me that in all areas that were troublesome to me, others were casually at ease. It was as if there was a divide that I could not cross, which made me envy their confidence. I could so easily have put it all down to sexual deprivation; but that would have been too simplistic. Mind you, although I was well out of my teens, this was still a serious enough problem in itself. But it could not be the cause of my feeling of isolation - merely an aggravation of it.

No, I believed then, and still do, that my confusion at that time went all the way back to my early years in Mearnskirk. That cloistered haven not only addressed my medical needs it protected me from the worst aspects of the insanitary grime and social conditions of that period. In doing so it also nurtured and instilled in me embryonic values that were not at one with the reality of subsequent years. Nevertheless these values grew over the years and unconsciously protected me from most of the excesses of the tenement culture. But not without cost. It left me with a difficulty in relating to people other than family and close friends. This expressed itself in a painful shyness. As 'Jean' would have said: I had acquired a frailty. "Stand up and deal with it. All you need is a helpful cuddle."

I remember well an occasion when I thought that I had found my "Eureka". My favourite subject at that time was Ancient Greece. And in the course of reading Plato and related works I came across an axiom that was reputed to have been uttered by Socrates to one of his students.
"Know thyself."

The Future - Exorcising the Past

Its simple profundity moved me and led me to believe that the answer was in my own hands. It was a joyous experience knowing that with careful introspection all would be revealed. But it was a fool's paradise. Wise and helpful as was that venerable advice I quickly came to know that wisdom without emotion has little meaning. Ergo, tell a blind man to be careful where he walks; tell an impatient lover that there is always tomorrow.

Nevertheless, this insightful dictum led me to consider how little I did know myself. In turn, it had me re-examine myself from another standpoint. Namely, why was I always looking back to Mearnskirk and Jean? Was I just being sorry for myself. Was it all just a spiritual crutch? These and other questions, I thought, could only be answered by revisiting their genesis.

I drove through the gates and parked my 'Mini' in the visitors car park. Ignoring the intrusion of the car park, my first impression after 23 years was one of little change. The gleaming red brick of the Pavilions had dulled to a warm orange colour and the white corner stones and architraves had lost their sheen. All down to weathering I thought. I walked along the main thoroughfare, which, owing to the greater use of the car, were wider than I remembered. I stopped in front of the main reception building. After some consideration I decided to leave it till later. I wanted to stroll through the grounds and have a look at the Pavilions. Again, apart from the weathering of their colour, they hadn't changed much. Coming to my own Pavilion the memories came back afresh.
The French doors fronting on to the veranda; the iron beds supported on their large wheels; the quiet of a summer day as we lay looking upwards at passing clouds

As I ambled past I could see the nurses busying themselves with their duties. The ridiculous thought that Jean might still be working there suddenly crossed my mind. It caused a feeling of self - consciousness to waft over me. It was so overpowering that I quickened my step and hurried past and out of sight.

The Future - Exorcising the Past

On returning to the main reception I paused on the lower step. Looking back at the beckoning gates some serious doubts began to form as to why I was here. Allied to this was the painfully self-conscious awareness of where I was standing and the unwelcome visibility it gave me. At that moment I could so easily have walked away but somehow I regained my self-control. Still with much unease I willfully made myself turn and with a degree of purpose I walked into the reception hall.

The internal appearance of the hall had little or no memories for me. To me it had always been what I would now call the control centre of the hospital. For this reason I chose to reacquaint myself with it. An information and inquiries counter was very prominent. I took comfort from this as it was clearly a ready source of information should I need it. The hall was also fairly quiet and hence I took up a position at its centre from where I allowed my eyes to randomly wander. As I stood there indulging my curiosity I still harboured the thought, or was it the hope, that Dr Dale, or Jean, would suddenly appear. 'What would I say if they did?', I surmised. 'Would they remember me?' I doubt it. As I indulged my daydream a woman, somewhere in her forties and dressed as a senior nurse or sister, came walking towards me. For a moment it was almost like a self-fulfilling wish.

"Can I help you, sir?" she asked. "You look as if you're searching for something"

"I'm just browsing", I diffidently answered.

She clearly empathised with my lack of confidence and smiled warmly at me in return.

"Have you been here before?"

"Yes, but many years ago."

"As a patient, I would say."

"Is it that obvious?" I responded with a little more confidence.

"No, not a bit. Occasionally we do get visits from former patients. How long is it since you were here?"

"Around 23 years ago."

The Future - Exorcising the Past

"The Hospital was a sanitorium at that time specializing in Tuberculosis." She said this with an assuredness that indicated she must have been a member of staff at that time.

I felt a sense of excitement at her knowledgeable links with the past and, wanting to hold her attention, I hurriedly let it be known that I had been treated by Doctor Dale and asked if she knew of him.

"Indeed I do", she answered with a restrained chuckle.

"At that time he would have been the Senior Orthopaedic Surgeon. But he's moved on a bit since then." She added. "Today he is the Superintendent of Mearnskirk." She openly chuckled when adding to her statement, "He's my boss".

I was inwardly elated at this news and a great sense of worthiness welled up in me. It was as if I had contributed in a small way to this great man rising to even greater heights. Naive vanity of course, but it left me with a great sense of pride and gratitude.

Pleased as she was at the pleasure she had given me, she made to take her leave. But I couldn't let this happen; I needed more from her - even at the risk of making her impatient with what could be construed as attention seeking. I shook her hand and gratefully thanked her for her time.

"Could you answer one last question for me?" To which she readily agreed. "Did you know a senior nurse at that time called Jean McDonald?"

"Very much so. And before you ask, she no longer works here."

In fear that she might lose patience with my line of question I quickly asked as to what became of her.

"She met a very nice Irish lad, a medical student, here at the hospital. They got married and soon after they went back to Ireland. They now have four lovely kids, the oldest of which would be around your age. We get a Christmas card each year from her. Just like you, she still has fond memories of her time here...I really must go now."

With that she turned and went about her business

Deep down in my subconscious, I realised that the vast importance that I had attached to my simple question had been instantly crushed by the reality of this simple answer. Its initial impact left me feeling absolutely empty. Soon after it would be replaced with a hunger to fill the void with some new spirit. My "Eureka" was up ahead. I only had to find it.

> You are no more my Bonny Jean
> Yet remain the stuff of lore
> For your family who come after
> They are blessed for evermore

Chapter VIII

The Future

Exorcising the Past

A Loss too far

Leave of Absence

The Future - A Loss too far

Working in the 'Fibreglass' was an experience not to be forgotten. Like all large factories it had an all-embracing culture that with familiarity and time; with regular income and habit; it would suck you into a dependency that was difficult to break. Not only that, it conditioned you into repressing the hellish conditions that existed. So much so that you had no qualms about helping others to join you. My brother Bert, who rose to become a union shop steward, was instrumental in having me work there. This was shortly followed by dad joining us as a lavatory attendant. It was not that he needed the income, although that was very welcome, it was simply that he had become bored with life since leaving the shop and mum felt that he needed something to fill his day. He certainly got that and more as he met and chatted with the workers as they to-and-fro'd from the lavvy on the back of any excuse. His retiring and chatty disposition soon made him popular and respected.

Fibreglass as a product was very much in demand at that time and as a consequence shift work was mandatory. This did not trouble dad but Bert and I hated it, especially the night shift. The only redeeming factor for me was that I could better organise my reading time at the Mitchell library, (the biggest public reference library in Europe and one of Glasgow's treasures). In addition to this I was able to spend more of my time in the company of dad. This was further helped by Bert, whose influence as a shop steward, ensured that all three of us were always on the same shift.

The late shift (3.00 to 11.00), and the night shift (11.00 to 7.00), fitted in well with dad's fondness for walking. This pastime probably emanated from his early days of pushing his handcart. By way of getting 'my head out of a book' he would always invite me to join him. More often than not I did. Especially when we were on late shift as mum would not be around in the mornings. She worked part time as a cleaner for the Mosshouse branch of the Clydesdale Furniture Company.

Our walks mostly took us up to the Keppochill playing fields, which sported around 12 football pitches. Dad was also fond of football and when we timed it right we would catch a few of the local schools playing 5 a side under the tutelage of their P.T. teachers. We would spend about an hour walking round the perimeter admiring the skills and hopes of Scotland's youth. From there we would make our way home. But not without stopping off at the local corner shop to buy our favourite treat - five of Jacob's chocolate biscuits. We both loved these biscuits with its thick chunky chocolate for our tea. Two each and one for mum. Mischievously, mum once asked him why we always bought five biscuits.

"We like tae fight over the extra one", he replied. "So tae avoid oor faw-oots wae decided tae let you hiv it."

I got very close to dad in this period. He loved talking about the old days. How he pushed his handcart through the streets hoping to find himself a niche where he could earn a few bob. He would recap on how difficult it was to earn a living in those days. But he would still laugh and joke about some of his memories as if they were yesterday. One of his hard luck stories came from the time when he switched from his normal wares to selling fruit. With the help of Granda, they pushed a barrow load of fruit up the Cathkin braes. "God, it almost killed us!"

As everyone knew there was hardly a flat piece of ground to be found up there. Yet it was very popular for trippers in those days. They would then chock up the wheels of the barrow and set out the fruit - mostly oranges and apples. They were doing a roaring trade when this woman, who was trying to chastise her kid for having too much fun, stumbled against the barrow. The chocks jumped out and, before they could get a hold on the shafts it tore off with them running after it. As it trundled down the slope one of the wheels hit something and pitched it on its back. As dad tells it, those oranges and apples that escaped the grasp of chasing kids ran all the way down the hill back to Glasgow. Granda was 'effing and blinding' and had he got hold of that woman (she was off like a sexed-up cat) there was no telling what he would have done. When he later told mum she nearly wet herself laughing. Mind you, he had sold most of the fruit before it happened. So he knew that all was not lost and that they still made a penny or two. As for the barrow, Jimmy Miller soon fixed it up good as knew.

In one of our chats I asked him how the shop came about and was told that it was mainly down to my mum. It was her drive and determination that made it happen. He went on to tell me that in the beginning it was not all plain sailing. That in those days there was only one way to hold on to your customers and that was to give them tick (credit). This meant that for a long time they were out of pocket. But for the stubbornness of my mum, he went on, he would probably have packed it in and gone back to pushing a barrow. But eventually they got ahead of the tick and started to earn a living out of it. But for a long time it was no more than that. There were people like Harry and Geordie, who envied them having the shop. But they were greedy fools who had no idea of how they had struggled to keep it. Even when they explained it to them, they couldn't care less. But he would sympathetically add that they didn't have far to search for their own problems as Granny and Granda well knew.

When asked if he missed the shop, he would always reply to the effect that he more missed the people than the shop. In the course of 40 years he had been drawn into the minds of his customers. He was part of their hardship and shared the good times and the bad times with them. He was proud of the respect they gave him. With a little prompting he would talk in great detail about the families who frequented his shop over the years. The Hargreaves, the Gillans, the Clohertys, and many more.

Despite the occasional misgivings, he was also very proud of his family. In particular he would praise Agnes for sharing the burden with mum in those early days despite her youth. As for Bill, his good nature and social ambition tickled him at times. "He dis git above 'imself", he would say with a smile. More to the point, though, he took great pride in Bill's success in billiards and golf. He was also taken by a few of his posh friends. Especially 'big Gill', who was a rising light in the Glasgow Police, but not above having some outrageous fun-and-games with mum.

The Future - A Loss too far

One day we were strolling round the Keppockhill playing fields when, 'out of the blue', he started to question me on what my hopes were for the future. Taken by surprise I was a bit lost for words. But typical of him he sensed that he might have embarrassed me and immediately changed the subject. He asked me how Michael was doing at Art College. I told him that I thought he was doing fairly well but that he would need to stick with it for a few more years to have any chance of getting qualified. He was 19 years old at that time. He was a typical fun loving Glaswegian (a bit like Bert) who would do anything for a laugh to the point of being a bit daft at times.

Having left school without any notable academic achievements (deja vu) I was always a bit concerned for his aimless (naughty-but-nice) pursuits. So much so that I picked up on his talent for drawing and tried to redirect some of his energy by encouraging him to practise more. I would even take him for the occasional trip to Loch Lomond and have him draw views of the Loch. Eventually I convinced him that he had talent and persuaded him to apply for a place at the Glasgow School of Art. He did and was accepted.

In the following few years he had many ups-and-downs and a few ins-and-outs. His biggest up was when he married Cathie, a pretty looking local girl with a big heart and a lot of tolerance - he certainly needed her. His big out was that he prematurely left the G.S.A. - a decision that we both later regretted. Another up from this episode was that Michael was no longer just my wee brother, he was now my friend.

Going over this with dad as we walked home he kept nodding and shaking his head as befitted his view.
"He wus a daft bugger. It wis a great opportunity lost. Wisn't it?" He asked. To which I had to agree but qualified it with the cliche, 'that we could all be wise after the event'.
At this point I deliberately swung the subject back to the question that begot it.

The Future - A Loss too far

"You asked me, dad, what my hopes were for the future. The answer is, at this point in time, that I don't really know. Maybe I will tomorrow." I concluded with a smile.

"Why don't yae take a break. Get yur heed oot o' those books and go'n take a holiday somewhere. Whit aboot goin' doon London for a while. Accordin' to yaer mum, Thistle and Gordon ur doin' well fur themselves doon there. Ahm sure they wid be gled tae pit yae up fur a while. Give 'm a ring."

"I'll think about it dad. But you are right; I do need a break."

****

I gave much thought to dad's suggestion and concluded that a trip down to London to visit Thistle and Gordon (her husband of 1 year's standing) was a good idea. Gordon and I got on well together and he assured me, when I spoke to him on the phone, that they were going to 'show me the town'. They were happy to have me and I arranged to go down in 2 weeks time. When I told mum and dad they were delighted, especially dad.

I rose for work the following morning feeling pretty good. We were on my favourite early shift. Having washed and shaved I joined mum in the kitchen. As she poured the tea she casually let it be known that dad was not keeping too well and that he was going to have a day in bed. This was not all that unusual as it was well known by the family that dad's working days were over and that he should retire. I popped in to see him before I left and he reassured me that he was ok and that his sinus, as evidenced by the red blotch on his lower forehead, was playing him up.

"Ah've jist taken an Askit Powder' fur it. An 'oors sleep will see me ok. You git off tae work."

With his assurance I gave it no more thought and took myself off to work.

In the course of the morning my thoughts kept returning to dad. I had noticed that he was getting more easily tired and that our walks were becoming shorter. But I told myself that this was only natural as he was getting on a bit. I kept dismissing these thoughts only for them to return. Around 1 o'clock, 2 hours before the end of my shift, I decided that I needed to know. I got clearance from the foreman to use the works telephone to ring home. I knew mum to be always unhurried when required to pick up the phone but in my impatience I impulsively hung up. "Git yir self hame, John", said the foreman who had clearly picked up on my body language. I briefly thanked him and left.

As I drove up to the close I spotted the familiar figure of our doctor getting into his car. He acknowledged me with a brief wave and drove off. As I opened the door I consciously tuned my ears to the smallest sound. The first thing I heard was a low moaning sound coming from mum and dad's bedroom. I hurried to the open doorway and fearfully froze with expectancy. The bedclothes were fully pulled back to reveal the naked body of dad lying lying on his side. Mother was kneeling on the floor behind him and looked to be inserting a suppository into his anus. A tear trickled down my cheek as I also saw for the first time the full extent of his ruptured groin. His truss had been removed and there, partly resting on the bed, was this large blood-red muscle enveloping his testicles. I stood there trembling with shock at this gruesomely painful image. This was my dad lying there and I had but the merest knowledge of his visibly long-term suffering. Mum was trying to soothe his pain as she attended his needs. What must have been only a few seconds it felt like I was frozen in time as my eyes continuously scanned to improve my ignorance. Eventually mum became aware of my presence. She put her finger to her lips to ensure my silence then gestured with her hand for me to leave.

I waited in the living room with all sorts of tortuous thoughts going through my head. When mum did appear she had her finger posted on her lips. In a low voice she told me that he was settled now and for me not to disturb him. I was a little tearful as I protested my ignorance of his true condition. She consoled me with the assurance that dad would not have had it any other way.

The Future - A Loss too far

"He cin be really stubborn", she said. "He wid rather suffer in silence than hiv anywan fussin' ov'r him. Ahm the only wan he'll talk tae. Ev'n the doecter his a hard time gettin' thru to him"

"How long has he been that way", I asked.

"Too long", she replied, as if to herself. I sat down beside her and put my arm round her shoulder. Tears welled up in both of us. She took my hand and looked at me.

"He also has bowel cancer", she said.

For me this was the final blow and, with both of us struggling not to have him hear, we quietly supported each others' tears.

****

Dad's condition continued to deteriorate and with dreaded expectation the family were seldom absent. As his condition worsened so did the doctor's visits increase. One such visit was destined to be the last. We were sat in the living room waiting for the doctor to report his assessment. Suddenly there was a drawn out shriek and mum ran into the room totally distraught.

"He's gone, John, he's gone", she kept repeating to me. I took hold of her and lowered her on to a chair. She looked up at me, her face soaked in tears, and in a plaintive voice she repeatedly asked:

"Who'se gonnae look efter us now? John, who's gonnae efter us?"

This was a deep-seated plea from the past.

As dad would have remembered.

Chapter VIII

The Future

Exorcising the Past

A Loss too far

<u>Leave of Absence</u>

The Future - Leave of Absence

The loss of dad had a serious impact on all of the family. Everyone rallied round in support; especially Agnes, who was an absolute stalwart. In this intense pool of emotion I was often at a loss in my efforts to support mum, and felt guilty for relying so heavily on the efforts of Agnes, who hid her own grief so well. I persuaded myself that mum's needs could be better served by Agnes; that female company had to be more comforting than mine.

In putting this to Agnes, she not only agreed but salved my guilt by assuring me that my feelings were understandable and that in certain matters she and May were better equipped than me to support mum. To this end she made the long trip from Castlemilk to visit her each day, often accompanied by May. From these visits the idea quickly took root that it would be better all round if mum and I relocated to Castlemilk.

With Agnes to the fore the Glasgow Housing Department was approached on compassionate grounds to have mum rehoused closer to her family. To our surprise the request was granted and to our added delight we were offered a house in Raithburn Road, Castlemilk. It was only a five minute walk from May's house and only ten minutes from Agnes. As an added pleasure for me, we were also only a five minute walk from Linn Park public golf course. In Glasgow, golf was second only to football in popularity. And at the bottom of our street it was all there. We were really going up in the world.

Having quit the Fibreglass (oh joy, outrageous joy), I soon found myself working for the Forth Caledonian Transport Company. They were the delivery arm of some of the largest manufacturing companies in central Scotland. I was employed as a load scheduler. It was not exactly a mind-stretching job and it paid significantly less than the Fibreglass. But was I caring? Soon my curiosity about the wider operations of the company (borne from a low threshold of boredom) got me noticed and I was fast-tracked as a senior clerk into the office that controlled the distribution of packed oil for the Shell

The Future - Leave of Absence

Oil Company. Initially the only difference I found, apart from a bit extra money, was that the office was a lot warmer than those on the loading bench.

There was one other surprise that extended my acceptance of the job a few weeks longer than my hopes. When I was being introduced to the other guys in the office there was one in particular that I took to immediately. His name was Willie Johnstone. He was a slim, fit looking man in his late fifties I would say. His head was bald on top with closely trimmed white hair on the sides and back. He was a quiet personable man who would readily smile when prompted. It was he who taught me the ins-and-outs of the job. He especially captured my job interest when he explained that the Shell Oil Company had a computerised administration system primarily based on punch cards. He talked of it as if it was a wondrously unique invention. He certainly made me want to know more about this new technology.

Willie was a very knowledgeable man and with his many references to other countries he also sounded a bit worldly. I soon got to know why. Arriving at work one Monday morning following a very good result by Celtic beating Rangers I was enthusiastically greeted by Willie and complimented on the result. Although I knew Willie to favour Celtic I was a little bit surprised at his exuberance. We fell into a conversation about the game in the course of which he revealed an amazing grasp of football and tactics. How do you know so much about the game, Willie? I asked.
"Because I used to be a trainer at Celtic Park."
"When did you leave?"
"Two years ago."
"You're kidding me."
"No. It's true."
"Then you must have known Jock Stein, Bobby Collins, Bobby Evans, Charly Tulley - the whole team in fact."
"Yes, except for Jock Stein. He had left for Dunfermline when I took over. I was also the trainer when we beat Rangers 7-1 to win the

The Future - Leave of Absence

League Cup in '57....Great players and easy to work with. I still see them now and again"
Such was my shock and joy at Willie's revelations all thoughts of me leaving the company were banished - temporarily.

****

Soon my feelings of frustration and isolation returned. This time not even the pleasure of sharing Willie Johnstone's memories would suffice. He was a wonderful man whose company I greatly enjoyed. But he also highlighted my deprivation. Namely, that there were far too few Willies in my world; and even fewer of my age. Reading was no longer a discovery; football and golf were my only diversion. I was now going on 32 years of age and drifting on the wind of chance.

"B'fore yaer dad died he told me that yae hid arranged to go an' visit Thistle and Gordon in London. Why don't yae take a break an' hiv yersel' a holiday?" Asked mum as we sat down to dinner.
"What brought this on?" I responded.
"Stop kiddin' yaerself. Yae know perfectly well whit ahm talkin' aboot. Ah hope yaer no deprivin' yaerself on account o' me?"
"You know I wouldn't leave you on your own, mum."
"Now yae are bein' daft. How the hell cin ah be on ma own when a've gote yur sisters jist up the road and good neighburs in the close."
We sat quietly for a few moments while I pondered. I knew that regardless of what she was saying I felt that there was still sadness hanging over her. Before I could resume, Agnes turned up and was immediately assailed by mum's views on my need for a holiday. Agnes, as expected, backed mum's view up to the hilt. Soon they both replaced my need for a couple of week's holiday with a couple of months. I couldn't do that I protested. Apart from leaving mum, what about my job?
"Ask fur leave of absence", said Agnes.

The Future - Leave of Absence

"Aye, yaer' right, Agnes." Mum hurriedly added. An' if they wulnae dae it, then quit. Yae cin always find anither jobe when yae git back."

There was no way back from this onslaught. There was to be no more debate; the subject was closed - I was going.
When Agnes left we sat quietly together for a while. I still was in need of reassurance that her grieving was under control. The silence was broken by mum.

"John, ah'm not a clever wumman; bit ah think ah know yae better than yae know yersel'....
Yae need tae find yaerself a companion in life....
An' when yae dae yae'll find yaer own tomorrow.
So nae mer thinking aboot it. Jist go an' enjoy yaerself"

****

Would that my absence help
To ease my mother's sorrow
And consummate her heartfelt quest
For me and my tomorrow